TALES FROM INDIAN HISTORY

D1860405

Owing to the antiquity and rarity of this book, certain pages are regrettably absent, and readability is compromised due to the blurring of the original text. If you possess any insights regarding the availability of these missing sections, kindly inform us. Your assistance is crucial in ensuring the completion of this significant work for the benefit of future generations.

TALES FROM INDIAN HISTORY:

BEING THE

Annals of India Retold in Narratives.

BY

J. TALBOYS WHEELER

GYAN

Published by

Gyan Publishing House
5, Ansari Road
Daryaganj, New Delhi-110002
Phone: 011-47034999, 9811692060
E-mail: books@gyanbooks.com

Distribution Network
gyanbooks.com
India, USA, Canada, UK, Australia

© Publisher

All rights reserved. No part of this work may be reproduced, stored, adapted, or transmitted in any form or by any means, electronic, mechanical, photocopying, micro-filming, recording or otherwise, or translated in any language, without the prior written permission of the copyright owner and the publisher.

ISBN: 978-93-6208-722-5 (PB)
First Published, 1881

2nd Impression 2024

Printed at: Gyan Press, Delhi.

The book is sold subject to the condition that it shall not, by way of trade or otherwise, be lent, resold, hired out, or otherwise circulated without the prior publisher's written consent.

TALES FROM INDIAN HISTORY
Author: J. TALBOYS WHEELER

TALES FROM INDIAN HISTORY:

BEING THE

Annals of India retold in Narratives.

COMPLETE IN ONE VOLUME.

BY

J. TALBOYS WHEELER,

LATE ASSISTANT SECRETARY TO THE GOVERNMENT OF INDIA IN THE FOREIGN DEPARTMENT,
LATE SECRETARY TO THE GOVERNMENT OF BRITISH BURMA,
ETC., ETC.

LONDON:
W. THACKER & CO., 87, NEWGATE STREET.
CALCUTTA: THACKER, SPINK & CO.
BOMBAY: THACKER & CO., Limited.
1881.

BY THE SAME AUTHOR.

HISTORY OF INDIA FROM THE EARLIEST AGES.

4 vols. 8vo., viz.:—

Vol. I. The Vedic Period and the Maha Bharata. 8vo, 18s.
(*Second Edition in preparation.*)
Vol. II. The Ramayana and Brahmanic Period. 8vo. 21s.
Vol. III. Hindu, Buddhist and Brahmanical. 8vo. 18s.
Vol. IV. India under Muhammadan Rule. 8vo. 24s.

These four volumes complete the history of India on a large scale down to the rise of British power. The history of the British Empire in India will probably occupy four more volumes. When finished the work will form a complete History of India in eight volumes. 8vo.

"No one can be said to know India, whether ancient or modern, who is unacquainted with the Maha Bharata and Ramayana, and we congratulate Mr. Wheeler on having performed a task which will earn him the gratitude of many readers, both in England and in India. He has given us something that has never been done before by any European scholar, and something which does not lose in value by the independent way in which it is carried out."—*The Times*, January 11, 1868.

"In his analysis and bold criticism of the Maha Bharata, Mr. Wheeler was, in England at any rate, first in the field. Readers who never studied a Sanscrit book, and who have not yet summoned up courage to face those ponderous tomes in which German erudition is slowly opening up the as yet unexplored wilds of Indian history and mythology, can appreciate Mr. Wheeler's lively style, and enjoy his brilliant analysis of one of the most interesting poems in the world. And to this task he brought a mind trained in Grecian and Roman history, familiar with Oriental modes of thought, and the practical acumen of the Government official, whose life is spent in close contact with the minds of the people whose ancient history forms the subject of his investigations. To these causes it is due that he should have elicited the applause of Orientals, and wrung from German *savants*, whose life is passed in the study of early Indian history, the tribute of sincere admiration."—Professor Goldstucker in *The Westminster Review.*

Trubner & Co., London.

A SHORT HISTORY OF INDIA AND OF THE FRONTIER STATES OF AFGHANISTAN, NIPAL, AND BURMA.

Complete from the Earliest Ages to the year 1880. With Maps and Tables. Crown 8vo. 12s.

"In this history there are nearly all the actual facts which an ordinary Englishman need know, and they are related by a man who has had exceptional opportunities for qualifying himself for dealing with them."—*Pall Mall Gazette.*

Macmillan & Co. London.

PREFACE.

The present work is a history of India in the form of tales or narratives, just as the history of Scotland is told in Sir Walter Scott's "Tales of a Grandfather." But it is not confined to mere history. It also tells the adventures of Indian heroes and heroines in legends of love and war; describes the village communities of India, their organisations and self-government; delineates the results of caste, infant marriages, and other Hindu institutions and usages, as seen in the family and social life of the people in villages and towns, as well as in courts and palaces. It also explains the circumstances under which the British government has been compelled at times to interfere in Native principalities, or has been forced to annex territories like the Punjab and Burma. It traces the development of political relations between the British government and Native states; and has something to say of the foreign relations with Persia, Russia, Turkey and China. The last chapter touches on the future prospects of India; the probable results of state education and increased communications with Europe and closer association with

Englishmen; and the possibility, if any, of introducing representative governments in India at some future time.

The work throughout has been written for the people of India, as well as for those of the British Isles. Twenty years ago the author taught the history of India to the higher classes of native students in the Madras Presidency College; and since then he has had large experiences of political affairs in the Secretariats both of India and British Burma. Consequently he is not only aware of what the rising generation of Hindus are anxious to be taught, but what it is desirable that they should know; whilst he has enjoyed special opportunities of acquiring the necessary knowledge, beyond what is available in libraries or record rooms.

In spite, however, of the authority of Sir Walter Scott's "Tales of a Grandfather," the present title of "Tales from Indian History" may be in some respects a misnomer. It possesses, however, the advantage of explaining that the work is meant to be interesting as well as instructive, whilst telling such facts as every Englishman ought to know about India, and which have hitherto been spread over bulky and voluminous publications, and in many instances have not been published at all.

WITHAM, ESSEX,
July 21*st*, 1881.

CONTENTS.

TRADITIONS OF THE RAJPUTS.

I. The War of the Maha Bharata (about B.C. 1500).

II. Legend of Rama (about B.C. 1000).

MUHAMMADAN RULE IN INDIA.

III. Three Conquering Sultans (A.D. 1000 to 1500).

IV. Akbar, the Great Moghul (1556 to 1605).

V. Reign of Jehanghir: Roe's Mission to India. (1605 to 1627.)

VI. Reign of Shah Jehan: Fratricidal Wars for the Throne.
(1628 to 1658.)

UPRISING OF THE MAHRATTAS.

HISTORY OF BRITISH INDIA.

XIX. Four Asiatic Empires: Persia, Russia, Turkey, and China (*ante* 1881).

XX. India: Past and Future.

TALES FROM INDIAN HISTORY.

TRADITIONS OF THE RAJPUTS.

I.—*The War of the Maha Bharata.*

About B.C. 1500.

THE Rajputs are, perhaps, the most interesting race in India. They are Hindus of the military caste; soldiers by birth and instinct; proud and sensitive after the manner of warriors of every age and clime, but somewhat toned down in the present day by the self-constraint of later civilisation, and the studied courtesy of Oriental society.

The Rajputs, or "sons of Rajas," might be described, in comparison with other Hindus, as the Hellenes of India. In ancient times they were a conquering race, descended from the old Aryan stock, which has been establishing thrones and dominions over aboriginal or pre-Aryan races ever since the dawn of history. They founded kingdoms in Hindustan with feudal institutions resembling those of Europe during the Middle Ages. The Raja was the independent ruler of his own State; but in later days he owed a certain allegiance to a Suzerain or Emperor, known as the Maha Raja, or "Great Raja," or "Raja of Rajas." Every Raja was supported by hereditary crown lands, known as the royal demesne. His kinsmen were nobles, or Thakurs, who had hereditary fiefs of their own, and attended on the Raja in time of war, like the feudal barons of olden time, taking the field with their armed retainers like the Thanes of Scotland with their kerns and gallow-glasses. The lands were cultivated by lower castes, immigrants and aborigines, who formed the peasant population known in the present day as Ryots, and who paid rent in money or kind to their feudal lord, Thakur or Raja. In some cases the Ryots were little better than serfs or slaves labouring for a bare subsistence, whilst the harvests and cattle were regarded as the property of their masters. In other cases they possessed hereditary rights in the soil, and made over a certain share of the produce, or maintained certain quotas of troops, in return for protection against brigands and cattle-lifters.

The characteristics and usages of the Rajputs are best told in their traditions. The earliest legend of all has been expanded into a national epic, in the Sanskrit language, known as the Maha Bharata, or "Great War of Bharata." It refers to a tremendous battle, said to have been waged three or four thousand years ago, in the neighbourhood of Delhi, between two branches of the house of Bharata, known as the Pandavas and Kauravas, and to have lasted, with occasional breaks in the night time, for the extraordinary term of eighteen days.

Bharata was one of those mythical heroes who flourished in the age of legend which preceded the Great War, and is said to have conquered all India. His story is of no more account in real history than the stories of Theseus or Hercules. His mother was the heroine Sakuntala, who was married to Raja Dushyanta, but was deserted by her husband before Bharata was born. The lady brought up her boy in the jungle, and one day as the Raja was hunting in the same forest, he saw Bharata playing with lions, and discovered that the lad was his own son. Accordingly the Raja became reconciled to his wife Sakuntala, and lived happy ever afterwards; and the whole story has been turned into a Sanskrit drama, by a poet named Kalidasa, of which translations have been published in English by Sir William Jones and Professor Monier Williams.

The story of the Great War opens at the city of Hastinapur, which was situated on the river Ganges, about sixty-five miles to the north-east of Delhi. Hastinapur was founded, nobody knows when, by a descendant of Bharata; and there was in the old dim aforetime a dynasty of Rajas of Hastinapur, of whom nothing is known beyond lists of names.

At last there was an old Raja named Santanu, who wanted to marry a young wife. The parents of the damsel opposed the marriage; but afterwards gave their consent, on the condition that her first born son should inherit the kingdom, or Raj. There was, however, a difficulty. The old Raja had a grown-up son by a former wife, who was the rightful heir to the throne. Fortunately for him this son was a model of filial piety, and sacrificed himself in order to gratify his father. He abandoned all claim to the Raj in favour of the unborn brother; and he bound himself never to marry, or to have any children, so as to prevent the possibility of any future contest for the throne. Accordingly, the old Raja married the young damsel, and became the father of a son; and the elder brother religiously kept his promise until the day of his death, and was always known by the name of Bhishma, or "dreadful," because of his dreadful vow.

Generations flitted by. The old Raja was gathered to his fathers, and was succeeded by the young Raja, who died in his turn, leaving two sons, namely, a pale-complexioned boy, who was named Pandu, and a boy who was blind from his birth.[1] Pandu died, leaving five sons, who were called the five Pandavas, of whom the three elder ones became famous, namely:—Yudhishthira, the wise; Bhima, the strong; and Arjuna, the gallant.

Meanwhile the brother of Pandu, known as the blind Raja, succeeded to the throne of Hastinapur. He was married to a princess named Gandhari, who is said to have been a princess of Candahar. She was betrothed before she knew that he was blind; but when she heard the truth, she tied a handkerchief over her eyes, so that she might have no advantage over her husband. Several sons were born of this union, who were known as Kauravas, after a celebrated ancestor, named Kuru; but the eldest, who became the most famous of all, was named Duryodhana.

The two families of boys, Pandavas and Kauravas, were brought up in the palace at Hastinapur, and were taught the Rajput accomplishments of riding horses, driving chariots, shooting the bow, and wielding swords, clubs, and spears. Their fathers had been trained by the faithful Bhishma, but he had grown too old for such duties, and a stranger had been engaged, named Drona. This Drona was a kinsman of the royal house of Kanouj, two or three hundred miles further down the river Ganges[1]. He had been driven into exile by some family feud, and was married to a young kinswoman of the house of Hastinapur, in order to secure his permanent residence with the family. He taught

---

[1] The ancient name was Panchala; but the Raj is best known as Kanouj, which was the name of the chief city. Both Hastinapur and Kanouj were seated on the Ganges. Delhi, as will be seen hereafter, was seated on the Jumna.

the use of every weapon, but was especially skilled in archery; and Arjuna, his favourite pupil, became the most perfect archer of his time. Meanwhile the fame of Drona was noised abroad, and many sons of Rajas flocked to Hastinapur to be taught the use of the bow.

In those days the aboriginal tribes of India were much the same as they are now: rude, ignorant, and barbarous. The Bheels, who dwelt in the southern hills, were faithful to their word, but addicted to robbing villages, plundering travellers, and carrying off horses and cows, and were not as yet skilled in the use of bows and arrows. Accordingly a young Bheel chieftain, who had heard of the fame of Drona, journeyed all the way to Hastinapur, and begged to be taught archery; but Drona refused, saying that it would be a sin to teach a Bheel the use of the bow. So the Bheel returned to his own country in great sorrow; but he made an image of Drona and worshipped it, and shot arrows before the image until he became an archer, and this story is told in Malwa unto this day.

Meanwhile, there was a jealous rivalry at Hastinapur between the Pandavas and Kauravas. It was the custom amongst the ancient Rajputs, as it was amongst the Hebrew kings of Judah and Israel, to appoint a son to the throne during the lifetime of his father. Henceforth this son was known as the Yuva Raja, or "Little Raja," and took his place in the administration; so that he was trained at an early age in the duties of a ruler, and secured the throne on the death of the Raja without any opposition from his brethren, uncles, or other rivals.

As the time approached for the appointment of a "Little Raja" at Hastinapur, the feud between the Pandavas and Kauravas grew exceedingly bitter. On one occasion, in accordance with Rajput usage, a public exhibition of arms was held at Hastinapur, resembling the tournaments of the days of chivalry. The young men engaged in mock combats and other games in the presence of the elders and ladies; and as they warmed to the work the Pandavas and Kauravas began to fight in downright earnest, and blood would have been shed had not Drona rushed into the arena and parted the young warriors by sheer violence, and thus put an end to the fray.

At last the question was settled. Duryodhana, the eldest son of the blind Raja, was appointed "Little Raja," and Yudhishthira and the other Pandavas were solemnly banished from the kingdom. The sentence of political exile is another Rajput usage. Whenever a prince was deprived of his birthright or declared an outlaw, he was clothed in black, and invested with a black sword, and placed on a black horse, and solemnly commanded to depart out of the Raj. Accordingly, the Pandavas went out of Hastinapur; and journeyed down the banks of the Ganges towards the city of Kanouj, hoping that the Raja, who was at feud with Drona, would help them in their feud against Drona and the Kauravas.

Now at this very time the Raja of Kanouj was sending proclamations to all the Rajas round about that he would give his daughter Draupadi in marriage to any Rajput of royal blood who should win the prize in an archery match. This custom was known as a Swayamvara, or "choice of the maiden;" for although the winner might claim her as his bride, it was necessary that she should throw a garland round his neck to show that she accepted him as her bridegroom.

In ancient times the Swayamvara was a national institution amongst the Rajputs, and Rajas and sons of Rajas flocked from the surrounding countries far and wide to compete for the hand of a royal bride. Sometimes the marriage was decided by other trials of strength or skill besides archery; and in later days it was settled by the maiden alone, who threw the garland round the neck of the bridegroom of her choice in the presence of her father and kinsmen and the assembled suitors. A relic of this primitive ceremonial still lingers in the courts of Europe; a virgin Queen is not supposed to be wooed until she has presented a flower in public to her favoured suitor. In Rajput courts the Swayamvara has died out, and royal marriages are arranged by the parents, as in other Hindu countries; but a gilded cocoa-nut is sent to the proposed bridegroom as emblematical of her choice, although she herself can have no voice in the matter.

The Swayamvara of Draupadi lasted many days, during which the assembled guests were encamped in the open plain, and passed the time in sports and feasting. The Pandava brothers were there, but they had disguised themselves as Brahmans, lest they should be discovered by Duryodhana and the other Kauravas. At last the all important day began to dawn. A golden fish was set up on a pole, and a quoit-shaped weapon, known as a chakra, was hung before it, whilst a huge bow and a heap of arrows were laid at the foot of the pole. A brother of Draupadi led her into the assembly, with the garland in her hand, and proclaimed that the first warrior who strung the bow, and shot an arrow through the chakra and struck the eye of the golden fish, might claim her as his bride.[1]

[1] The chakra of the Rajputs resembled the discus of the Greeks, and was probably the same weapon. The native soldiers of the Punjab use it as a weapon to this day, and many of the Sepoys in Sikh regiments display great skill in whirling it at an enemy. It was set up at the archery match in order to render the task of striking the eye of the fish more difficult to the competitors.

Then the whole plain was filled with commotion. The warriors gathered round the pole and gazed curiously at the golden fish, or shook their heads at the ponderous bow. Some tried to lift the bow, and failed, and then ran off, to escape the laughter of the lookers-on; and at last one and all began to doubt whether any mortal man would succeed in striking the golden fish and winning the hand of the daughter of Kanouj.

After a while a young warrior named Karna entered the lists, and lifted up the bow and strung it. Now Karna was a strong man and an archer of renown, but he was not a true Rajput. His father was only a driver of chariots, and consequently the son could not claim a higher calling. Accordingly Draupadi held him in scorn, and cried out that she would not accept him as a bridegroom. So Karna threw down the bow and left the assembly, but he had much ado to hide his rage and shame.[1]

At this moment the Pandavas began to show themselves, but they were still disguised as Brahmans. The eldest, Yudhishthira, would not compete because he was better skilled in the use of the spear than in that of the bow; whilst Bhima, the second Pandava, held back because he could only fight with a club. Arjuna, however, the third Pandava, was one of the best archers of the time, and few could come near him, excepting Karna. Accordingly Arjuna stepped forward and bent the bow, and fixed an arrow to the string. The

---

[1] The story of Karna is obscure. Chariot-driving and chariot-racing were favourite sports of the ancient Rajputs, just as they were of the ancient Greeks; but the Raja who drove his own chariot ranked higher than a common charioteer, just as a nobleman who drives a four-in-hand is of higher rank than an ordinary coachman. The story, however, has another explanation, which will appear hereafter.

multitude looked on him with wonder and admiration, for he was as strong and handsome as the god Indra. The Brahmans, however, who had flocked to the Swayamvara to collect alms, were aghast at seeing a young man of their caste attempting to compete for the hand of a daughter of a Raja. They feared that the Rajas would be offended, and give them nothing; and they entreated Arjuna to desist. The young warrior laughed them to scorn, and drew the bow with all his might, and shot an arrow through the chakra into the eye of the golden fish. At this sight a roar of acclamations rent the air. The Brahmans forgot their fears, and waved their scarfs in triumph. The beautiful Draupadi cast her eyes on Arjuna, and her heart thrilled with love; and she threw the garland round his neck, and suffered him to lead her away as her lord and bridegroom.

But the Rajas were hot with rage at seeing a damsel of royal blood about to marry a Brahman. They would have killed Arjuna on the spot, only that it was a deadly sin to shed the blood of a Brahman; but they threatened to slay every man of the house of Kanouj, and to burn Draupadi on a funeral pile, rather than she should marry any man who was not a Kshatriya.[1] But the commotion was soon over. Arjuna threw off his disguise, and made known his name and lineage; and there was no one to say, amongst all that host of angry Rajas, that a true Kshatriya of the house of Hastinapur was not a fitting bridegroom for a daughter of Kanouj.

---

[1] The Rajputs claim to be Kshatriyas, the soldier caste amongst the Hindus, just as the Brahmans form the caste of priests. The caste system is explained hereafter in the "Legend of the Ramayana." Some have doubted whether the Rajputs of the present day are really descended from the ancient Kshatriyas, but the matter is of no moment

The marriage of Arjuna was followed by the marriages of his four brethren, and then the blind Raja and the elders of the house of Hastinapur began to relent towards the Pandavas, and gave them all the jungle land on the banks of the river Jumna, where the city of Delhi now stands, which was known as the wilderness of Khandava. So the Pandavas went to the jungle, and burnt down the forest and cleared the land, and drove out the people of the jungle, who were called Nagas,[1] and divided the land into five districts, which they portioned amongst themselves. They also built a fortress, which was called Indra-prastha, and the ruins are to be seen to this day along the road from the city of Delhi to the tomb of Humayun, the father of Akbar.

Now, when the Pandavas began to dwell in the wilderness of Khandava, they hunted the deer of the forest and lived on the venison. After a while many cultivators, or Sudras, came to that country, and sowed the lands and reaped the harvest; and the Pandavas took a share of the harvests for themselves and their retainers, and stored up the grain in their fortress of Indra-prastha; and they protected all the people round about from robbers and evil-doers. Thus Indraprastha became the capital of a famous Raj, and the Pandavas gave a great feast to all the Rajas round about, which was known as a Raja-suya, or "royal sacrifice to the gods;" for the feast was a sign to all men that the Pandavas had established their sovereignty over all that realm.

When the Raja-suya was over, the Kauravas became more

---

[1] The Nagas are literally serpents; but they are also an aboriginal people who worshipped serpents, and are sometimes identified with serpents. They were more civilised than the Bheels. Their memory still lingers in the name of Nagpore, the "city of Nagas."

jealous than ever of the Pandavas, and tried to work them mischief. They had an uncle named Sakuni, who was the brother of their mother, and lived with them at Hastinapur; and this uncle was the most skilful gambler in all that country. So Duryodhana plotted with his uncle to challenge the Pandavas to a gambling match at Hastinapur; and Sakuni was to play with Yudhishthira in the name of Duryodhana, and to secretly make use of loaded dice, until Yudhishthira had gambled away all his possessions.

Accordingly the Kauravas set up a tented pavilion hard by the palace at Hastinapur, and invited the Pandavas to a gambling match; and when the guests were assembled in the pavilion Duryodhana challenged Yudhishthira to a game, but Sakuni was to throw the dice. Yudhishthira was loth to play, but would not refuse the challenge; and he sat down and gambled with Sakuni until he had lost all the possessions of himself and his brethren to Duryodhana, including their Raj, their household goods, and all their cattle and horses.

By this time Yudhishthira was mad with excitement. His brethren dared not restrain him, as he was the first-born, and the others were bound to respect him as their father. He staked his brethren one after the other to be slaves to Duryodhana, and he lost them all. He then staked himself, and again he lost. Then Duryodhana said,—"Draupadi, the wife of Arjuna, has come with her husband to Hastinapur, and is staying at the palace; you can stake her if you please against all you have lost: If you win I will give you back your Raj and all your possessions, and you and your brethren will be free men; but if Sakuni wins Draupadi must be my bond-maid." So Yudhishthira played the game, and lost. Bhishma and Drona, and all the kinsmen present, looked on and said nothing, for the match was over, and no one could interfere but the blind Raja, and he had been kept away from the pavilion.

After a while Duryodhana broke the silence, and sent a younger brother, named Duhsasana, to the palace to bring Draupadi to the pavilion. When Draupadi heard what had taken place, she cried out that Yudhishthira had become a slave before he played the last game, and that no slave had the right to gamble away a free woman. Duhsasana heeded not her words, but seized her by her hair, and dragged her into the pavilion; and Duryodhana called to her to come and sit upon his knee.

At this moment the blind Raja was led into the pavilion, and every voice was hushed. He had been told of the quarrel which was breaking out between his sons and their cousins, and hastened to the spot. The whole assembly stood before him with joined hands whilst he questioned the Pandavas and Kauravas, and then pronounced judgment. He declared that neither the five brethren, nor the wife of Arjuna, could be treated as slaves; but that the Pandavas had lost their Raj and all their possessions, and must go into exile for a period of thirteen years, in order to avert a war.

Thus ended the gambling match at Hastinapur. The Pandavas went away to the jungles in great sorrow, whilst their hearts were burning for revenge. The Kauravas rejoiced at having won the Raj of Khandava, but Duryodhana mourned over the loss of Draupadi, for he cared more for her than for all the lands of the Pandavas.

Thirteen years passed away, and the exile of the Pandavas was brought to an end, and they thought to return to Indraprastha; but the Kauravas were as jealous as ever. Bhishma and Drona prayed them to restore the Raj of Khandava, but Duryodhana and his brethren were deaf to all their prayers.

Envoys were sent to and fro between the Pandavas and the blind Raja, and their messages were delivered by word of mouth, and debated in the Councils on either side; but no peace could be made. The blind Raja entreated the Pandavas to return to Hastinapur, and promised to provide for them, and reconcile them to the Kauravas; but they saw that he was only seeking to beguile them, and that if they once entered the palace at Hastinapur every man of them would be slain.

Both sides now began to prepare for war. The rival kinsmen took the field with their respective friends and retainers on the plain of Kuru-kshetra, which may be seen to this day about two days' journey to the north of Delhi. On the morning of the battle they abused each other with the foulest epithets, until they were lashed into fury, and rushed against each other like wild beasts of the jungle fighting for their prey. They fought, kicked, and wrestled, and buffeted with their fists, and tore each other with their nails, or shot arrows from a distance, or threw stones, or fell-to with clubs and swords; and when a man got the better of his adversary, he cut off his head and carried it about in his hand, as a terror to all the others. Bhishma was slain by Arjuna, and Drona by the brother of Draupadi; and Bhima, the strong Pandava, fought against Duhsasana, the Kaurava, who dragged Draupadi into the gambling pavilion; and Bhima overcame him and slew him, and cut off his head, and drank his blood with cries of savage exultation.

At evening time the darkness put an end to the fighting; but next morning the survivors rushed upon one another as fiercely as ever; and thus they fought on for the eighteen days of the War of the Maha Bharata. But as the battle was drawing to a close they fought more savagely than ever, and they were so maddened with the bloodshed that the darkness could not stop them, and every man took a torch in one hand and fought with the other, until they were so weary that they fell upon the earth and slumbered until the rising of the moon, when they rose up and began to slaughter one another as before.

At last on the eighteenth day of the war, all the Kauravas had been slain except Duryodhana, the "Little Raja," whose hatred of the Pandavas had caused all the mischief and wrong-doing. Duryodhana was sorely troubled at the slaughter of his brethren and kinsmen, and knew that the Raj had passed away from him, and he made his escape to a lake in the middle of the plain of Kuru-kshetra; and when Bhima and other Pandavas challenged him to single combat, he refused to come out of the water. But Bhima taunted him with bitter words that stung his inmost soul; and he came out of the lake with his club in his hand, but looking as grim and ghastly as if he had been dead. Then the two warriors fought for life or death, knowing that one or both must be slain, until Bhima struck Duryodhana a foul blow on his thigh, and the shattered Kaurava fell down upon the earth and gave up the ghost without a groan.

Thus the Pandavas gained the victory over the Kauravas, and recovered their Raj of Khandava, and established their dominion over Hastinapur. The blind Raja and his wife Gandhari came out to meet the conquerors, but were broken-hearted at the loss of their sons, and could do nothing but weep and scream; and they went away into the jungle and lived in a hut on the bank of the Ganges, and never returned to the old home at Hastinapur.

After this Yudhishthira slaughtered a horse and roasted

its flesh before the fire, and gave a great feast to all the Rajas round about. This feast was known as the Aswamedha, or "horse sacrifice," and was a sign to all men that Yudhishthira had become a great Raja, or Raja of Rajas, and was sovereign over all the lands of Hastinapur and Khandava.

II.—*Legend of Rama.*

About B.C. 1000.

THE legend of Rama, the mythical sovereign of Ayodhya or Oude in the centre of Hindustan, is told in another famous Sanskrit epic, known as the Ramayana. It is divided into two parts, namely, the exile of Rama from Ayodhya, and the wars of Rama in Southern India against an ancient Raja of Ceylon. The exile is the result of a domestic catastrophe, not unlike the story of Bhishma, in the beginning of the Maha Bharata; but it reveals a more advanced stage in civilization and caste, whilst the plot and characters open up a new phase in Rajput history.

The early scenes in the Ramayana are laid at the city of Ayodhya or Oude, on the banks of the river Gogra. In the present day it is represented by heaps of mounds, extending for miles; but in the Ramayana it is described as a city of streets and temples, groves and gardens, palaces, perfumes, and ponds of water. Banners were waving in the air, and Brahmans were chanting Vedic hymns, and musicians were playing in honour of the Maha Raja. The walls, towers and city gates were manned with archers and stored with weapons. Brahman sages were teaching their disciples in the porticoes of the temples. Kshatriya warriors were training their troops in the use of swords, spears, and bows, in the presence of the Maha Raja. The Vaisyas, or merchants, were bringing merchandise from all parts of the earth and seas; while the Sudras, or cultivators, were tilling the lands round about, or waiting on the Brahmans as their servants.

Such were the four great castes of the Hindus, namely, the Brahmans, Kshatriyas, Vaisyas and Sudras,—or priests, soldiers, merchants and cultivators.[1] Outside these four castes, there were many orders of common people, who were all lower than the Sudras, but yet were all divided into castes of their own. There were jewellers and artificers, singing men and dancing women, charioteers and footmen, potters and smiths, painters and oilmen, and sellers of flowers and betel nut. Every son, from the highest to the lowest, followed the calling of his father, and was married to a girl of his own caste, so that there was no mixture or confusion.

The Maha Raja dwelt in his palace in the centre of the city, and was praised to the skies as the greatest sovereign in all the world. He was versed in the sacred books, known as the four Vedas, and the sciences, known as the six Vedangas.[2] He was a famous conqueror, and a perfect archer and charioteer. He was beloved by all his subjects and knew everything that was coming to pass. He took tribute from his subjects, but only to return it in other ways. His

---

[1] In the legend of the Maha Bharata the Brahmans appear in an inferior rank to the Kshatriyas, who are represented by the Rajputs of modern times. In the Ramayana, however, which is essentially a Brahmanical epic, the Brahmans appear in the very highest rank of all. The Vaisyas are represented in the present day by the Banians of Western India and the Bunneahs of Bengal. The Sudras are no longer cultivators of the servile caste, but form the great middle class of Hindus. Indeed, many Rajas of the present day are Sudras.

[2] The six sciences of the Brahmans comprised pronunciation, metre, grammar, explanation of words, astronomy, and ceremonial.

ministers were wise, devoted, and capable of understanding a nod. He had eight special counsellors, and his charioteer was the chief man amongst them.[1] He had two chosen Brahmans as his priests and spiritual advisers; and the greatest of the two was Vasishtha.

The Maha Raja of Ayodhya was married to four queens, by whom he was the father of four sons. The first queen was the oldest, and her son, Rama, was the firstborn, and consequently the rightful heir to the throne. Accordingly, he was educated by Vasishtha, the Brahman, and taught the six sciences as well as the use of arms. At the age of sixteen he was married to Sita, the daughter of the Raja of Mithila, a territory to the eastward, between Oude and Bengal.[2]

The marriage of Rama and Sita is a favourite story with Hindu readers, but the original Rajput legend has been altered to suit Brahmanical ideas. The Rajputs delighted in Swayamvaras, where grown-up warriors competed for grown-up brides; they were anxious to marry their daughters to husbands who were strong and able enough to protect them. But the Brahmans were astrologers and cast nativities, and were employed by parents to arrange marriages according to the horoscopes of their sons and daughters. Therefore nuptials are celebrated when bridegrooms and their brides

---

[1] In ancient times the charioteer was often the minister and confidential adviser of the Raja or Maha Raja. But in the legend of the Maha Bharata Karna is said to have been of inferior birth because his father was a charioteer. It should, however, be borne in mind that the Sanskrit epics were composed by Brahmans; and as the Brahmans of later times sought to act on all occasions in the same capacity of ministers or confidential advisers of the sovereign, they depreciated charioteers whenever they had a chance as men of inferior standing.

[2] The Raj of Mithila lay to the north of Patna, and answered to the region now known as Tirhut.

are still boys and girls, and before love or romance can stir up any rebellion against the union.

The Raja of Mithila celebrated the Swayamvara of his daughter Sita by proclaiming that she was to be given in marriage to the Kshatriya who could bend and string an enormous bow. But a Brahmanical tone is imparted to the legend. Rama is said to be only sixteen years of age, although he strings the bow which no one else could raise from the ground. The marriage was arranged by his father, the Maha Raja, and the father of Sita; and he was not permitted to see the face of his bride until the ceremony was over. In other respects the marriage rites were celebrated in the old Aryan fashion, which has survived the crash of empires and religions. The bridegroom and his bride were placed before the sacred fire which was kindled on the altar, and the bridegroom took the hand of his bride in the presence of the fire as the symbol of the divine presence, whilst the happy pair were sprinkled with water which had been consecrated by the utterance of Vedic hymns.

The marriage of Rama was followed by a popular movement in favour of his installation as "Little Raja." The Maha Raja was growing slothful and self-indulgent in his advancing years, and notwithstanding the praises lavished in the Ramayana on his wisdom and foresight, he was neglecting his duties as a sovereign, and shutting himself up in the palace with his queens. Accordingly, the ministers and counsellors, together with the chieftains of the Raj, proceeded in a body to the palace, and prayed that Rama might be appointed "Little Raja," and even hinted that the Maha Raja would do well to resign the cares of sovereignty and devote the remainder of his days to his religious duties.

The Maha Raja was exceedingly angry at this demonstration. He asked what evil he had done that they should be anxious for the elevation of Rama. They replied, with Oriental politeness, that they were all devoted to him, but also had a great regard for Rama, and wished to see him installed as "Little Raja."

The Maha Raja had another cause for disquietude. His youngest queen was his favourite consort, and he was infatuated with her beauty. She was the mother of a boy named Bharata, and the Maha Raja knew that she was bent on excluding Rama from the throne, and securing the Raj for her son Bharata. In his perplexity he got Bharata out of the way by sending him on a visit to his maternal grandfather, the Raja of Giri-vraja.[1] He then convened a general assembly, or parliament of all his ministers, counsellors, and chieftains, to discuss in public the question of appointing a "Little Raja," whilst the officers of the army and the people of the city gathered together in like manner to express the popular sentiment in favour of Rama.

The debates that followed were of an Oriental type. The nation was anxious for the installation of Rama, as a settlement of the succession; but it was known that the favourite queen was plotting for the elevation of her son Bharata, and for her own ultimate aggrandisement as Regent-mother, and that she had a large number of secret partisans, who were expecting promotion and profit in the event of her gaining her ends. Nothing, however, was said in the Council-hall about the boy Bharata. The speakers were content to extol Rama as a hero and demi-god, whilst they overflowed with flattery and devotion towards the Maha Raja. At last it was

[1] Giri-vraja was the old name of Rajagriha, the modern Rajghir in Behar, to the south-east of Oude.

decided that Rama should be appointed "Little Raja," and the announcement was received with a storm of acclamation and applause.

The Maha Raja gave his assent, but he was sorely troubled in spirit. He tried to escape from danger by fixing next morning for the installation; but he ordered Rama, who was living in a separate mansion with his wife Sita, to keep on the watch throughout the night, lest there should be any insurrection in the city in favour of Bharata. At the same time the Maha Raja hoped to keep matters quiet within the palace by passing the night in the chambers of his favourite queen.

But fate was against the Maha Raja. A slave girl of the favourite queen had ascended to the roof of the palace, and seen that the city was in a blaze of illuminations; and she had then heard that Rama was to be installed on the morrow, and had run off to tell her mistress the unwelcome news.

When the Maha Raja entered the presence of his favourite, he was seized with horror and despair. The floor was strewed with her jewels and ornaments; and she herself was lying in the midst, shrieking like a mad woman, with her long black hair hanging dishevelled over her face and shoulders, and everything else in horrible disorder. The Maha Raja was as helpless as a child. He tried to coax and caress her, but his attempts were rejected with fury. He could do nothing but wring his hands, and weep and moan, whilst his beloved queen raged like a tigress, and called him a liar and coward, until he could hold out no longer, and was forced to let her have her way.

Next morning at early dawn the city of Ayodhya was astir with preparations for the coming ceremony. The golden throne was set up, surrounded by all the insignia and accompaniments of royalty;—the white umbrella or canopy, the whisks of white hair for keeping off the flies, the tiger's skin, the bow and scimitar, the elephants, the chariots with four horses harnessed to each, and the sacred fire, which was kept constantly burning. The temples and sacred trees were hung with garlands and banners. The roads were watered and strewed with rice and flowers. Tables were set out in the open streets, and covered with provisions and sweetmeats for all who pleased to take their fill. Musicians were filling the air with sweet harmonies; whilst dancing girls, play-actors, and show-men of all descriptions were arranging their performances for the day. The crowds were increasing every moment, for the country people from the villages round about were flocking into the city to take a part in the festivity and rejoicing. Even the little children, who were playing in the courtyards and under the porticoes, were constantly crying out that Rama was to be installed that day as "Little Raja."

At this auspicious moment the charioteer of the Maha Raja, who was also his chief counsellor, was sent to bring Rama to the palace. The young hero took his leave of his wife Sita, and ascended his chariot lined with tiger's skin, accompanied by a younger brother named Lakshmana, and drove off to the palace, followed by horses. and elephants. The musicians played louder than ever, the bards sang his praises, and the women appeared on the verandas of the houses in their brightest attire, and threw down flowers upon his head. All classes hailed him as their future Maha Raja, and looked forward to his installation as "Little Raja" with exultation and joy.

Rama was soon ushered into the presence of his father and

the favourite ; but the Maha Raja was speechless with grief, whilst the queen was radiant with triumph. Rama saw that the Raj was lost, but bent himself to the ground with the utmost respect, and awaited his doom with calm serenity. The queen pronounced his sentence with a cruel and malicious smile. "It is the Maha Raja's orders," she said, "that you depart out of Ayodhya, and go into exile in the southern forest for a period of fourteen years; and that my son Bharata be installed as "Little Raja."

Rama listened without a murmur or a tear. He dared not reproach his father, and he would not bandy words with his step-mother. Once more he made his obeisance, and then left their presence. But whilst his countenance was serene his heart was sinking within him. He could not leave the palace without telling all to his mother ; and he must take a last farewell, without a hope of seeing her face again.

All that night the mother of Rama had been worshipping the god Vishnu with sacrifices and thanksgivings. When she heard that her son was to be banished, and Bharata installed in his room, she was almost beside herself. She declared that the Maha Raja had lost his senses; that he had become the slave of his youngest wife. She called on Rama to seize the throne, and told him that he might slay his father without remorse. His brother Lakshmana joined in her entreaties. But Rama was adamant. He would not rebel against his father; he would not even deliver his mother from the insults of her rival, by taking her with him into the jungle. Both were bound to obey the commands of the Maha Raja.

Rama then returned to his own house to break the news to his wife Sita. But Sita was only grieved because her husband was sorrowful. She cared not for the loss of the

Raj, nor the pains and privations of the jungle, so long as she was permitted to share his exile. She feared not serpents or tigers, thorny ways, or rough resting-places; she longed to roam in the forest with Rama, and to see the lakes and rivers, the flowers and water-fowl. At last Rama consented to take her, and his brother Lakshmana was also permitted to accompany them.

The departure of the exiles was a painful ceremony. All three walked with bare feet to the palace, amidst the cries and tears of the people of the city, to take their leave of the Maha Raja. Rama was stripped of all his ornaments, and arrayed in sorrowful garments made of the bark of trees. All three were placed in the chariot of the Maha Raja, and driven away to the southern frontier. They then left the chariot, and made their way on foot to the city of Prayaga, at the junction of the rivers Ganges and Jumna, which is now known as the city of Allahabad. Still they went on further and further to the south, until they came to the hill Chitra-kuta, in the jungles of Bundelkund; and there they built a hut of leaves and branches of trees, and lived on venison, fruits, and wild honey.

Meanwhile there was great tribulation in the city of Ayodhya. On the night that followed the departure of the exiles the Maha Raja was gathered to his fathers. According to the Ramayana, he died of grief at the loss of Rama, and no one was present but the mother of Rama. But the truth seems to be that the Maha Raja was murdered, and that the mother of Rama was guilty of the crime.

On the morning after the catastrophe palace life began as usual. Nothing was known of the death of the Maha Raja. The men servants brought in jars of water. The handmaids began to carry food and flowers to the different chambers. The Brahmans prepared their morning sacrifices and chanted invocations to the gods. The bards filled the air with the praises of the Maha Raja, so that he might waken to the sound of pleasing words. Suddenly the screams of the women heralded the fatal news. The cry ran through the verandas and corridors that the Maha Raja was dead. The whole palace was filled with confusion and dismay. The Ministers called a Council of the Chieftains, and debated what was to be done in the emergency, for every son of the dead Maha Raja was absent from Ayodhya. Nothing was said about the recall of Rama. He had been placed under a ban, and could not return to Ayodhya. Messengers were accordingly dispatched to the city of Giri-vraja to bring Bharata in all haste to Ayodhya to perform the funeral ceremonies of his father; and the royal corpse was placed in a bath of oil to be preserved until the arrival of Bharata.

Meanwhile, nothing could be done as regards the succession to the throne. Bharata obeyed the summons of the Council, and took his leave of his grandfather, and set off with all speed for the city of Ayodhya. There he was told that the funeral ceremonies must be performed, and the days of mourning be accomplished, before any steps could be taken for the installation of a new Maha Raja.

The royal obsequies were celebrated with great pomp, but no widows were sacrificed on the funeral pile. Bharata and his remaining brother placed the body of the dead Maha Raja on a litter, and covered it with garlands, and strewed it with incense and perfumes, crying aloud,—"O! Maha Raja, whither art thou gone?" Then the procession was formed in the courtyard of the palace for conducting the litter to the place of burning on the banks of the river, outside the city. The bards marched in front singing the praises of the dead

Maha Raja. The musicians played sad and solemn harmonies. The widowed queens, with hundreds of slave girls, walked with bare feet, weeping and wailing, with their long black hair hanging over their faces and shoulders. The litter was carried after the women by the servants of the Maha Raja, but Bharata and his brother walked behind, and held on to the back of the litter. The ensigns of royalty were held aloft, and the sacred fire was carried along on an altar, and kept continually flaming. Last of all, the other servants were driven in chariots, and distributed alms of money and food to the multitude.

When the procession reached the place of burning, the corpse of the Maha Raja was placed on a pile of fragrant woods, and Bharata brought a lighted torch from the altar and set the pile on fire. The lamentations of the mourners then broke out afresh, and they all cried out:—"O! Maha Raja, why have you departed from among us, and why have you left us here?"

When the burning was over, Bharata and his brother dried their tears, and went with the other mourners into the river, and bathed in the stream; and Bharata poured water out of the palm of his hand, to refresh the soul of the dead Maha Raja in the world of shades. Having thus performed the rites of fire and water, they all returned to the city of Ayodhya.

The further ceremonies performed by Bharata for his dead father are precisely the same as those which are performed on like occasions in the present day in every Hindu household. The son mourns apart for the space of ten days, and then purifies himself and returns to domestic life. On the twelfth day he performs a Sraddha, or solemn feasting of the dead—an expression of filial piety which has been handed down from a very remote antiquity, and is associated not only with the obsequies of the deceased, but with every family gathering of joy or sorrow.

The Sraddha was unknown to the Hebrews, but the usage was familiar to the ancient Greeks, and is still practised by the Chinese. Amongst the Hindu people it consists in offering funeral cakes to the soul of the deceased father, or near kinsman. It is performed on the twelfth day after a death, or whenever the news arrives of a death. The cakes are offered with certain ceremonies, and are then thrown into water or fire, or given to be eaten by cows and Brahmans, and either process is supposed to be equivalent to their being eaten by the ghosts to whom they are offered. A Sraddha is also celebrated every month in propitiation of paternal ancestors, and on the occasion of a marriage or other important ceremony. It is accompanied by a feast to the Brahmans, and is sometimes carried out on a large and costly scale, alms of food and money being given, not only to Brahmans, but to all classes of the community.

The Sraddha of the dead Maha Raja calls for no special notice. On the following day Bharata proceeded to the place of burning, and threw the relics of the funeral pile into the river. This last act brought the funeral ceremonies to a close.

The Sanskrit epic of the Ramayana is highly prized by the Hindu people, but chiefly on account of its religious character, which is beyond the scope of the present volume, and the legend loses much of its interest after the banishment of Rama, and the obsequies of the Maha Raja. Bharata is said to have been unwilling to accept the throne of Ayodhya, and to have gone to Chitra-kuta with a large army, and offered the Raj to Rama. Rama is then said to have refused to return to Ayodhya until the term of his banishment should have expired.

After this, Rama and Sita, accompanied by Lakshmana, wandered through the southern jungle, which was known as the Wilderness of Dandaka. During their wanderings they visited the hermitages of many Brahman sages, and were received with great honour. Meanwhile the sages were frequently attacked by a hostile people known as Rakshasas, who tried to put a stop to the sacrifices of the Brahmans. Accordingly, Rama made war upon the Rakshasas, and thus appears as the champion of the Brahmans against their persecutors.

It is generally thought that these Rakshasas were aborigines of the country; it is possible, however, that they were a Buddhist people, as Buddhists were opposed to the worship of the gods, and to the sacrifices of the Brahmans, and the Rakshasas in question are described as the enemies of the gods and Brahmans. Moreover, Ravana, the king of the Rakshasas, is said to have taken up his abode in a strong fortress in the island of Lanka, or Ceylon, which is a Buddhist country.

According to the Ramayana, Ravana carried off Sita to his fortress, and tried to persuade her to become his wife. The story of what followed resembles that of the abduction of Helen by Paris, and the siege of Troy by the Greeks, as told by Homer. But the legend is swollen out with supernatural details and Oriental exaggerations. Rama is said to have formed an alliance with Hanuman, the king of the monkeys, who joined him with large armies of these animals. The monkeys are then said to have brought huge rocks from the Himalaya mountains, and to have built a bridge across the straits which separate India from Ceylon; and huge boulders are pointed out in the Straits of Manaar which are fondly believed by the Hindus to be the remains of this marvellous undertaking, and are known as Rama's Bridge to this day. Eventually, Ravana was captured and slain; Sita was delivered from captivity; and as the term of banishment was expired, Bharata abdicated the throne, and Rama and Sita returned in triumph to Ayodhya, and reigned in great glory over the whole Raj.

One sad episode is told at the end of the Ramayana. The Rajputs have always been extremely sensitive of the honour of their wives, and Rama, after his return to Ayodhya, began to doubt whether Sita had not been deluded into a tender regard for Ravana. Accordingly, he sent her away into the jungle, in charge of his brother Lakshmana; but she found her way to the hill of Chitra-kuta, and was entertained at the hermitage of a Brahman sage, named Valmiki, and gave birth to two sons—Lava and Kusa.

When the lads were grown, Rama became reconciled to Sita, just as Raja Dushyanta became reconciled to his wife Sakuntala. Valmiki composed the poem known as the Ramayana, as far as the triumphant return to Ayodhya, and taught the two boys to chant it. One day as Rama was sojourning in the jungle he heard the boys singing the verses. Then he knew that they were his sons, and he took Sita once more to his bosom, and brought her and the boys to the city of Ayodhya, and passed the remainder of his days in peace and joy. Lava the elder was the ancestor of the Ranas, who to this day are respected by all Rajputs; whilst Kusa the younger was the ancestor of the Rajas of Jeypore.

MUHAMMADAN RULE IN INDIA.

III.—*Three Conquering Sultans.*

A.D. 1000 to 1500.

BETWEEN the tenth and twelfth centuries of the Christian era, the old Rajput kingdoms of Hindustan were frequently invaded by the Muhammadans of Central Asia. Turks, Afghans, and others, who had been conquered by the Arab Caliphs of Damascus and Bagdad, and converted to the religion of the Koran, were bent upon compelling the Hindus to abandon the worship of idols, and to become the followers of God and the prophet Muhammad.

The Muhammadans in those days were much stronger men than the Hindus. They had been nurtured in the snows of the Western Himalayas, or the bleak winds of the steppes of Tartary. The horsemen rode on powerful steeds from the banks of the Oxus, and were armed with scimitars and maces. The footmen were archers whose ancestors had been practised in the use of the bow from the days of Darius and Xerxes. The Hindus, on the contrary, had been bred beneath the burning heats of Hindustan, and were weak and effeminate. The Rajputs were brave and warlike as of old, but they had become luxurious, and were, moreover, divided amongst themselves.

The greatest Muhammadan Sultan of that age was a Turkish warrior, known as Mahmud of Ghuzni. His father had founded a kingdom in Cabul, and fixed his capital at

Ghuzni, about half-way between the cities of Cabul and Candahar. Mahmud was a soldier from the nursery; he had accompanied his father in his campaigns from his early boyhood. At thirty years of age he succeeded his father as Sultan of Ghuzni. Within thirty years more he had conquered the Punjab, Bokhara and Persia. He paid homage to the Caliph of Bagdad, as the Pope of Islam, but in all other respects he was an independent Sultan. Ghuzni was the metropolis of his empire, and after every expedition he always returned to Ghuzni with the captives and spoil.

The first invasion of Mahmud made a great stir in Hindustan. He marched an army from Ghuzni to the plain of Peshawar, and prepared to cross the river Indus into the Punjab. The Raja of the Punjab sent for help to the Rajas of Hindustan, and they all responded to the appeal. A vast host of men and elephants was moved through the Punjab towards Peshawar; whilst the Rajput women sold their jewels, or spun cotton, in order to keep the armies in the field. But there was no standing against Mahmud. The elephants were blinded by the arrows of the Muhammadan archers, and driven mad by fire-balls, until they turned round and trampled down the masses of Hindu infantry. The Muhammadan horsemen took advantage of the confusion to charge the panic-stricken host, with wild cries of "God and the Prophet!" They scattered the Rajput armies, and then went through the Punjab into Hindustan, plundering and destroying. They broke down the idols, stripped the temples of their gold and jewels, slaughtered the Brahmans in the porticoes, carried off thousands of men, women, and children as slaves, and then returned to the city of Ghuzni.

Mahmud made twelve expeditions into India, but they are nearly all alike. He annexed the Punjab to his empire, but left Hindustan under the rule of the Rajas. The plunder he carried away from the temples of India is beyond all calculation, whilst his captives were so many that Hindus were sold at two rupees each in the slave markets at Ghuzni.

At last Mahmud resolved to plunder the great temple of Somnath, on the southern coast of the peninsula of Guzerat, in Western India. The Rajputs made no attempt to oppose his march, but the garrison at Somnath fought desperately for three days, and then fled to their boats and escaped by sea.

Mahmud entered the temple with his victorious generals, and found it as gloomy as a grave. The idol was a huge pillar, which had been set up in an inner chamber. The Brahmans of the temple wanted to pay a ransom for it, but Mahmud declared that he came to destroy idols, not to sell them. He raised his mace, and broke the pillar asunder, and a great heap of rubies and diamonds fell upon the floor. The Brahmans had stored their richest gems within the idol pillar, and but for the mace of Mahmud would have saved them from the conqueror.

The expedition, however, ended in disaster. Rajputs and Brahmans were bent on revenging Somnath. Mahmud returned in triumph to Ghuzni with the sandal-wood gates of Somnath; but he was harassed by Rajput armies, and led astray by treacherous guides into the desert of Sinde, where there was no water. The guides turned out to be Brahmans in disguise, and were put to death with great torture. But the mischief was done. The soldiers of Mahmud went mad with heat and thirst. Thousands perished in the sands, and only a feeble remnant reached the city of Ghuzni. Mahmud died in 1030, and the gates of Somnath were placed at the entrance to his tomb outside the city.

Mahmud was of the middle height, athletic and well proportioned, but disfigured by smallpox. He was the contemporary of Sweyne and Canute, and in some respects was not unlike them. Thomas Moore has drawn a vivid picture of Mahmud in his poem of "Paradise and the Peri" in "Lalla Rookh":—

> "Land of the Sun! what foot invades
> Thy pagods and thy pillar'd shades—
> Thy cavern shrines and idol stones,
> Thy monarchs and their thousand thrones?
> 'Tis he of Ghuzni: fierce in wrath,
> He comes, and India's diadems
> Lie scatter'd in his ruinous path.
> His blood-hounds he adorns with gems,
> Torn from the violated necks
> Of many a young and loved Sultana;—[1]
> Maidens, within their pure Zenana,
> Priests in the very fane he slaughters;
> And chokes up with the glittering wrecks
> Of golden shrines the sacred waters!"

But Mahmud was not a mere brigand. His memory is associated with poetry and learning, with beautiful mosques, and famous schools and colleges. He expended the wealth of India on his capital. He built a mosque at Ghuzni of marble and granite, and furnished it with rich carpets, candelabra, and ornaments of gold and silver, so splendidly that it was known throughout Muhammadan Asia as the "heavenly bride." He founded a university at Ghuzni with a collection of curious books in various languages, and a museum of natural curiosities; and he set aside large sums of money for allowances to students and professors, as well as

---

[1] Moore was not well versed in Oriental matters. A Sultana was the queen of a Muhammadan Sultan. A Hindu queen was known as a Rani. It was the Hindu princesses who suffered from the invasion of Mahmud, not the Muhammadan Sultanas.

for pensions to learned men. His nobles imitated his munificence, and lavished so much wealth on palaces and public works, that the city of Ghuzni was provided with mosques, porches, fountains, reservoirs, aqueducts, and cisterns, beyond any other Oriental capital.

Ferdusi, the Persian poet, was engaged by Mahmud to compose the poem known as the Shah Namah, which should tell the exploits of the old Persian kings. The poem teems with supernatural details of demigods, griffins, and monsters; of extravagant amours, miraculous weapons, and impossible battles. A beautiful princess falls in love with a charming prince, whose hair is as white as silver. She appears on a balcony, and unloosens her long tresses, to enable him to climb up and join her. The pair are married in time, and become the parents of the famous Rustam, the Hercules of Central Asia, the hero whose name is to this day a household word throughout Persia, Afghanistan, Turkistan, and Hindustan. Immediately after his birth he drank the milk of ten cows; at three years of age he rode on horseback, and at five he consumed as much victuals as a full-grown warrior.

But whilst the Shah Namah overflows with legends of idolaters, it has little or nothing to say of Muhammad or the Koran; and Mahmud was so aghast at this enormity that he would only pay Ferdusi the weight in silver which he had promised to give in gold. Ferdusi is said to have died broken-hearted at the loss. The Sultan relented, and sent the gold, but the offending bard had already breathed his last, and the money was eventually paid to his daughter.

The gates of Somnath, which formed the entrance to Mahmud's tomb, have had a strange destiny. At the close of the first Afghan war, in 1842, they were brought away as trophies by the order of Lord Ellenborough, who thereupon issued a bombastic proclamation to the Muhammadan and Hindu princes of India, boasting that the insult of eight hundred years was avenged, and that the gates of Somnath had become the proudest record of their national glory. But Muhammadans could not rejoice over the restoration of gates which had been carried away from an idol temple by the followers of the Prophet, and Hindus could not rejoice on the restoration of gates which had been rendered impure by contact with a tomb. To crown the absurdity, the gates were a sham. They were made of sandal wood, and the originals must have perished long before the expiration of eight centuries, whilst those brought from Ghuzni to India were comparatively fresh and new.

Towards the end of the twelfth century, or about a hundred and fifty years after the death of Mahmud, there were great changes in Central Asia and India. Turks were driven out of Ghuzni by the Afghans, and an Afghan dynasty of Sultans reigned over Cabul and the Punjab. Meanwhile the Rajas in Hindustan were at war amongst themselves, and a feud broke out between Delhi and Kanouj, which threw open Hindustan to the Afghan invaders, and led to disasters as tragical as those of the Maha Bharata.

The Maha Raja of Kanouj was proud of his dignity as a "Raja of Rajas." He appointed a day for his solemn inauguration, at which all the Rajas who attended played the part of servants, as an acknowledgment of his supremacy. This ceremony was in accordance with old Rajput usage. Something of the kind still lingers in the courts of Europe, where nobles of high rank are engaged on state occasions in personal attendance upon the sovereign. It is to be found, however, in childlike simplicity amongst some of the hill tribes of India who claim to be of Rajput descent; one chieftain playing the part of a horse and carrying the Suzerain into the hall; another playing the part of a throne, and making himself into a seat for the suzerain; whilst all the others are more or less engaged in the service of the new Maha Raja.

The Maha Raja of Kanouj held out a tempting bait to the Rajas. He proclaimed the Swayamvara of his daughter, and ordered that it should be held immediately after the ceremony of enthronement. Accordingly the Rajas flocked from all parts of Hindustan to the installation of the Maha Raja, in the hope of subsequently winning the hand of his fair daughter at her Swayamvara.

The Raja of Delhi was deeply in love with the daughter of Kanouj, but he refused to act as a servant to the Maha Raja. On the appointed day there was a great gathering of Rajas in the assembly hall at Kanouj, but nothing was to be seen of the Delhi Raja. Accordingly the Maha Raja made a clay image of the Delhi Raja, and placed it in derision at the outer door of the hall to serve as a door-keeper. Then the ceremonies of installation were duly performed, and all present paid homage to the Maha Raja.

When all was over the daughter of Kanouj was conducted from the palace into the assembly hall with the garland of betrothal in her hand. Every Raja was enraptured with her beauty, and burning to be the bridegroom of her choice; but she moved gracefully through them all with proud disdain, without a word or a smile. Presently she approached the door, and all present looked on and marvelled, when she threw the garland round the image of the Delhi Raja, and thus chose him to be her lord and bridegroom.

At that moment the Delhi Raja appeared at the door, and carried off his bride in the face of all the Rajas. The whole assembly was in an uproar. Swords were drawn and the air was filled with clamour. But the bridegroom had vanished with the bride. The Delhi Raja had played the part of young Lochinvar. His steed was ready at the door, and he galloped off to Delhi with the daughter of Kanouj, leaving the Maha Raja and the suitors to rage and storm.

The Rajas of olden time had strange ideas of honour. The Maha Raja of Kanouj was so angry with his daughter and her lover that he sent secret messengers to the Sultan of Ghuzni to tempt him to march against Delhi. An army of Afghans was soon tramping through the Punjab, but the Delhi Raja took no heed; he cared for no one but his beautiful bride, and turned a deaf ear to all tidings from afar. Presently the host of horse and foot was thundering at the gates of Delhi, and the bridegroom awoke from his dream of felicity. His queen girded on his sword. She bade him remember that he who was slain in battle was translated to the heaven of Indra; and she vowed that if he perished on the field she would follow him to the celestial mansions. There was a roar of war outside the city walls, the clashing of arms and horses; and then the palace was filled with gloom. The Raja had been cut off in the pride of youth and love, and the widowed queen ordered the pile to be prepared, and threw herself upon the flames, in the hope of being united with her lord on high.

The Maha Raja of Kanouj had soon reason to repent his treachery. The Afghans founded a dynasty of Sultans at Delhi, and then pushed down the valleys of the Ganges and Jumna to the cities of Kanouj and Allahabad. The Maha Raja of Kanouj was defeated and slain; his body was found in the Ganges, and recognised by his false teeth fastened with gold wire. His empire fell into the hands of the Afghan conqueror; and his son went away to the south, and founded the Raj of Marwar or Jodhpore, between the desert of Sinde and the Aravulli mountains.

A column of victory was raised by the Afghans in memory of the triumph of Islam over the idol worshippers of Delhi and Kanouj. It is to be seen to this day, garnished with texts from the Koran, and towering above the ruins of old Delhi. It is known as the Kootub, and was begun by the once famous Kootub-ud-deen, who was originally a slave, like Joseph, but ultimately ascended the throne of Delhi as Sultan of the Punjab and Hindustan. Kootub-ud-deen died in 1210; he was a contemporary of King John.

Another century passed away, and Ala-ud-deen, a contemporary of Edward the First, was Sultan of Delhi. Ala-ud-deen carried the Muhammadan arms into the remote south, and opened up new scenes and incidents to the invaders.[1]

By this time the Rajputs had abandoned their ancient seats on the Jumna and Ganges, and were settled in different kingdoms in Rajputana and Guzerat, as far south, perhaps, as the Nerbudda river. Their Suzerain, or "Raja of Rajas," was known as the Rana, and claimed descent from Lava, the elder son of Rama, the hero of the Ramayana. The Rana held his court at Chitor, in the centre of Rajputana; and the fortress of Chitor, with its palaces and temples covering several miles, still frowns from the summit of a precipitous rock which commands the surrounding country.

Southward of Rajputana was the Mahratta country, under the sway of a Mahratta Raja. The Mahrattas were Hindus,

---

[1] Every reader of the "Arabian Nights" will remember the story of Aladdin and the Wonderful Lamp. The name is the same as that of the Delhi Sultan, and should be pronounced, Alá-ud-deen.

but were regarded by the Rajputs as an inferior race, vulgar and base-born. Consequently there were no alliances or intermarriages between the Rajputs and the Mahrattas.

Sultan Ala-ud-deen was bent on the conquest of Chitor, but he made his approaches slowly, and sought to conquer the country round about before striking at the heart of Rajputana. Before he came to the throne he led a body of horsemen across the Jumna near Allahabad, and made his way through the jungles of Bundelkund to the Nerbudda river, and thence into the Mahratta country. The Raja of the Mahrattas fled into a fortress, but found that it was provisioned with nothing but salt, which had been stored up by mistake for grain; and he was consequently obliged to surrender to the Muhammadans, and to make over the greater part of his treasures to Ala-ud-deen.

When Ala-ud-deen became Sultan at Delhi, he sent an army to conquer the Rajputs of Guzerat. The Raja of Guzerat abandoned his kingdom to the invaders, and fled away into the Mahratta country, taking with him a little daughter, named Dewal, and leaving his queen behind. The Muhammadan general carried the Rajput queen to Delhi, where the Sultan fell in love with her and married her. But she grew sad and lonely in the palace, and the Sultan tried to comfort her by sending messengers to bring her little daughter Dewal to Delhi.

Meanwhile the Raja of Guzerat found a refuge in the Mahratta country, but was soon placed in a dilemma. The Mahratta Raja was eager to arrange a marriage between his son and the daughter of the Guzerat Raja; but although the latter had lost his kingdom, he was as proud as ever, and refused to give his daughter in marriage to a Mahratta.

The Guzerat Raja was soon obliged to change his mind.

The messengers from Ala-ud-deen demanded the surrender of his daughter. He was powerless to resist the Sultan; but the thought of sending his daughter to Delhi, where she might possibly marry a Muhammadan, was more opposed to his Rajput sentiments than giving her in marriage to a Mahratta. So he came to terms with the Mahratta Raja, and sent his daughter with a procession of young maidens to marry the Mahratta prince.

At that moment a troop of Muhammadan horsemen fell in with the wedding train, and carried off the bride, and conducted her to Delhi. She was only eight years old, and was soon reconciled to her fate, whilst her mother rejoiced at the sight of her daughter, and became better pleased with her life in the palace of the Sultan.

Now the Sultan had a son by an older queen, who was ten years of age, and he wished to betroth the boy to the little Dewal. Accordingly the children played together in the palace, and amused the ladies and hand-maidens with their gambols; and at last grew so warmly attached to each other that they could never bear to be separated.

All this while the mother of the boy was very jealous. She wanted to marry him to a daughter of her brother; and she set the Sultan against the match with Dewal, and persuaded him to send Dewal to another building known as the Red Palace. Her son broke out in a rage, tore his clothes, and became frantic with grief, but all to no purpose. Dewal was sent to the Red Palace, but the prince met her on the way, and gave her a lock of his hair, and she in return presented him with a ring.

The prince loved Dewal very dearly, but his mother laughed at his passion, and coaxed him over to marry his cousin. He yielded at last, but his happiness was gone.

He received a letter of reproaches from Dewal, and began to pine away. His mother relented at the sight of his distress, and as Muhammadans are permitted to marry four wives, she prevailed on the Sultan to allow the prince to marry Dewal as a second partner, and the nuptials were accordingly celebrated with great rejoicings.

After this the Sultan marched a vast army into Rajputana and laid siege to Chitor. The operations lasted many months. The Rajputs resisted until they were starved out, and there was no alternative but to surrender or die. At last they resolved to perform a terrible rite of self-sacrifice, which was not unfrequent in ancient times, and was known as the Johur. Huge piles of timber were raised up in a declivity and set on fire. The women approached in a funeral procession and threw themselves into the flames. The men arrayed themselves in saffron coloured garments, and rushed out of the fortress sword in hand. Most of the warriors were cut to pieces, but a few escaped through the Muhammadan lines and made their way to the Aravulli mountains. The flame and smoke of the horrible sacrifice was still rising above the hecatomb of female victims, when Ala-ud-deen made his way through the heaps of slaughtered Rajputs into the old rock fortress of Chitor.

After the capture of Chitor, Ala-ud-deen sent his armies to the remotest parts of India. His generals collected tribute from the Rajas of the South, and plundered palaces and temples as far as the coasts of Coromandel and Malabar. The riches of the South were beyond all telling. The palaces were built of wood, and thatched with leaves and bamboos; but the treasuries were overflowing with gold, silver, and precious stones. The Rajas were black barbarians, wearing nothing but a cloth about their loins; but they were loaded with bracelets and anklets of gold and jewels, and wore necklaces of rubies, diamonds, emeralds and pearls. Every Raja was attended by Brahmans, and had a multitude of wives and concubines. The temples were built of brick or stone, and covered with plates and tiles of gold. The idols were made of gold and silver; they were decked with jewels like the Rajas, and were served in like manner by Brahmans and dancing girls.

All this while the Sultan was in constant fear of rebellion. Tidings of his death, whether true or false, might drive an army to revolt; whilst the destruction of an army might lead to an outbreak at Delhi. Accordingly, every army was connected with Delhi by a line of posting-stations, with relays of horses and runners. Every day news of every army was carried to Delhi, and news of Delhi was carried to every army.

Ala-ud-deen had married a Rajput queen, and from that time he ceased to be a good Muhammadan. He punished drunkards as sinners against Islam, but he cared nothing for the Koran if it opposed his will. The lawyers and divines, —the Cazis and Muftis,—dared not thwart him, lest they should arouse his anger; they told him that he was breaking the law of the Koran, but that his acts might possibly be politic and wise.[1]

---

[1] The Cazis were judges, and decided law cases; the Muftis were officers appointed to enforce the observance of religious duties. But law and religion are so closely associated in the ordinances of the Koran that lawyers are often divines, whilst divines are often lawyers. The collective body of lawyers and divines at the capital, including Cazis and Muftis, is known as the Ulama, and often exercises a strong check upon the Sultan. It will be seen, however, that Ala-ud-deen defied the Ulama.

Ala-ud-deen died in 1316—two years after the battle of Bannockburn. After his death there was an insurrection of Hindus at Delhi, and the rebels set up idols in the mosques, and seated themselves upon Korans. For five months the city was at the mercy of the Hindus. At last the Turkish governor of the Punjab, named Tughlak, captured the city, and stamped out the rebellion with great slaughter. He was known as the saviour of India. He ascended the throne of Hindustan, and was the first Sultan of the Tughlak dynasty.

The Tughlak Sultans would not reign at Delhi; they held their court at Tughlakabad, about an hour's ride from the ruins of old Delhi. The remains of the city may be seen to this day. The fortifications of solid masonry, the gates, bastions, and underground galleries, bear witness to the strength of the metropolis of the Tughlak Sultans. The streets and bazaars, the palaces and gardens, may still be traced, but the inhabitants have passed away, and the country round about is a desolation of desolations.

The second Sultan of the new dynasty, named Muhammad Tughlak, brought the Muhammadan power in India to the verge of ruin. He was either mad, or acted like a madman. He sent an army of a hundred thousand men over the Himalaya mountains to conquer China, and nearly every man is said to have perished. He had heard of China paper money, and he coined copper counters, and made his people use them instead of gold money; but the Hindus made copper money for themselves, and Hindustan was flooded with copper, whilst gold and silver seemed to have vanished from the land. Then followed a terrible famine, and the people of Delhi perished by thousands, as no man would sell food or grain unless it was paid for in gold or silver. The Sultan was so moved by their sufferings that he ordered the whole population of Delhi—men, women, and children—to go seven hundred miles off, across the Vindhya mountains and river Nerbudda, to the city of Deoghir, in the Mahratta country. The memory of that march lingered in the land for centuries afterwards. Thousands perished of toil and hunger by the way; or were blighted by the bleak winds of the Vindhya mountains; or were drowned in the waters of the Nerbudda river. Even when they reached Deoghir there was no provision for their maintenance, and they still continued to die; and the Sultan could only order them to depart out of the Dekhan and return once more to the city of Delhi in Hindustan.

At last the people and army broke out in rebellion, and the Muhammadan empire of Hindustan and the Punjab was dismembered into different kingdoms under different Sultans. Muhammad Tughlak died of a broken heart. Fifty years after his death Timour the Tartar invaded Hindustan, and reached the city of Delhi; then followed a blank. For a century and a quarter,—from the reign of Richard the Second to that of Henry the Eighth,—there is little to tell of India beyond dynastic changes and forgotten wars.

IV.—*Akbar, the Great Moghul.*

1556 to 1605.

THE Emperor Akbar, better known as the Great Moghul, is perhaps the most illustrious sovereign that ever reigned in Hindustan. But his genius was Oriental. He tried to behave like a Persian, whilst his instincts were those of a Tartar. When he was at his best he appeared to be a wise and gracious prince, especially towards Europeans; at other times he was hasty, passionate, and greedy of flattery. He was a contemporary of Queen Elizabeth, and not unlike her in temper. He began to reign in 1556, two years before the death of Queen Mary; and he died in 1605, the year of the Gunpowder Plot, and just two years after the accession of James the First.

Baber, the grandfather of Akbar, was a descendant of Timour the Tartar, and claimed by the female line to be a descendant of Chenghiz Khan. Like Mahmud of Ghuzni, he had been familiar with war from his boyhood; but Baber was more jovial, fond of drinking bouts, with singing, story telling, recitations, and *repartées*. When still a boy he inherited the kingdom of Khokand to the northward of the Oxus; but afterwards he lost it, and was forced to fly to Cabul, to the southward of the Oxus. In Cabul he founded another kingdom, and then invaded Hindustan. He defeated and slew an Afghan Sultan, who was reigning at Delhi, and then he routed a Rajput army under the Rana of Chitor. He died in 1530, in the latter half of the reign of Henry the Eighth.

Humayun, the son and successor of Baber, inherited the new Moghul empire in Hindustan; but he was one of those luckless princes who are born to disaster. When he succeeded to the throne at Delhi, Hindustan was harassed by Afghans, who occupied fortresses, levied blackmail, and were the terror of all the villages round about. One Afghan, named Shere Khan, held the fortress of Chunar, which overhangs the river Ganges between Allahabad and Benares. Humayun marched against him, but was flattered and cajoled into permitting Shere Khan to keep the fortress. Next he was inveigled into invading Bengal during the rains, and lost an army by fever and dysentery, and was eventually compelled to fly towards the Punjab, and leave Hindustan and Bengal in possession of the Afghan.

During this flight Humayun fell in love with a Persian girl, and persisted in marrying her in spite of the remonstrances of his friends and followers. The honeymoon was spent in the burning desert of Sinde, where Mahmud of Ghuzni lost his army; and there, amidst horrible privations and sufferings, his young wife gave birth to Akbar. Eventually Humayun reached Cabul, where he left his wife and son in charge of a brother, and made his way to the court of Persia to seek for help from the Shah.

After an exile of fifteen years Humayun returned to Hindustan with an army, and recovered possession of his throne. But fortune was still against him. One evening he ascended the stairs outside the palace at Delhi in order to say his prayers on the roof, when his foot slipped, and he fell lifeless on the pavement. He was buried in the grand mausoleum between Delhi and the Kootub tower, which may be seen to this day, standing in a large quadrangle of terraces, fountains, and gardens, surrounded by cloisters for the accommodation of holy men, who read the Koran over his remains.

Akbar was a boy of fourteen at the time of this disaster. He ascended the throne at Delhi under the guardianship of a minister named Bairam. At this period he received very little schooling, excepting in fighting and field sports. He could not read or write, for, like Baber and Mahmud, his childhood had been spent in war.

Akbar, however, was by no means wanting in craft. For some years he played the part of a mild and modest youth, who left everything to his minister. By so doing he probably saved his life, for Bairam never left him, but took him on every campaign, and was scheming to usurp the throne. When, however, Akbar was eighteen years of age, he pretended that his mother was sick, and left the camp in order to visit her. Then he suddenly proclaimed to the army that he had assumed the sovereignty, and that no one's orders were to be obeyed but his own.

Bairam was taken aback by this proclamation. The reins of power had slipped from his hands into those of Akbar. He tried hard to keep the post of minister by working on the feelings of the young Padishah;[1] but Akbar was immovable. At last Bairam prepared to go on a pilgrimage to Mecca, but was stabbed to death by an Afghan on the eve of embarkation.

The wars of Akbar have lost their interest in the present day, but they ended in the establishment of a Moghul empire which endured for two centuries, and was greater

[1] The term Padishah was the Moghul equivalent for Emperor.

than that of the first Napoleon. It extended over the whole of Hindustan, and included the Punjab and Cabul at one end and Bengal at the other. His rapid marches were the wonder of the age. He moved his troops on the backs of dromedaries with such swiftness that when his enemies thought that he was at the other end of Hindustan, they would be thrown into a panic by the thunder of his kettle drums. He was tall, handsome, and strong; very long in the arms, with a nut brown complexion. He would spring on the back of an elephant who had killed his keeper, and compel it to do his bidding; whilst his skill as a marksman was known to all India.

One war created a great change in Akbar. At the age of twenty-six he conquered the princes of Rajputana. The Rana of Chitor gave him some trouble. The women performed the same rite of self-sacrifice which had been carried out when the place was besieged by Ala-ud-deen. The Rana escaped to the Aravulli mountains and founded the city of Oodeypore. But Akbar destroyed the city of Chitor, and never allowed the Rana to return. All the other Rajas made their submission to Akbar, and were each required to give him a daughter in marriage.

These Rajput marriages were a matter of policy. The Rajas of the Rajput league had hitherto given their daughters in marriage to the Rana of Chitor, as the living representative of Rama. Moreover, they had, one and all, aspired to wed a daughter of the Rana, in order to ennoble their respective families. But Akbar was resolved to be the Suzerain of the Rajputs in the room of the Rana. Accordingly he took the daughters of the Rajas in marriage; and in after times a custom grew up of giving the daughters of the Padishah by his Rajput brides in marriage to the Rajas.

The number of Akbar's wives far exceeded the four which were permitted by the Koran; but Muhammadan lawyers and divines were looking out for promotion as magistrates and judges, and no one cared to raise an outcry against such breaches of the law on the part of the Padishah. The fact that the new wives were Hindus, and consequently worshippers of idols, would have been far more scandalous in the eyes of the orthodox; but the mischief was averted by a show of conversion. Every Rajput bride, before she entered the zenana of the Padishah, was required to utter the formula of Islam—"There is but one God and Muhammad is his Prophet." But this soon proved to be an empty form. Akbar grew very fond of his Rajput brides, and permitted them to engage Brahmans, and worship idols and offer sacrifice after their own fashion; and at last they turned his heart after strange gods, and he, too, began to burn incense and offer sacrifices like Solomon of old.

Up to this period Akbar had been a Muhammadan. He built a mosque at Ajmere, the heart of Rajputana, as a silent invitation to all the surrounding Rajas to embrace the religion of the Koran. On one occasion, when his eldest son Jehanghir was born, he walked on foot from Agra to Ajmere, a distance of two hundred miles, to offer prayers and thanksgivings at the shrine of a Muhammadan saint in accordance with some vow. But neither Akbar, nor his father Humayun, nor his grandfather Baber, were strict Muhammadans. They indulged in wine. They practised divination with burnt mutton bones. They performed mystic rites belonging to the old Sabæan worship of the sun, moon and planets, which had flourished since the days of Job and Abraham. They were inclined to be liberal and tolerant, like their famous ancestor Chenghiz Khan, the conqueror of Asia, who respected every religion provided that it taught the worship of one God.

Meanwhile there was a strange movement going on amongst Muhammadans generally, which corresponded in some respects to the Reformation in Europe. There was a growing disgust amongst earnest believers at the worldliness of orthodox lawyers and divines. Fervent preachers denounced the ungodliness of the age, and ascribed it to the pharasaic pride, the vain learning, and the greediness for promotion to office, which prevailed amongst the holy men who professed to teach and expound the religion of the Koran; whilst all classes, high and low, Hindus as well as Muhammadans, were constantly complaining of the insatiable thirst for presents and bribes which prevailed amongst magistrates, judges, and all officers concerned in the administration of the law.

To add to the excitement, large numbers of Muhammadans believed that a Millenium was approaching. A thousand years had nearly passed away since the flight of Muhammad from Mecca to Medina; and a new prophet was expected to appear, in the shape of the Imam Mahdi, the "Lord of the period," who was to convert the world and usher in a new era. The coming of this Millenium was to be heralded by the decay of Islam; and consequently every lamentation on the wickedness of the times was a sign that the Millenium was at hand.

Amidst this turmoil the whole machinery of Muhammadan fanaticism was put in motion. Zealous believers abandoned their daily occupations and formed themselves into brotherhoods, holding property in common or living upon alms. They met every day to rant and pray, and sought to rouse sinners to repentance and prepare the world for the coming of Mahdi. False Mahdis began to appear in all directions, followed by crowds of enthusiasts, who often created dangerous tumults; whilst Cazis and Muftis were only too glad of an opportunity to punish and persecute the zealots, who were not only schismatics and heretics, but were holding up orthodox lawyers and divines to the hatred and contempt of the masses.

About this time Akbar became acquainted with a scholar named Abul Fazel. This extraordinary man was a Muhammadan Sufi of the advanced type, who had a special liking for religious speculation. He had studied the religions of the Brahmans, the Buddhists, and the Parsi fire worshippers, until he had mixed up the doctrine of the transmigrations of souls, and the pantheistic idea of the Sun as the soul of the universe, with the religion of the Koran. He had a special spite against the lawyers and divines of the Ulama, because in years gone by they had persecuted his father, and driven the family into exile. At the same time he was burning with ambition, and bent upon making Akbar the stepping stone to his own advancement.

Akbar had already become half a heathen in the hands of his Rajput wives. He was ignorant of books and sciences, but was fond of listening to readings in history, and was especially desirous of learning something of the principal religions of the world. At the same time he was very susceptible of flattery and anxious to be thought learned.

Accordingly Abul Fazel fooled the Padishah to the top of his bent. He organised evening assemblies at the palace, where the lawyers and divines of the Ulama were invited to discuss questions of law and religion in the presence of Akbar, so as to enable the Padishah to decide who was right and who was wrong. He then artfully drew the Ulama into hot controversies, in which they excited the contempt of

Akbar by their abuse of one another, or roused his wrath by expressing their doubts of the legality of his marriages, or otherwise tried to set their own authority as the exponents of law and religion above that of Akbar, who aspired to be the sovereign ruler in things spiritual as well as in things temporal.

By this time Abul Fazel had become the minister of Akbar, and was ever at his side as prompter, flatterer, and confidential adviser. Akbar lost his temper with the Ulama, and eventually determined, like Henry the Eighth, to throw off the ecclesiastical authority, and to become himself the head of the Muhammadan church, the Pope or Caliph of Islam.

Meanwhile, however, Akbar was brought under higher and brighter influences, and was almost persuaded to declare himself a Christian. He married a Christian wife, known as Miriam or Mary; and he built a palace for her at Futtehpore, which is to be seen to this day, and was characterised by refinements which in those days were only known to Europeans. He entertained Christian Fathers from the Portuguese settlement at Goa. He permitted them to build a Catholic chapel and set up an altar within the precincts of his palace at Futtehpore; to carry the Cross in procession through the streets, and to preach Christianity wherever they pleased.

The circumstances which led to the marriage of Akbar and Miriam, and the events of their married life, are unknown to history. Possibly Miriam was a Portuguese maiden, educated at Goa, who had become the wife of Akbar in the hope of converting him to the Christian faith, and bringing the Moghul empire in India under the rule of the Catholic religion. Possibly she may have been an instrument in the hands of the Christian Fathers from Goa, and a fellow labourer in the work of conversion. Something, however, of

Miriam and her surroundings may be gathered from a glance at the state of society in Goa, and the nature and extent of the labours of the Catholic Fathers in the court of Akbar.

The little island of Goa lies off the western coast of India, about half way between Guzerat and Cape Comorin, and was in those days very far removed from the empire of the Great Moghul. It was only twelve miles long and six broad, and was separated from the main land by an arm of the sea, in which ships lay at anchor. Up to the fifteenth century it was a nest of pirates, who scoured the Indian seas from Malabar to the Mozambique; but one of the Muhammadan Sultans of the Dekhan drove the pirates out of the island, and replaced them by Muhammadan traders. In the early years of the sixteenth century, the Portuguese, under Albuquerque, took the island by storm, expelled the Muhammadans, raised forts and fortifications, and founded the city of Goa, which was destined to become the capital of the Portuguese empire in the East, and the Venice of the Oriental world.

Goa has been immortalised by the poetry of Camoens and the missionary labours of Francis Xavier. The early Portuguese adventurers were heroes burning with the spirit of Crusaders, who fought for the honour of Portugal and the triumph of the Cross. But Goa also became an emporium of trade, which extended over the coasts of India and Burma, and far away through the Straits of Malacca to China and Japan. Portuguese East Indiamen of large burden sailed every year from Lisbon to Goa laden with soldiers of fortune, priests, and European wares. Every year the same ships returned to Lisbon with cargoes of silks, spices, jewels, pepper, pearls, and porcelain, which had been brought in smaller craft from every quarter of the Indian seas. In the course of two or three generations Goa overflowed with the riches of Europe and the East. Strangers gazed with wonder and admiration at the convents, churches, and colleges, swarming with priests; the stately palace of the Viceroy, crowded with officials; and the private mansions of the wealthy, with gardens and orchards behind them surrounded by lofty walls.

The Portuguese of Goa were remarkable for the haughtiness of the men, and the Oriental seclusion of the women. Every man, excepting the priests, wore a sword and claimed to be a soldier, whilst the meanest soldier from Portugal claimed to be a gentleman. Every one greeted a fellow countryman with the utmost courtesy, and removed his hat with the gravest politeness; and if any man, from the Viceroy downwards, failed to return these greetings, the neglect would be regarded as an insult, and revenged sooner or later by maiming or murder. Every gentleman was attended by numerous slaves; and even the common soldier was followed by a slave boy to hold an umbrella over his head, and carry his cloak and rapier, or the cushion on which he knelt at mass. Every Portuguese man in Goa, from the Viceroy down to the common soldier, was engaged in trade or money changing; and every morning, except Sundays and Saints days, was spent in a broad street, known as the Exchange, where every kind of commodity was sold at public outcry, and male and female slaves from all parts of Asia and Africa were offered for sale.

The Portuguese of Goa were very jealous of their wives and daughters, and consequently the ladies were almost as secluded from the society of the opposite sex as if they had been shut up in a zenana. They dawdled away their hours in the inner rooms and gardens, making confections, eating sweetmeats, playing on the lute, or listening to the gossip of their slave girls. They had no literature but religion; no amusement but love stories and marriages; and no occupation, beyond attendance at the church and confessional, or gazing from the balconies on festival days and holidays at the religious shows and processions which were the special amusement of the people of Goa.

The wonders of Goa, especially the big ships, the huge cannon, and the strong forts and walls of the Portuguese, must often have reached the ears of Akbar. He had taken several Europeans into his service as gunners and artisans, and he was extremely fond of talking to them about the marvels of Western civilisation, with that mixture of curiosity and pride which has always characterised enlightened barbarian princes of similar stamp. He admired the physical strength of Europeans, their energy and self reliance, and innate love of honesty, truthfulness, and manly courage; and he could not understand how such men could be tempted to indulge in intoxicating drinks, until he arrived at the amusing conclusion they could not live without wine any more than fishes would live without water. It is thus easy to imagine that the fair form of some Christian girl, the daughter it may be of some European in his own employ, may have attracted his admiration, and inclined him to make her his wife.

It is not, however, so easy to conjecture the thoughts and feelings that were stirring in the heart of Miriam. She may possibly have learned to admire and love Akbar; for he certainly was handsome and imposing; and if she had been educated amidst such surroundings as those of Goa, she could scarcely have objected to a married life of Oriental seclusion. Again, there was every outward sign of pomp and magnificence which could dazzle the imagination of a girl. Akbar was the puissant sovereign of Hindustan and the Punjab, whilst his exploits as a warrior and conqueror were noised abroad throughout Europe and Asia. Domestic circumstances may also have reconciled Miriam to such a marriage. She may have lost her mother, and been troubled by a native stepmother; whilst her father may have hoped to profit by the marriage of his daughter to his imperial master, and even supposed that by so doing he was promoting her future happiness and welfare.

But Akbar was to all appearance a Muhammadan, and was already married to Muhammadan and Rajput wives; and, under such circumstances, few European girls of Christian education, to say nothing of feminine instinct or refinement, would willingly have wedded the greatest prince that ever reigned. But there was one ambitious vision which would have overpowered even these considerations. The Portuguese of Goa were eager for the conversion of the so-called infidels and heathens to the Catholic faith; and if the imagination of an enthusiastic girl was fired by the same hopes and aspirations, no sacrifice would have been too great for such a glorious triumph. It was easier for Miriam to become the wife of Akbar than for Esther to become the wife of Ahasuerus; whilst the conversion of the Great Moghul, and extension of the Catholic faith over the Moghul empire, would raise her to the highest rank of saints and heroines throughout the whole world of Christendom.

Such may have been the dream of Miriam, and something of this kind may be gathered from the real experiences which befel Akbar. The Padishah sent a letter to the Viceroy of Goa, requesting that learned Fathers might be sent to his court at Futtehpore to instruct him and his courtiers in the truths of Christianity; and may we not believe that the

Christian wife, the mysterious Miriam, played a part in this letter? The receipt of the epistle threw the religious world at Goa into the wildest excitement. Every priest in the island prayed humbly and fervently to God and the Virgin, that he might be chosen as the humble instrument for converting and baptising the Great Moghul.

Three Fathers were at last dispatched on the toilsome journey. They were animated by a faith which rendered them superior to pain or privation, and they confidently looked forward to another Pentecost in Hindustan. Akbar awaited their arrival with his customary impatience, and received them with every mark of favour. They delivered their presents from the Viceroy of Goa with fear and trembling, for they knew not how a Muhammadan sovereign would receive things that were sacred in Christian eyes. They handed up a Polyglot Bible in four languages, and to their joy and wonder the Great Moghul placed the holy book upon his head as a sign of respect and reverence. Next they produced images of Christ and the Virgin Mary, which Muhammadans would have regarded as idols; but Akbar kissed the images with devotion, as a sign of worship and adoration. Would Akbar have done these things had he not been previously instructed by Miriam?

For a long time the Christian Fathers imagined that they had converted the Great Moghul. After the first audience, Akbar kept them the whole night discussing the doctrines of Christianity, and the lives and teachings of Christ and his Apostles. He gave them lodgings within the precincts of his palace. He not only permitted the Fathers to build a chapel and an altar, but he himself entered the chapel, and fell prostrate upon the ground before the image of Jesus. To crown all, he ordered his minister, Abul Fazel, to prepare with all speed a translation of the Gospels into the Persian tongue.

There can be little doubt that for a while Akbar was a Christian at heart. A Muhammadan historian who wrote his life, pronounces pious curses on the Christian Fathers, and complains that they seduced Akbar into becoming a Christian. But Akbar was never baptized. Palace influences were too strong. His mother, the Persian lady who won the heart of Humayun, was a staunch believer in the Prophet until the end of her days. All his wives, excepting Miriam, must have been still more hotly opposed to his becoming a Christian, for they dreaded being put away in favour of one only. For a long time, however, Christianity was a kind of fashion. A younger son of Akbar was sent to the Fathers to be educated in the Christian religion and European sciences. Even the minister Abul Fazel avowed himself a believer in Christianity, but in reality he was a deist who professed to seek after God in every temple, and was equally ready to worship him in a Christian church, a Muhummadan mosque, or a Hindu pagoda.

But a day arrived when Akbar began to diverge from Christianity. The Fathers saw that his conversion was hopeless. The influence of Miriam passed away, and possibly she herself had passed away into another world; for Akbar began to indulge in vagaries which could not have been possible so long as a Christian wife was guiding his thoughts and ways, and was only possible under the combined seductions of Muhummadan and Rajput queens, and the fulsome flattery of an unscrupulous minister like Abul Fazel.

In the first instance, Akbar was induced to believe that he was himself the "Lord of the period," the prophet or Imam, who was to usher in the Millenium, and teach a new Islam. This was the work of Abul Fazel and the Muhammadan queens, and would have made him equal to the Prophet himself. Next he was puffed up by the idea that he was an incarnation of Vishnu or the Sun, like Rama and Krishna, and as such was the sovereign ruler of Hindustan, in the room of the Rana of Chitor. This was the work of Abul Fazel and the Rajput queens, and would have made him equal to the deity. The last idea prevailed. Akbar appeared every morning at a certain window and publicly worshipped the Sun; and the people below worshipped Akbar as a "ray of the Sun's rays."

A profound craft was at work under these proceedings. Like the Roman Cæsars, Akbar was anxious to establish a divine right to the throne of Hindustan by playing the part of God, and thus uniting in himself the functions of deity and sovereignty.

Akbar died in 1605, at the age of sixty-three. He was buried in the garden of Secunder, about four miles from Agra, where his tomb may be seen to this day. In spite of the religious vagaries of his latter years, crosses were set up around the spot; but whether in memory of his wife Miriam, or as a relic of the teachings of the Christian Fathers, is a mystery for all time.

V.—*Reign of Jehanghir: Roe's Mission to India.*

1605 to 1627.

IN 1615, just ten years after the death of Akbar, Sir Thomas Roe was sent by James the First, King of England, as Lord Ambassador to the Great Moghul. The East India Company had been formed in London in 1599. Sixteen years had passed away, and several English ships had been sent to India, whilst a factory, comprising a warehouse and offices, was established at Surat; a port on the western coast of India, immediately opposite the peninsula of Guzerat, and near the mouth of the river Tapti. Surat belonged to the Great Moghul, and was very convenient for trade. One road, available for waggons, ran to Delhi and Agra; another road ran to the city of Ajmere in the heart of Rajputana. Surat was a capital situation for a depôt where English goods, such as sword blades, knives, and broad cloth, might be sold to the native merchants, and cargoes of Indian goods, such as silk and cotton, pearls, spices, pepper, and precious stones, might be provided for shipment to England.

But the English merchants could not get on at Surat. The Moghul officials were insolent and grasping. They not only levied Custom duties on all goods landed or shipped at Surat, but the Nawab, or governor of the place, took what he pleased for his own use, and paid for it or not as he thought proper. Heavy transit duties were also exacted on the different roads, and fines were levied without just cause. Moreover, the usages of the Moghuls were very different from those of civilised countries. The Padishah inherited the property of all his subjects, and took possession of all ships and cargoes that were wrecked upon his coast. Accordingly, if an Englishman died in Hindustan, his effects were seized in the name of the Padishah, and if a ship was wrecked it was confiscated in like manner. Many petitions had been sent to the Padishah, but no redress had been obtained; and at last the East India Company sent a Lord Ambassador in the name of the King of England, in the hope that the Great Moghul would pay some attention to the complaints if sent direct from a fellow sovereign.

Sir Thomas Roe was born in Essex in 1568, being the tenth year of the reign of Queen Elizabeth. He was educated at Oxford and the Inns of Court; and was familiar with courts as well as colleges; with government and diplomacy as well as with history and law. In a word, he was a man of the Elizabethan era; fond of politics, pictures, and plays; and intimate alike with the Archbishop of Canterbury and the Chairman of the East India Company.

Sir Thomas Roe sailed from the Downs in February, 1615, and reached Surat the following September. He landed in great state, as befitted a Lord Ambassador. The English ships in the river were decked out with flags and streamers. A hundred sailors were sent to form a guard of honour, and a salute of forty-eight guns was fired in honour of Roe, who was forty-eight years of age. But the Moghul officials at the Custom House were worrying to the last degree, and wanted to search the whole party. Roe insisted on his right of exemption as a foreign ambassador, but he could not prevent them from opening all his boxes, including those which contained the English presents for the Great Moghul. He was, however, provided with a house, and began to make preparations for a journey to the Moghul court, which at this time was at Ajmere, in the heart of Rajputana, about six hundred miles to the north-east of Surat.

But Roe was doomed to trouble. On the day of his landing his English cook got drunk in the shop of an Armenian wine seller, and in this condition met the brother of the Nawab of Surat on horseback, and drew his sword and called out, "Come on, thou heathen dog!" The Muhammadan grandee did not understand English, and asked the man what he was saying. The cook made a slash at him, but was immediately arrested and carried off to prison. Roe wrote a note to the grandee, saying that he would leave the cook to be punished in any way that might be thought proper. The grandee, however, sent the man home without doing him the slightest injury.

Roe was delayed more than a month at Surat. The Moghul officials were to furnish carts for carrying the presents to Ajmere; but they procrastinated from day to day until Roe was getting exasperated. At last carriage was provided, but only as far as Burhanpore, about 250 miles to the east of Surat. But Burhanpore was the head-quarters of the Moghul army of the Dekhan, and Roe was told that he could procure fresh carriage from the general in command.

Roe was fifteen days on the journey to Burhanpore, and was disgusted with the desolate state of the country. The towns and villages were built of mud; there was not a house fit for an Englishman to lodge in, and he and his party were compelled to sleep at night in their tents. At one place a body of horsemen and musketeers were sent to guard the ambassador and his presents, because of the Rajput brigands in the neighbouring mountains—the subjects of the Rana of Chitor, who was still unconquered by the Moghul. At Burhanpore a Moghul officer, known as the Kotwal, came out to meet him with sixteen horsemen carrying streamers, and conducted him to a house built of stone with an imposing front, but with only four small rooms as hot as ovens, so that the party slept in tents as before.

The Great Moghul at this period was Jehanghir, the eldest son of Akbar. Before his accession to the throne he was known as Selim; and the loves of Selim and Nur Mahal on the lake of Cashmere are duly celebrated in Moore's poem of "Lalla Rookh." But Moore has toned down the character of Jehanghir. He tells us that the lovers became estranged by "a something light as air, a look, a word unkind or wrongly taken;" and tells a pretty story of how they became reconciled at the Feast of Roses.

History tells a different story. Jehanghir was a jovial Moghul, fond of strong drink and the flesh of the wild boar. He had several wives and four sons, who will appear hereafter; but he fell in love with a Persian girl named Nur Mahal; and Akbar stopped all scandal by sending the girl to Bengal, where she was married to somebody else. When Akbar was dead, his son Jehanghir succeeded to the throne and sent for Nur Mahal. The Moghul governor of Bengal hinted to the husband of Nur Mahal that his wife was wanted, and was promptly stabbed to death for his inconsiderate suggestion. The husband, however, was cut to pieces by the guards, and Nur Mahal was sent to Agra, but declined to speak to Jehanghir; and this was the estrangement so delicately mentioned by Thomas Moore.

Ambition, however, got the mastery of the lady's wrath. Nur Mahal forgot her deceased husband, and became the principal queen of Jehanghir, whilst her brother, Asof Khan, was appointed prime minister. Henceforth she was known by the fancy name of Nur Mahal, or the "Light of the Harem," and afterwards as Nur Jehan, or the "Light of the World." She will appear hereafter as a virago, the firebrand of the palace; and in his calmer moments Jehanghir had reason to regret the reconciliation at the Feast of Roses; although it must be said to her credit that she did her best to repress his indulgences in strong drink, to which he had always been prone.

Jehanghir had left Agra and gone south as far as Ajmere, because he was getting anxious about the Moghul army of the Dekhan. This army had been originally sent to Burhanpore by Akbar, who had planned the conquest of the Muhammadan Sultans of the Dekhan. Jehanghir had placed it under the nominal command of his second son Parwiz, and had appointed an experienced general, known as the Khan Khanan, to carry on operations. But the army was doing nothing. The Khan Khanan was being bribed by the Sultans of the Dekhan, who sent him presents of gold and jewels so long as he kept the army quiet at Burhanpore.

When Roe reached Burhanpore the Kotwal told him that Parwiz was curious to see him. Accordingly Roe went to the palace of the prince at the early morning, accompanied by the Kotwal; for he was anxious to learn something of Moghul etiquette, and also to establish an English factory at Burhanpore for the sale of sword blades and scarlet cloth to the Moghul army. A body of horsemen was drawn up outside the gateway waiting for the prince to come out; but Roe passed through the gateway and entered the court-yard of the palace. There he saw Parwiz sitting with great pomp in a gallery overlooking the court-yard; whilst his grandees stood beneath him on a raised platform with their hands joined in the attitude of supplication. The officers in waiting wanted Roe to prostrate himself, but he declined doing so, on the score of being an ambassador. He was allowed to ascend the three steps leading to the platform, and to make his way through the grandees to the gallery, and then he made his bow; but he was refused admittance to the gallery. The prince condescended to return his bow, and to tell him that he was welcome; but he added that neither the Shah of Persia nor the Grand Turk would have been permitted to enter the gallery.

All this, however, was mere Moghul arrogance and bombast, and otherwise Parwiz was very gracious to Roe. He ordered carriage to be supplied for the journey to Ajmere, and granted permission for the establishment of a factory at Burhanpore. He received some presents which Roe laid before him with smiling delight, and was so softened at the sight of a case of cordials that he told Roe to wait a few minutes, and they would have a private talk together in another place. Parwiz then left the gallery, and Roe waited in vain upon the platform. At last Roe was told that he might take his leave and see the prince some other day. It turned out that in the interval Parwiz had helped himself so freely to the cordials that he was too drunk to see anybody.

That same night Roe was struck down with fever. Nine days afterwards he began his journey to Ajmere, but was still very ill. He stopped, however, at Mandu to visit the ruins, which filled him with wonder and admiration.

Mandu was a city and fortress, which had been built by the old Afghan Sultans of Malwa on the summit of a table mountain of the Vindhya range. It was nearly thirty miles in circumference, and was cut off from the surrounding country by a deep ravine, which, during the rainy season, was filled with water. The only approach to the city was a causeway stretching across the bottom of the ravine, and a narrow path winding up the mural face of the rock. Mandu had been the capital of an Afghan empire in days of yore, and the amours of the Sultans, and their wars with the Rajputs, are to this day lingering in country ballads and traditions. The Afghan empire had been overthrown by Akbar fifty years before Roe's visit, and the city and fortress had been dismantled. But the remains of palaces, colleges, mosques, and tombs, mostly of white marble from the banks of the Nerbudda, are still standing as relics of the bygone age of Afghan dominion.

Twelve days after leaving Mandu, Roe and his party reached Chitor—the once famous capital of the Ranas. The city was a magnificent ruin. There were a hundred Hindu temples of carved stone, with many towers, domes, and pillars, as well as innumerable houses; but there was not a single inhabitant. The ruins are to be seen to this day, and are striking specimens of ancient Hindu architecture, without any Muhammadan intermixture, and resemble in some respects the old Egyptian style.

The Rana, named Oodey Singh, had fled from Akbar to the Aravulli mountains and founded the modern city of Oodeypore, or "the city of Oodey"; but he was now dead, and his son Pertab Singh inherited his title of Rana, and to this day Pertab Singh is the hero of the house of Oodeypore. When the Moghul army took the field against him, Pertab Singh was flying from rock to rock on the Aravulli mountains; when the army retired he descended into the plains, and carried death and desolation far and wide, whilst plundering every caravan that attempted to pass between Surat and Agra. His privations were severe, for his children were often crying for food, but he would not submit to the Moghul, or give him a daughter in marriage, and he never forgot Chitor. He vowed that neither himself, nor his children after him, would twist their beards, or sleep in a bed, or eat from gold or silver until they returned to Chitor. The memory of this vow is preserved to this day, for his descendants have never returned to Chitor. The Rana of Oodeypore never twists his beard; he sleeps on a bed, but there is a litter of straw below; and he eats from gold and silver, but leaves are always placed beneath the dishes.

At Chitor Roe met with a wandering Englishman named Tom Coryat, who had boasted to his boon companions in a London tavern that he would go to Hindustan, see the Great Moghul and ride upon an elephant, an animal which in those days had never been seen in Europe since the days when they were paraded in the circus at Rome. Coryat kept his word. He made his way to Jerusalem, and then walked on foot through Turkey in Asia, Persia and Candahar to the cities of Lahore, Delhi and Agra, where he saw the Emperor Jehanghir, and succeeded in riding on an elephant. According to his own account his travelling expenses did not exceed a penny a day; but he seems to have been regarded as a madman, and Muhammadans have a respect for such unfortunate individuals, and give them food as alms. On one occasion, when a holy man cried out "There is but one God and Muhammad is his prophet," Coryat cried out in the same language, "There is but one God, and Jesus Christ is His Son, and Muhammad is an impostor." Such a proceeding in any other Muhammadan country would have been fatal to the speaker; but Coryat was safe under the tolerant rule of the Moghul, especially as he was thought to be a madman. At Mandu, Coryat took leave of the Ambassador, and went on to Surat, where he died from indulging too freely in sack, which was given to him by the English factors.

Roe reached Ajmere at Christmas, but so ill that he was obliged to keep to his bed. In a few days, however, he was much better, in consequence, probably, of the cold season which was now at its height; and on the 10th of January, 1616, he had his first audience with Jehanghir.

The daily life of the Great Moghul was spent in a regular routine, and the palaces at Agra and Ajmere were arranged to correspond with it. The palace enclosure was a large area surrounded on all sides with high walls and fortifications. The lofty gateway in front opened inside upon a court, and at the further end of this court was the hall of audience, or Durbar, which was open to the public. Hard by was a smaller chamber, known as the Ghusal Khana, where the Moghul held evening assemblies; but none were admitted to these assemblies unless they had been specially invited.[1]

The whole of the palace area, beyond the Durbar and Ghusal Khana, was set apart for the Padishah and his wives and their attendants; and no one else, excepting women or eunuchs, or occasionally a prince of the blood, was permitted to enter these sacred precincts. At the back of the palace were gardens and fountains; and at the further end of the gardens was a little pavilion, where the Padishah slept, and a window to this pavilion looked out upon the surrounding country. This window was known as the Jharokha; and

[1] The term Ghusal Khana signifies literally the "bathroom," and a large golden bath, studded with precious stones, was kept there for the use of the Padishah.

here it was that the Emperor Akbar appeared every morning and worshipped the sun, whilst he himself was worshipped by the crowd below. The guards of the palace were composed of Tartar or Calmuk women, armed like Amazons with bows and arrows, and also with swords and daggers. These women had high cheek bones, and eyes very far apart; and were always ugly, and often fierce and terrible. The captain of the Tartar guard was also a woman, and ranked with the Ameers of the empire.

When the Great Moghul awoke in the morning, he appeared at the Jharokha window, and received salaams or petitions, or administered justice, or reviewed the parade of troops and elephants. At nine or ten o'clock he retired within his palace, and took his breakfast and a siesta. At noon he appeared again at the window, and was amused with animal fights, or combats between gladiators and wrestlers, or between men and tigers. Every afternoon about three or four o'clock he appeared in the Durbar hall and took his seat in a gallery. His grandees were stationed below him on a platform three steps from the ground, and were railed off in three sections, according to their rank. At the Durbar the Padishah received strangers of distinction, and transacted business of importance, whilst every thing that was said or done was written down by one or other of the royal scribes. Outside the platform was a miscellaneous crowd of people who formed the general public.

In this Durbar hall at four o'clock in the afternoon, Sir Thomas Roe was introduced to Jehanghir. He describes the scene as representing a London theatre, at a time when a play was being acted in the presence of the King. The Great Moghul sat in state in a gallery overlooking the whole. The grandees on the platform beneath him were the actors who played their parts on the stage. The crowd of people outside the platform were the audience or commonalty who looked on.

Roe had arranged before hand that he would show the same respect to the Padishah as he would to his own sovereign, but that there was to be no prostration. He ascended the three steps to the platform, and was led through the three ranks of grandees, making a reverence at each rail, and at last found himself amongst the Ameers, Rajas, and Ministers of the highest order. Jehanghir received him with courtly condescension, referred to the King of England as his royal brother, looked curiously at the letter which Roe had brought from King James, and regarded the presents with a gracious smile. The gifts were not costly; they included a little piano of the period known as a virginal, a rich sword, an embroidered scarf, some knives, and an English coach. The coach was too large to be brought into the hall, and was left in the outer court.

Whenever an Englishman comes in contact with an Oriental prince, there is generally something ludicrous. Jehanghir was bothered with the little piano; but a musician in Roe's train played it before the Durbar, and the Great Moghul professed to be highly gratified. He could not see the coach, but he sent some officials to look at it, and describe it to him. He politely asked after Roe's health, offered to send his own physicians to attend him, and advised him to keep within his own house until he was strong. He then dismissed the English ambassador, and Roe went away charmed with his reception.

When the Durbar was over, Jehanghir ceased to be high and mighty, and became an inquisitive Moghul. He went into the outer court to look at the coach, and got inside, and was drawn about by his servants. In the evening he entertained a party of grandees according to custom; and at ten o'clock at night Roe was roused from his slumbers, and requested to send an English servant to array the Padishah in the scarf and sword. The servant was dispatched, and Jehanghir was girt with the scarf and sword in English fashion, and then strutted about and brandished his sword to his own entire satisfaction. He complained, however, of the poorness of the presents, and said that if the King of England had been a great sovereign, he would at least have sent some precious stones and pearls.

In spite of the reception Roe's mission was a failure. Jehanghir would promise anything so long as presents were forthcoming; but neither he, nor his ministers, nor his great men, were at all inclined to bind themselves by any treaty. Roe often attended the afternoon Durbar, and was frequently invited to the evening assembly; but he could not get a treaty. Jehanghir, however, was always ready for a gossip with the English ambassador. He wanted a horse from England, but was told that such a thing was impossible. An English horse could not be brought overland through Turkey and Persia, because of the wars; and if sent by sea it would certainly perish in the storms off the Cape. Jehanghir, however, suggested that if six horses were placed on board a ship, one at least would survive the passage; and that if it arrived in a lean condition, it could be easily fattened after it was landed. Accordingly Roe promised to make a note of the suggestion, and to send it home to the Directors of the East India Company. Jehanghir was also a great toper, and generally got drunk at the evening assemblies. He was consequently anxious to know what the English ambassador drank, how much, and how often. He was curious to know all about beer, and he asked if Roe could not brew a cask in India for his especial drinking.

Jehanghir's birthday was in September, and was kept in Moghul fashion. The Padishah was weighed in golden scales in the Durbar hall against a variety of good things, including gold and silver coin, all of which were afterwards given to the poor. This ceremony is a curious relic of antiquity. Hindu Rajas are sometimes weighed in like manner, and the good things in the opposite scale are given to the poor, or to the Brahmans. Strange to say, the mother of Thomas à Becket, the martyr of Canterbury, is said to have piously weighed her son in similar fashion, and distributed the good things as alms to the poor.

In the evening there was a lively entertainment in the Ghusal Khana. Although Jehanghir was notorious for his drunkenness throughout Hindustan, it was the law of the Ghusal Khana, probably instituted by Akbar, that no one was to be admitted to the evening assemblies whose breath smelt of wine; and if Jehanghir heard that any of his grandees had been drinking, he would order them to be flogged in his own presence, without any regard to rank, or previous services. On certain occasions, however, Jehanghir commanded his guests to drink, and then every one was bound to obey.

At ten o'clock on the night of the birthday, Roe was roused from his bed to attend the Padishah in the Ghusal Khana; and he was especially requested to bring with him the picture of an English lady, which Jehanghir knew that he possessed, but had never seen. This picture was associated with a sweet romance in the life of Roe. He had dearly loved the original, but the lady had been dead several years; yet, although Roe was verging on his fiftieth year, he took her picture out with him to India; and the fact was no doubt communicated to Jehanghir by some spy in the ambassador's household.

Roe was much nettled at being required to produce the picture of his lady love to the Great Moghul; but he was obliged to obey. He took the picture to the palace, together with two or three others, in the hope of distracting the Padishah's attention. He found Jehanghir sitting cross-legged on a little throne, with a table of gold before him, covered with vessels of gold studded with pearls and precious stones, whilst large flagons of different sorts of wine were standing around. The Great Moghul had ordered his grandees to drink, and they were obeying the mandate. Under such circumstances Roe's little ruse proved a failure. Jehanghir at once pitched upon the idolised portrait, and admired it with drunken enthusiasm. He insisted upon keeping it, and declared that he should prize it above the richest jewel in his palace; and Roe with a sad heart was compelled to leave the picture of his departed lady love in the possession of the Great Moghul.

By this time Jehanghir and his grandees were getting glorious, and Roe was forced to drink to the health of the Padishah, and drown his sorrows in a cup of liquor that made him sneeze, and threw the Padishah into a fit of laughter. Presently Jehanghir began to fling new rupees amongst the crowd of natives outside, and then to scatter gold and silver almonds for his grandees to scramble for. The assembly degenerated into a drunken revel, but Roe saw that Asof Khan, the minister, and two or three of the older courtiers, kept aloof from the uproar, and he wisely followed their example. At last Jehanghir dropped off into a heavy slumber, and the lights were put out by the order of Nur Mahal, and the whole party had to grope out of the Ghusal Khana, and find their way as best they could to their respective homes.

A few evenings afterwards there was another scene in the Ghusal Khana, which led to still more unpleasant consequences. An ambassador from the Shah of Persia was amongst the guests, and Jehanghir ordered every one to drink wine, but was so drunk at the time that he afterwards forgot that he had given the order; every name, however, was taken down by the court scribes and entered in a register according to custom. Next day at the afternoon Durbar some one alluded to the drinking, and Jehanghir threw himself into a rage, and asked who had given the command. No one dared to tell the truth, and Jehanghir ordered the register to be brought, and every grandee who had drank to be mercilessly flogged in his presence. These orders were carried out on the spot; the Persian ambassador got off scot free, but some of the grandees were left for dead, whilst many were carried out grievously mangled.

By this time Jehanghir was exasperated beyond all bounds at the inactivity of the army of the Dekhan. He recalled his son Parwiz and sent him to command the army in Bengal. He recalled the Khan Khanan, the real offender, but the Khan Khanan refused to come. This was a serious matter, as it was feared that the Khan Khanan would break out in rebellion. Jehanghir thought it best to make a show of reconciliation by sending a dress of honour to the Khan Khanan; but a kinswoman of the refractory general, who was living in the imperial zenana, plainly told the Padishah that the Khan Khanan would never wear the dress lest it should have been poisoned. "Twice," she said, "you have given poison to the Khan Khanan, and twice he has escaped by putting it into his bosom instead of swallowing it." Jehanghir could not deny the charge. Accordingly he sent his third son, Shah Jehan, to Burhanpore, to take the command of the army of the Dekhan, and he determined to follow with all his court as far as Mandu.

Roe did not like Shah Jehan. This prince was not a toper like his father, but he was proud, jealous and ambitious. All along he had been intriguing to supersede Parwiz and the Khan Khanan. He had married the daughter of Asof Khan, the minister, and this young lady bore a close resemblance to her aunt, Nur Mahal. She was known by the name of Taj Mahal, or the "Crown of the Harem."[1] She was exceedingly beautiful and fascinating, but vindictive to the last degree; bigoted to the Muhammadan religion and hating Christians and Rajputs. As long as she was alive, her influence over Shah Jehan was nearly as unbounded as that of Nur Mahal over his father Jehanghir, although, as in other Muhammadan households, she could not prevent him from marrying other wives.

All this while the eldest son of Jehanghir, named Khuzru, was kept in the back ground. Khuzru was supposed to be a Christian, and he so far carried his Christianity that he would only marry one wife. He had been the favourite of his grandfather Akbar, and consequently had excited the jealousy of his father Jehanghir. At the beginning of the reign he fled to the Punjab in terror for his life, and raised a rebellion; but he was brought back in silver fetters and kept in close confinement in charge of a Raja of Rajputs. His adherents, however, were punished with merciless cruelty—flayed alive, crucified, or trampled to death by

---

[1] The correct name of the daughter of Nur Mahal was Mumtaz Mahal, but she was widely known as Taj Mahal, and her tomb at Agra is still known as the Taj, or "Crown."

elephants, and Khuzru was led amongst the dying men, and forced to hear their cries and witness their agonies.

Shah Jehan was always afraid lest Jehanghir should become reconciled to Khuzru. One day when Jehanghir was drunk, he was cajoled by Nur Mahal into removing Khuzru from the charge of the Rajput, and placing him in that of Asof Khan. Every one at court expected that the prince would be murdered; but the sister of Khuzru, and other ladies in the imperial zenana, raised a terrible outcry, and threatened to kill themselves if anything happened to the prince. Nur Mahal tried to soothe them, but they refused to listen to her. Roe reported these circumstances to England, as a warning against establishing too many factories in the interior. If Khuzru obtained the throne, all would be well; but if Shah Jehan gained the day, the English in India would be in sore peril.

Roe was present at the Durbar when Shah Jehan took leave of his father at Ajmere, preparatory to his going to the Dekhan to take the command of the army. The prince was dressed in cloth of silver, embroidered with pearls and diamonds. When he had made his salaam, he drove away in a coach built on the model of the English coach which had been given to Jehanghir; and as he went along he threw handfuls of silver money amongst the people, corresponding in value to English sixpences.

The following day was fixed for the departure of Jehanghir; and Roe went to the palace at early morning, in order to get a sight of the Great Moghul at the Jharokha window. Roe ascended the platform underneath the window where the grandees were standing, and saw that the Padishah was giving and receiving presents. What he gave he let down by a string which ran upon a pulley; and what he received was pulled up in like manner by an old woman who was decked with gimcracks like one of the Hindu idols in a pagoda. Roe saw also that two of the queens were sitting on one side at a window covered with a matting of reeds, where they were making holes in the matting in order to peep at the English ambassador. They had fair complexions, and glossy black hair; and they glittered with diamonds and pearls. When Roe looked up they retired from the window, but were so merry that he thought they must be laughing at him; as no doubt they were; for the costume of an ambassador in the time of James the First must have been as ridiculous in the eyes of Oriental princesses as that of English gentlemen in the reign of Victoria.

Going into camp was always attended with great pomp and show. The tented pavilions of the Padishah and his grandees were sent on in advance, and pitched at a short distance from the city, so that the first day's march from the palace to the camp was a pageant procession. A vast crowd assembled round the palace to see the Great Moghul take his departure, followed by the ladies of the zenana, and accompanied by all the grandees at court. Jehanghir appeared in the Durbar hall in travelling bravery. His coat was of cloth of gold. His boots or buskins were embroidered with pearls. His turban was plumed with heron's feathers, and had a ruby as big as a walnut on one side, a large diamond on the other, and an emerald shaped like a heart in the centre. His sash, necklaces, and armlets were radiant with pearls, rubies and diamonds. His sword, buckler, and bow and quiver were richly mounted, and inlaid with precious stones.

Thus accoutred, Jehanghir descended the Durbar steps and entered his coach, amidst a roar of acclamations from the mob as loud as cannon. The coach was built on the model of the one from England, but it was covered with gold velvet, and the coachman was as gaudy as a play actor. Two attendants on either side carried gold maces, and whisks of white horse tails to sweep away the flies. Before him went drums, trumpets and other loud music, together with canopies, flags, standards and other imperial insignia. Behind were led horses and golden palanquins, covered with crimson velvet embroidered with pearls, with borders of rubies and emeralds, and long fringes of pearls. Nur Mahal followed in the English coach, but Roe could scarcely recognise it, as the lining had been taken away, and the coach was covered with gold velvet and decorations. The ladies of the zenana were mounted on elephants, and peeped through the golden wires of their howdahs like parroquets in gilded cages. The grandees of the court walked on foot. The procession wound up with long lines of elephants covered with costly velvets, and carrying flags of satin and silver.

Camp life was an institution with the Great Moghuls. Both Akbar and Jehanghir were nomads at heart, like their Tartar ancestors, Timour and Chenghiz Khan; and their progresses to remote provinces of the empire was one of the elements of their power. Two sets of tented pavilions were always in use by the Padishah and his grandees, one for the camp during a halt, and one in advance to await the arrival of the camp. A large army accompanied the court to overawe the Rajputs. There was also a miscellaneous following of artisans, dealers, and common people; but these people would not move out of Ajmere, and it was not until Jehanghir ordered their huts to be burnt down, that they could be induced to follow the camp.

On the first night of the march Roe was taken aback at the magnificence of the scene. The tented pavilions of the

Padishah were set up on the same plan as the imperial palaces at Ajmere and Agra. There was the courtyard leading to the Durbar hall and Ghusal Khana; and beyond these pavilions was the palace proper, including the apartments of the Padishah and his ladies, and the Jharokha window at the back. The whole was surrounded by walls and fortifications, with a lofty gateway in front. But the pavilions and fortifications were all made of canvass stretched upon canes and supported by rods with brass knobs; and all were painted outside of a bright scarlet, which was the imperial colour of the Moghuls. Round about, at a respectful distance, were the pavilions of the grandees, painted white, green, and blue; whilst shops were arranged in long streets like the bazaars at Ajmere and Agra. In a word, the Moghul camp was a tented city, and covered an area of twenty miles.

The life of Jehanghir in camp was not, however, so public as the life in the city. No one was allowed to approach within pistol-shot of the imperial quarters without special invitation. Jehanghir showed himself every morning at the Jharokha window, but no one was allowed to speak to him. He rarely held a Durbar, but spent the time in hunting and hawking. No business was transacted except at the evening assemblies in the Ghusal Khana, and by that time Jehanghir was generally too drunk to attend to anything.

Roe rode on in advance to pay a visit of ceremony to Shah Jehan, but found him somewhat distracted. The prince had just received a visit from Nur Mahal, who had given him a cloak embroidered with pearls, diamonds and rubies. Roe fancied there was some love affair between the two, but discovered afterwards that Nur Mahal wished him to marry her only daughter, who had been born before her marriage to Jehanghir. Roe also thought that he himself was being treated with disdain, and took his leave in a huff; but Shah Jehan tried to smooth him down by giving him a cloak of cloth of gold. Roe accepted the gift, but he did not relish it. He was required to wear the cloak, and it made him look like an actor on the stage playing the part of Timour the Tartar. Moreover, the porters and other servants were so pressing for money, that he parted with half as much as the cloak was worth before he could get away from the prince's quarters.

Roe's experiences of the march of the Moghul camp were far from favourable. At one place a hundred thieves were executed in the fields. At another place he fell in with a string of camels bringing the heads of three hundred rebels from Candahar. As the camp moved further south, the route lay through forests and mountains that were haunted by Rajput brigands and outlaws. Sometimes the inhabitants of a town or village would fly away to the jungles in mortal alarm at the approach of the Great Moghul; and on such occasions Jehanghir would order the place to be destroyed as a punishment. Indeed, there was often a great scarcity of provisions or water in consequence of such stampedes; and whilst the Padishah and his grandees might be well supplied, the soldiers and poor people were subjected to great privations.

Public affairs were not propitious. Jehanghir had been persuaded by Nur Mahal and Asof Khan, that the news of his advance towards the south would soon bring the Sultans of the Dekhan to submission. But the Sultans were combining against the Moghul. They packed off all their treasures to a distance, and sent a large army to the frontier, being probably in collusion with the Khan Khanan. Accordingly Shah Jehan took fright, and would not march further south than Mandu; whilst Nur Mahal urged her husband to turn the expedition into a hunting party, and go back to Agra.

Jehanghir, however, refused to go back, and said that his honour was at stake. He summoned levies from distant provinces, and sent such large reinforcements to Shah Jehan, that the prince took heart, and began his march to Burhanpore.

About this time Roe fell in with Khuzru, the captive son of Jehanghir. When the Padishah left Ajmere he took Khuzru under his protection, and it was thought that he would soon be reconciled to his eldest son. Roe says that Khuzru was a handsome man with a cheerful countenance; but his beard hung down to his waist, as a sign that he was out of favour with his imperial father. Khuzru, however, was so ignorant of public affairs, that to Roe's surprise and disgust, he had not even heard of an English ambassador.

Some months afterwards Khuzru lost all hope of becoming reconciled to his father. Shah Jehan obtained a splendid victory over the Sultans of the Dekhan, and returned in triumph to his father's camp at Mandu, and was soon in greater favour with his father than ever. In reality the victory was a sham. Shah Jehan had come to an understanding with the Khan Khanan, and had married his daughter; and the intriguing old Khan Khanan had given a hint to the Sultans, and thus secured a great show of success for his new son-in-law.

Meanwhile Roe had been much exasperated against Shah Jehan and his father. He had been expecting a number of chests from Europe, which contained presents for the Great Moghul, and a number of miscellaneous articles, curiosities and rarities, which he purposed to use as occasion required as presents to Nur Mahal and other ladies, as well as to

Asof Khan and other grandees. The chests were all locked and sealed; and Jehanghir had given his word of honour that none of them should be stopped or opened, but that all should be made over to Roe. Shah Jehan, however, had stopped the chests, in spite of the Englishmen in charge, and had secretly sent them to Mandu, where Jehanghir had opened them and taken whatever pleased his fancy. Roe went one evening to the Ghusal Khana to complain, but Jehanghir was more than half drunk, and would only talk about the laws of Moses and Muhammad, and boast of his friendship for Jews and Christians.

In one way Roe was revenged. Amongst other things, Jehanghir had opened a box of pictures, and taken out a painting of a Venus leading a Satyr by the nose. He admired the Venus, who was pretty and white complexioned, but he was sorely troubled at the horns and black complexion of the Satyr. At last he jumped at the conclusion that the picture referred to his domestic relations; that he himself was the Satyr and that Venus was Nur Mahal leading him by the nose. He must have been very angry, but he feigned to accept the picture as a present from Roe, and nothing more was heard of the painting.

Roe resided nearly three years at the court of the Moghul, but his mission was a thankless task. The Moghuls knew nothing of Europe, but were kept in awe by European ships and guns. On one occasion Roe presented Jehanghir with a map of the world on Mercator's projection, but it was returned to him afterwards, as neither Jehanghir nor his wisest Mullahs could make anything of it. At last Roe begged that he might be dismissed, with a reply to the letter which he had brought from King James. After a long discussion respecting seals and forms of address, a royal letter was composed, of which the following paragraph will serve as a specimen:—

"When your Majesty shall open this letter, let your Royal heart be as fresh as a sweet garden; let all people make reverence at your gate; let your throne be advanced higher amongst the greatest of Kings of the Prophet Jesus; let your Majesty be the greatest of all Monarchs, who may derive their counsel and wisdom from your breast as from a fountain, that the law of the Majesty of Jesus may revive and flourish under your protection. The letters of love and friendship which you sent me, and the presents (tokens of your good affection toward me) I have received by the hands of your ambassador, Sir Thomas Roe, who well deserves to be your trusted Servant; delivered to me in an acceptable and happy hour. Upon which mine eyes were so fixed, that I could not easily remove them to any other object, and have accepted them with great joy."

Jehanghir left the Dekhan, and eventually went to Lahore, and began to spend his winters at Lahore and his summers amongst the mountains of Cashmere. Outwardly he was as jovial as ever, and equally as devoted to his beloved Nur Mahal. But his first-born, Khuzru, whom he loved, was an object of jealousy and suspicion to the different members of his family; and Nur Mahal became the plague of his life during the remainder of his days.

Nur Mahal was fiercely ambitious for the advancement of her daughter. She no longer cared for her niece Taj Mahal, the wife of Shah Jehan. She had tried to persuade Shah Jehan to marry her daughter, and had been bitterly disappointed when he chose to marry the daughter of the Khan Khanan. She now wanted Khuzru to marry her daughter; and she purposed to reconcile Khuzru to his father, and secure

G 2

his succession to the throne. But Khuzru refused to take a second wife. His prospects were desperate, and even the wife whom he so dearly loved urged him to redeem the past by marrying the daughter of Nur Mahal; but he was not to be persuaded, and deliberately threw away his chance of a throne rather than sacrifice his wife to the pretensions of a rival.

Nur Mahal was exasperated beyond measure at such blind obstinacy. She was bent upon marrying her daughter to one of the sons of Jehanghir, and placing the bridegroom on the throne of Hindustan. But Khuzru would not take the lady; Parwiz was a drunkard and out of favour; and Shah Jehan had already married more wives than was becoming in a good Muhammadan. There was no prince left but the boy Shahryar, the youngest son of Jehanghir; and she accordingly betrothed her daughter to Shahryar, and sought to pave his way to the throne by the destruction of his three elder brothers.

Shah Jehan, however, was equally as ambitious and unscrupulous as Nur Mahal, and was backed by his two powerful fathers-in-law—Asof Khan, the father of Taj Mahal, and the crafty Khan Khanan. The war in the Dekhan broke out afresh, and Shah Jehan was ordered to march against the Sultans; but he refused to go unless he was allowed to take Khuzru with him. Nur Mahal furthered this scheme, for she was anxious to get rid of Khuzru at all hazards; and Jehanghir in a weak moment was induced to yield to her wishes. The unfortunate prince was conducted to Burhanpore, accompanied by his devoted wife. Suddenly it was told at Burhanpore that Jehanghir was dying at Lahore; and the tidings sealed the doom of Khuzru. He was barbarously strangled at midnight, and his broken-hearted widow charged Shah Jehan and the Khan Khanan with the crime.

An avenging Nemesis fell on the murderers like a thunderbolt. Jehanghir recovered from his sickness, and was furious at the loss of his eldest son; and he resolved that the son of Khuzru, a boy named Bulaki, should succeed him on the throne of Hindustan, to the exclusion of all his own surviving sons. Bulaki and his mother were summoned to Lahore, and treated with the respect due to their change of fortune, whilst Bulaki was publicly nominated to be the future Padishah of the Moghul Empire.

At this moment Asof Khan planned a desperate scheme for the salvation of his son-in-law. He persuaded Jehanghir to remove the imperial treasures from Agra to Lahore, and he secretly advised Shah Jehan to cut off the treasure party. Had the plot succeeded Shah Jehan would certainly have gained the throne, for the vast accumulations of gold and precious stones would have sufficed to buy over every officer and man in Jehanghir's armies. The firman of the Padishah for the delivery of the treasures was carried to Agra, but the treasurer was troubled by forebodings. He was obliged to obey orders, but his heart misgave him as he drew the precious packages out of the vaults of the fortress at Agra, and loaded them on the backs of camels to be carried to the remote city of Lahore. At this moment he heard that Shah Jehan was advancing from the Dekhan, and at once the truth flashed upon his mind. He promptly carried the gold and jewels back to the vaults, and dispatched messengers on dromedaries to Lahore to inform the Padishah of what he had done.

If Shah Jehan had not been so impetuous he would have captured the treasures on the way to Lahore; but no Oriental army in those days could have captured the fortress at Agra, except by starving out the garrison. Shah Jehan took possession of the city and committed horrible atrocities on the inhabitants, but the fortress defied his efforts, and he was soon called away from the walls by the news that Jehanghir was on his way to Agra at the head of an overwhelming army. Accordingly, he fled to Bengal, in the hope of procuring men and money for carrying on the war.

The battles and surprises that followed the flight of Shah Jehan are as bewildering as the scenes in a pantomime. He called on the commandant of the Portuguese settlement at Hughly to furnish him with cannon and soldiers, but was told that Christians could not help a son to rebel against his father, and that the Portuguese would not violate their allegiance to the Padishah of Hindustan. He swore to be revenged if ever he had the power, but meanwhile his affairs were desperate. His own father-in-law, the Khan Khanan, had nearly betrayed him to his brother Parwiz, but Shah Jehan suspected his design, and made his way to the south to find a refuge in the courts of the Sultans of the Dekhan.

All this while the Moghul empire was troubled by antagonisms between Rajputs and Muhammadans. Nur Mahal displayed a bitter spite against Rajputs, and they broke out in revolt, and on one occasion carried off Jehanghir as their prisoner. Nur Mahal recovered her husband, and restored him to power; but the story is obscured by romantic details, which were more or less invented by the poets of the court to glorify the beautiful Nur Mahal as the saviour of the devoted Jehanghir.

Suddenly startling news thrilled through the empire. Jehanghir had died near Lahore, and Bulaki, son of Khuzru, had been hailed by the army as the rightful successor to his grandfather, and was enthroned at Delhi by Asof Khan as the Padishah of Hindustan. Nur Mahal tried to set up Shahryar, but Asof Khan arrested both her and her son-in-law. He then placed his sister in close confinement, and destroyed the hopes of Shahryar by putting out his eyes with a hot iron. Meanwhile, Parwiz had died of drink, and nothing remained to ensure the peaceful reign of Bulaki but the submission of Shah Jehan.

The craft of Orientals is beyond all fathoming. Asof Khan had placed Bulaki on the throne to quiet the army, but he was still bent on winning the empire for Shah Jehan. He advised Bulaki to send a trusty grandee to the Dekhan to call upon Shah Jehan to make his submission. The grandee found Shah Jehan at Burhanpore, vomiting blood in large quantities, and evidently on the point of death, and he at once sent off a courier to report the matter to the new Padishah. Shortly afterwards he was told that Shah Jehan was dead, and requested to ask the Padishah to permit the remains to be buried in the tomb of Akbar. Bulaki joyfully consented. He was only too glad to hear of his uncle's death to raise any difficulty as regards the burial.

All this while Shah Jehan was alive and well at Burhanpore. He had filled a bason with the blood of a goat, and taken some into his mouth, in order to deceive the emissary from Bulaki. Asof Khan was weeping sham tears over the death of his son-in-law, and advising Bulaki to go to Agra and attend his uncle's funeral. An empty bier was conducted in sad procession to Agra, accompanied by Shah Jehan and a large army. Bulaki appeared with a small escort, but was thunderstruck at seeing the plains covered with horsemen, and at once suspected treachery, and galloped off to Lahore. He was only just in time. He heard the noise of the trumpets and kettle-drums proclaiming the accession of Shah Jehan as Padishah of Hindustan; and presently a roar of acclamations announced that Shah Jehan had entered the fortress of Agra, and ascended the throne of the Great Moghul.

The fate of Bulaki is a mystery to this day. It was said by the Muhammadan historians of the time that he was murdered at Lahore, together with Shahryar and a host of other princes of the house of Akbar. Ten years afterwards some ambassadors, who had been sent to the Shah of Persia by the Duke of Holstein, met an exiled prince in Persia who was called Bulaki. At the same time ambassadors from Shah Jehan were requesting the Shah of Persia to deliver up the exile, which the Shah refused to do. Whether the man in question was Bulaki or an impostor is a problem which will perhaps never be solved.

VI.—*Reign of Shah Jehan: Fratricidal Wars for the Throne.*

1628 to 1658.

SHAH JEHAN began to reign in 1628, three years after the accession of Charles the First. As Roe had foreseen, he was bitterly disposed towards Christians. He was bent on revenging the refusal of the Portuguese of Hughly to help him with guns and soldiers. His wife Taj Mahal was still more exasperated against them, for two of her daughters had become Christians, and found a refuge amongst the Portuguese, and possibly married Christian husbands. Moreover complaints were sent up from Bengal that the Portuguese kidnapped the people of the country, and carried them to Goa, where they were converted and baptised. Accordingly Taj Mahal vowed that Hughly should be destroyed, and that every Portuguese prisoner taken at Hughly should be brought to Agra and cut in pieces.

Every Englishman in Bengal is familiar with the town of Hughly, which is situated on the river of the same name, about twenty-six miles above Calcutta. The cathedral, built by the Portuguese in the reign of Akbar, is still standing, and to this day a quaint Catholic air lingers about the spot. But in the early years of the seventeenth century Hughly was a trading emporium—imposing, wealthy, and full of busy life. Portuguese ships of large burden, and native craft of every description, plied up and down the river between Hughly and the Bay of Bengal, and traded with Pegu, Malacca and Goa. The city was surrounded with fortifications and towers, mounted with cannon, as a protection against the pirates of Chittagong; and the Muhammadans in Bengal were complaining that the Christian dogs were growing insolent behind their walls and guns, and buying slaves of the very pirates whom they were bound to destroy.

The city of Hughly was doomed to a fate as bitter as that of Jerusalem in the hands of Nebuchadnezzar. All the native boatmen in the service of the Portuguese, to the number of three thousand, fled from the settlement at the first tidings of attack. A vast host of Moghul soldiery was brought down the river from Burdwan; and all way of escape by the sea was blocked up by a Muhammadan fleet at Serampore. Moreover the hot season was at its height, and the Portuguese ships, which might have broken through the blockade, were unable to move from Hughly through want of water.

The siege of Hughly lasted four months, and its horrors were beyond all telling. There was a burning anxiety amongst the Portuguese for the safety of the women and children, but nothing could be done beyond fighting day and night upon the walls. One ship, with two thousand Christian men and women on board, would have fallen into the hands of the Muhammadans, but the magazine was fired and every soul perished. At last all was over. The fortifications were mined and blown up, and many only escaped the fire to perish in the river. The survivors, to the number of six or seven hundred, were carried away as prisoners to

Agra. Taj Mahal was dead, or all would have been slaughtered. As it was, some turned Muhammadans to save their wives and families; others to escape being trampled to death by elephants, or some other horrible martyrdom. Boys were forced to embrace Islam, and to serve as pages in the houses of Muhammadan masters; whilst the younger and fairer women were condemned to a destiny worse than death in the zenanas of Shah Jehan and his grandees.

Taj Mahal died at the age of forty, and Shah Jehan spent the treasures of the empire in building a mausoleum for her remains, which is standing to this day. It is a hall of marble, with a dome, towers, and pavilions surrounded by gardens and terraces. The walls on the outside are of dazzling whiteness; but inside they are inlaid with precious stones of different colours to represent birds and flowers; whilst the doors of the pavilions are thin slabs of white marble curiously perforated like bridal veils. The whole structure, with galleries and windows looking down on groves and fountains, is a retreat for lovers, but the silence of death hangs over all. The soul is gone, but the memories of loveliness are lingering round the tomb.

Shah Jehan however soon forgot his beloved Taj Mahal. He married other wives, and became the patron of gladiators and dancing girls. He lounged away his winters at Agra and his summers at Cashmere, leaving his generals to subdue rebellious Rajas, and keep the peace in distant provinces. One of his amusements created a host of secret enemies. At festival times the wives and daughters of grandees were invited to hold a fancy fair in the palace gardens; and the Padishah and his princesses went from stall to stall, bargaining for brocades, embroideries, and fine muslins, whilst husbands and fathers were rigidly excluded. But a day of reckoning came for Shah Jehan; a day when his own sons rebelled against him, and there was no one to draw a sword in behalf of his sovereign or risk his life in defence of the throne.

Shah Jehan had four sons by his deceased wife Taj Mahal, namely, Dara, Shuja, Aurangzeb and Murad. Dara was the first-born, and consequently the heir apparent, but he was the most unpopular of the four. He offended Muhammadans by despising the Koran. He offended Hindus by insulting the Rajas. He talked much with Catholic Fathers, and took many Europeans into his service as gunners and engineers, but he could not be persuaded to be a Christian.

When Shah Jehan was growing old he left the cares of government to Dara. He was more avaricious than ever, and spent a great part of his time in counting his treasures. He left the Viceroys of provinces to commit any tyranny, and almost any villany, so long as they sent him presents of gold and jewels. He appointed his three younger sons to be Viceroys of the outlying provinces. Shuja was sent to Bengal; Aurangzeb to the Dekhan; and Murad to Guzerat. There they maintained themselves at the expense of the people; whilst the distance between them was so great that they were unable to plot against each other, or assassinate each other, as they would have done had they remained at court.

Dara was puffed up with his sense of power, and the flatteries of the very parasites who hated him for his insolence. He is suspected of having murdered his father's minister; and he certainly excited the jealous alarm of the Padishah by his overbearing demeanour at court. At the same time he was jealous and alarmed in his turn at the proceedings of his third brother Aurangzeb, who was to all appearance intriguing in the Dekhan in the hope of making it a stepping-stone to the possession of Hindustan. Accordingly Dara was trying to set his father against Aurangzeb, whilst Shah Jehan was trying to set up Aurangzeb as a check upon the ambitious designs of Dara.

Aurangzeb was the cleverest and craftiest of all the four sons of Shah Jehan, and has often been compared with his famous English contemporary, Oliver Cromwell. He professed to be a strict Muhammadan, zealous for God and the Prophet; and he sought the support of the old Muhammadan party, who had been out of court favour ever since Akbar had over-ridden the Ulama. He was spare in figure, abstemious in diet, plain in his dress, and full of pious discourses on the law of Muhammad, and affected yearnings for a life of penitence and prayer. He fixed his headquarters at a town which was called Aurangabad, or "the city of Aurangzeb;" and he was often to be seen carrying a Koran under his arm, and praying aloud in the streets of Aurangabad, like the Pharisees of old.

At this time the Moghuls had conquered the northern part of the Dekhan, but the southern region as far as the river Kistna was occupied by the two Muhammadan kingdoms of Bijapore and Golkonda. Aurangzeb belonged to the Sunni sect, and he hated the Sultans of Bijapore and Golkonda because they were both Shiahs.[1] He was anxious

---

[1] The antagonism between Sunnis and Shiahs is an important element in the history of Islam; almost as much so as the antagonism between Catholics and Protestants in the history of Christianity. After the death of Muhammad, four Caliphs reigned in succession as Popes of Islam, each having been elected or accepted in turn by the congregation at Medina. The Shiahs urged that the line of succession could not be rightfully settled by the suffrages of the body of believers, but ought to have been restricted to the family of the Prophet. Muhammad had left no son, but he had adopted a boy, named Ali, and married him to his own daughter Fatima. Accordingly

in the first instance to conquer their territories and annex them to the Moghul empire, and then to cross the Kistna river, and conquer the Hindu Rajas of the Peninsula.[1]

Meanwhile a boy Sultan was reigning over Golkonda, and a Persian adventurer, named Ameer Jumla, obtained the post of Vizier, partly by bribes and partly by making love to the Sultan's mother. Subsequently Ameer Jumla found that his life was in danger, and he invited Aurangzeb to invade Golkonda. The proposal was gladly accepted. Aurangzeb gave out that he was going to Bengal to betroth his son Mahmud to the daughter of Shuja; but he took another direction, and suddenly appeared with an army before the walls of Golkonda, where he was joined by Ameer Jumla. The Sultan saw no way of escape from their united forces, and was about to surrender, when Aurangzeb received orders from the Padishah to raise the siege of Golkonda and

---

the Shiahs reject the first three Caliphs—Abubaker, Omar, and Othman—as not being of kin to the Prophet; and they accept Ali the fourth Caliph, and his two sons, Hassan and Hussein, as the only rightful successors of Muhammad. In the present day the Sunnis and Shiahs are still cursing and reviling each other; and as arguments are of little avail, the disputants occasionally resort to fisticuffs, cudgels and swords, in the vague hope of settling the controversy by force of arms.

[1] It may be as well to bear in mind that India is divided into three regions or zones, namely, Hindustan, the Dekhan, and the Peninsula. Hindustan lies north and south between the Himalaya mountains and Nerbudda river, having the Punjab on the north-west and Bengal on the south-east. The Dekhan, properly so called, lies to the south of Hindustan, between the Nerbudda and the Kistna rivers; it is a broad causeway of table-land running from Hindustan towards the Peninsula, bounded on the west by the mountain chain known as the Western Ghats, and on the east by the jungles of Ghondwana and Orissa. The Peninsula lies to the south of the Dekhan, between the Kistna and the sea, tapering off to a point on the south known as Cape Comorin; it was at this period parcelled out amongst Hindu Rajas, whose little kingdoms had often been invaded and plundered by the Sultans of Bijapore and Golkonda, but had never as yet been conquered by the Muhammadans.

return to Aurangabad. Aurangzeb knew that Dara was his enemy, but he was compelled to obey orders. Accordingly he patched up a peace, and married his son Mahmud to a daughter of the Sultan, on the understanding that Mahmud should be declared heir apparent to the kingdom of Golkonda.

Aurangzeb then returned to Aurangabad, accompanied by Ameer Jumla; and costly presents were sent to Shah Jehan to induce him to agree to the conquest of Bijapore. Shah Jehan readily assented, for he saw that the united armies of Ameer Jumla and Aurangzeb might protect him against the ambition of Dara. But Dara was again at work, and Ameer Jumla was ordered to send his wives and daughters to court as pledges of his fidelity, whilst Aurangzeb was ordered to remain at Aurangabad, and to take no part in the campaign against Bijapore. This arrangement checkmated Ameer Jumla. He began operations against Bijapore, but he could not help Aurangzeb in the event of any rebellion, because his wives and daughters would be at the mercy of Dara.

Suddenly rumours reverberated through the empire like the roll of thunder or rumblings of an earthquake. It was noised abroad in bazaars and caravanserais, in mosques and pagodas, in resting places beneath trees and groves, by wells, tanks and rivers, that Shah Jehan was dead or dying, and that his four sons were about to fight for the succession to the throne of Hindustan. In Bengal, Shúja was making hot preparations for marching an army towards Agra. Elephants were dragging artillery; arms and ammunition were served out at the arsenals; couriers on horses and dromedaries were riding to and fro; whilst every soldier looked to his weapons and accoutrements, and every street and highway resounded with the noise and hubbub of war.

Shuja left Bengal with a great host, declaring that the Padishah had been poisoned by Dara, and that he was going to avenge the murder. Aurangzeb remained a while longer in the Dekhan to mature his plans. He told his officers that he was going to avenge the sacred Koran which Dara had insulted; and he wrote to Murad, in Guzerat, saying:—"Dara is an infidel; Shuja is a heretic Shiah; whilst I myself am a Fakir; and if I can place you on the throne as Padishah of Hindustan, I will retire from the world, and spend the remainder of my days in contemplation and devotion at the tomb of the Prophet."

All this while Shah Jehan was really alive, but he was very ill and closely shut up in the palace, for Dara was jealous of his own son Soliman, and afraid that Shah Jehan would nominate Soliman to be his successor on the throne. But Dara was equally alarmed at the advance of Shuja. He issued proclamations that Shah Jehan was alive and recovering, but no one believed them. He persuaded the old Padishah to show himself in the Durbar hall, but the grandees would not trust their eyes, and whispered that the apparition was a sham. At last Dara sent the flower of the army into Bengal under the command of Soliman, and thus hoped to repel the advance of Shuja, and get Soliman out of the way of his grandfather.

For some days there was a lull, and then the tidings reached Agra that Aurangzeb and Murad had united their forces, and were marching through Rajputana towards the capital. Dara dared not leave Agra, but he sent a mixed army of Muhammadans and Rajputs to oppose the rebel princes. The Muhammadan generals, however, were in secret communication with Aurangzeb, and during the battle which ensued, the Muhammadan soldiers held aloof from the fighting whilst the Rajputs were cut to pieces.

Dara was frantic at the disaster. He waited in vain for the return of Soliman from Bengal, and at last was compelled to take the field at the head of a vast mob of raw levies. But he was doomed to suffer for his pride and insolence. He was deserted by his own officers in the midst of the battle, and compelled to fly to the Punjab with a mere handful of followers.

Aurangzeb and Murad advanced to Agra and surrounded the palace with their armies. Shah Jehan pretended to forgive them, and invited Aurangzeb into the inner apartments of the palace; but Aurangzeb was warned that if he put himself in the power of the Pádishah he would be murdered by the guard of Tartar Amazons. Shah Jehan then tried to win over Mahmud, by promising him the throne if he would only turn against his father Aurangzeb. But Mahmud was staunch, and Shah Jehan was shut up in the inner apartments, and kept there as a state prisoner for the remainder of his days.

Thus ended the great rebellion of the four sons of Shah Jehan. Aurangzeb was master of the situation, and gained the empire of Hindustan by the destruction of his three brethren. Murad was tempted to a carouse in the tent of Aurangzeb, and then exposed to the Muhammadan officers in a drunken state, as a prince who had forfeited all claim to the throne by his violation of the law of the Koran. He was sent in silver chains to the fortress of Gwalior, and was condemned to die by the bite of a cobra. Dara was betrayed to Aurangzeb, and barbarously paraded before the people of Delhi, clothed in tattered garments, and mounted on the sorriest elephant that could be found. He was then murdered by assassins in a private chamber, declaring in his last moments that he put his faith in Christianity. Shuja escaped with his family to Arakan, but every one of the party is said to have been miserably slaughtered by the king of that country.

Mahmud, the eldest son of Aurangzeb, met with a pitiable fate. In early life he was to have been betrothed to a daughter of Shuja; but he was married at Golkonda to the daughter of the Sultan. Subsequently Aurangzeb sent him with an army to fight against Shuja. He kept back Mahmud's young wife on pretence that she was unfit to go to the war, but in reality as a pledge for the fidelity of her husband. The result was that Mahmud, being deprived of his Golkonda princess, began to think of the young lady in Bengal to whom he was to have been betrothed; and eventually he ran away to Shuja, and married his fair cousin. After awhile Mahmud repented of his alliance with Shuja, and returned to his father, but Aurangzeb never forgave; and the son was condemned by his own father to imprisonment for life in the fortress of Gwalior.

Soliman, the eldest son of Dara, met with a similar fate. He had escaped from Bengal to Cashmere, but was betrayed by a Raja and sent to Aurangzeb. He was bound in golden chains, and brought into an inner hall of the palace before Aurangzeb and his grandees; whilst the ladies of the zenana sat behind a lattice to see the young prince, whom many of them had known from his infancy. Bernier, the French physician, was an eye witness of the scene, and describes it as pathetic to the last degree. Some of the grandees were moved to tears, whilst there was doleful weeping and wailing amongst the ladies behind the lattice. The young man was tall and handsome, and profoundly reverential. He was in terror lest he should be forced to drink poust, a horrible mixture of hemp and night-shade, which destroyed the brain, and turned the strongest man into a babbling idiot. "Kill me at once," he said, with a pleading air, "but do not compel me to drink poust!" Aurangzeb himself was moved by the spectacle, and promised in a loud voice that no poust should be given to him. Next morning the prince was sent away to Gwalior, and it is to be hoped that Aurangzeb kept his word; but nothing more was heard of Soliman.

The fratricidal wars between the sons of the Padishah for the succession to the throne are types of the wars in other countries which have prevailed from the earliest times. The rivalry between Jacob and Esau, Solomon and Adonijah, William Rufus and Robert of Normandy, had a similar origin. Such wars are guarded against in Europe in the present day by the force of public law; whilst they have ceased in India ever since the establishment of the British government as the paramount power.

VII.—*Reign of Aurangzeb: Persecution of Hindus.*

1658 to 1707.

AURANGZEB was established on the throne at Delhi in the palace of the Great Moghul. He had triumphed over all his enemies, but he was haunted by a skeleton night and day. His father was a state prisoner in the palace at Agra, and at any moment might be delivered from captivity and restored to his throne and empire. Where would he be then? Condemned, strangled, poisoned, or at the best a prisoner or an exile.

Meanwhile the surroundings of Aurangzeb were perhaps more magnificent than those of any of his predecessors. A new Delhi had been founded by Shah Jehan, and is known to this day as Shah Jehanabad, or the "city of Shah Jehan;" and still, when seen from a distance, it is one of the loveliest cities in the world. Domes and towers, mosques and fortifications, peer through a paradise of trees and gardens; whilst glimpses of the river Jumna, and of the great palace of red sandstone which stands between the river and the city, will carry the imagination of the pilgrim far back to the Moghul capital as it was in the days of the Emperor Aurangzeb.[1]

---

[1] It will be remembered that Moore's poem of "Lalla Rookh" turns upon the marriage of the youngest daughter of Aurangzeb, the "Lalla Rookh" in question, with the Sultan of Bucharia or Bokhara. It is

Delhi was never a great metropolis like London or Paris: it was a camp turned into a capital. There were broad streets and narrow lanes, but the bulk of the houses were mud huts, little better than common tents; and even the mansions of the grandees, with their imposing gateways and courtyards, were mostly built of clay whitened with lime: very few were built of brick or stone. When the Padishah was at Delhi the city was full of people; but when he was away in camp the streets were silent and bare.

The aristocracy of the Moghul, the grandees of the empire, were of the same evanescent character as the buildings. The princes of Rajputana, who dwelt at court, were the only hereditary nobles with landed possessions, and they might build houses of stone at Delhi or Agra, which might last for generations. But the Muhammadan grandees, whether Persians or Turks, were creatures of a day. Their rank, their wealth, their honours and their offices or commands, depended solely on the personal favour of the sovereign, and were not inherited or derived from landed estates or family titles of any sort or kind. All the lands of the empire belonged to the Padishah; and although the rents or revenues of these lands were sometimes assigned in Jaghir in lieu of

---

sad to destroy illusions, but the plot of the poem has no foundation in history. Aurangzeb had good reasons for hating the Sultan of Bokhara, and he had no daughter named Lalla Rookh; whilst a marriage between such a daughter and the rude Uzbeg Sultan of Bokhara was as unlikely as the minstrelsy of Feramorz or the criticisms of Fadladeen. The following bit of Moore's prose introduction is however worth quoting:—"The day of Lalla Rookh's departure from Delhi was as splendid as sunshine and pageantry could make it. The bazaars and baths were all covered with the richest tapestry; hundreds of gilded barges floated on the Jumna, with their banners shining in the water; while through the streets groups of beautiful children went strewing the most delicious flowers around, till every part of the city was as fragrant as if a caravan of musk from Khotan had passed through it."

military pay, or as a reward for particular services, the lands still belonged to the Padishah, and the rents might be resumed at any moment at the will or whim of the Padishah.

Under Moghul rule in India, a fair white complexion was the chief claim to nobility, and, if combined with intelligence and courtly tact, would enable the humblest individual to rise to the highest position in the empire next to the princes of the blood. Ameer Jumla, the Vizier of Golkonda, and friend of Aurangzeb, was the son of a Persian oil dealer, who originally entered the service of the Moghul, and owed his fortune to his complexion.[1] But this fairness of countenance, which has always been regarded as a stamp of nobility in Oriental countries, often disappears in India after two or three generations, and all claim to distinction disappears in like manner. The grandfather of a Muhammadan family might be a minister, a viceroy, and an Ameer of the first water; but his son could only be a captain, whilst his grandson, born perhaps of a still duskier mother, might be obliged to serve as a common soldier.

The fact was that in the palmy days of the Moghul empire the Muhammadan grandees had no territorial influence. They were mostly adventurers of Persian or Turkish origin, and their incomes were nothing but military pay on a liberal scale, and the profits of their respective commands. When a grandee died all his wealth was inherited by the Padishah. Gold and jewels might sometimes be concealed for the benefit of the family, and small pensions were often given for the support of widows; but the harpies of the Padishah seized

[1] The first chapter of the Book of Daniel contains a curious illustration of the idea of fair complexions, combined with stoutness of form, which prevails in India to this day.

all they could, and the sons of the wealthiest Muhammadans had no alternative but to enter the service of the Padishah. It was not until later days, when the Moghul sovereigns had dwindled into pageants, that estates and even commands became hereditary in families.

The court life in Delhi centred in the palace on the river Jumna, but the city life centred in the great square between the palace and the city proper. This square was a bazaar for traders, a parade ground for troops and horses, and a general place of resort. Wares of every kind were offered for sale, from shawls and jewellery down to pottery and brass lotahs. Mountebanks and jugglers amused the crowd with their performances; whilst astrologers sat on pieces of carpet, with books and mathematical instruments, and told the fortunes of any man or woman who chose to consult them. Here the unfortunate Dara was paraded before his execution, in order that the people of Delhi might not be deluded on a future day by any impostor bearing his name.

The magnificent gateway of the palace faced the square, and was guarded by two huge elephants of stone, each having a colossal statue of a Rajput warrior on its back. Passing through the gateway, the visitor entered a series of streets of palace shops and offices leading to the Durbar hall and other buildings. There were also workshops for embroiderers, goldsmiths, artists, tailors and dressmakers, who were kept constantly at work for the Great Moghul and his ladies. There also were quarters for the Muhammadan grandees, who kept watch and ward day and night in rotation, whilst the Rajput princes kept guard in like manner in the square outside.

The Durbar, or grand hall of audience, was built at the far end of a large quadrangle surrounded by arcades. The ceiling was of white marble, supported by thirty marble columns. The whole surface was decorated with gold and colours, whilst a golden inscription ran round the cornice—"If there be an Elysium on earth, it is this!" The throne was in a recess at the back of the hall, and over the throne was a peacock constructed of gold and jewels, valued at many millions sterling. The peacock is an emblem of the sun, and was no doubt symbolical of the legend that the Great Moghul was descended from the sun through Chenghiz Khan.

Beyond the Durbar hall was the haram or zenana, known as the Mahal. It was a Muhammadan heaven of pavilions, gardens, and houries, guarded by Tartar Amazons. Queens, princesses, and concubines were kept secluded in these retreats, under the control of duennas and governesses, to swell the pomp and dignity of the Great Moghul. They were all dressed in the same fashion, arranging their hair in tresses, and glittering with jewels; but every day each one wore a new dress of a different colour. Some, like Nur Mahal and Taj Mahal, interested themselves in affairs of state, or strove to promote the welfare and advancement of fathers and brothers outside the palace walls; but the majority dawdled away their time in listless languor, and admiring themselves in the little mirror which every lady carried with her, hanging from her thumb by a ring. Zenana life was pleasanter in camp, and especially when the Great Moghul moved with all his court to the cool mountains of Cashmere. As Thomas Moore sings:—

> "If woman can make the worst wilderness dear,
> Think, think what a heaven she can make of Cashmere!"

Aurangzeb, with all his strictness, cared little about the religion of his wives, and may have thought that women had no souls. His first wife was a Rajput princess, and is said to have worshipped idols in her own apartments. His favourite was a Christian girl of Circassia, who had been sold as a slave to Dara, and after his death became the wife of his conqueror; but she must have been unlike the Christian wife of Akbar, for she is said to have smuggled wine into the zenana, and to have indulged pretty freely whenever she had an opportunity.

Aurangzeb was still ambitious of establishing the Muhammadan religion throughout his empire; but for some years he was chary of persecuting Hindus, lest he should drive the Rajas to liberate Shah Jehan. Accordingly, he contented himself with improving the morals of Muhammadan grandees by punishing drunkenness, and prohibiting the performances of musicians and dancing girls. The musicians did not give in without a protest. One Friday, as Aurangzeb was going to mosque, he fell in with a mob of mourners following a bier, and filling the air with bitter wailings. On enquiring what was the matter, he was told that they were going to bury their mother, whose name was "Music," and who had been put to death by the Padishah. Aurangzeb smiled grimly, but only told them to bury her deep, as she must never rise again.

About this time Aurangzeb was much annoyed by Sivaji the Mahratta. This man was a Hindu brigand, who had revolted against the Sultan of Bijapore, and founded an independent principality in the mountains of the Konkan, to the eastward of the modern city of Bombay. He possessed several fortresses, mostly built on the tops of mountains, with one winding ascent cut in the precipitous sides. When Aurangzeb was Viceroy of the Moghul Dekhan, he formed an alliance with Sivaji, and ceded certain territories, with the view of taking refuge in these fortresses in the event of any disaster during his wars for the throne. When, however, he was established on the throne at Delhi, he appointed his uncle Shaista Khan, a brother of Taj Mahal, to be Viceroy of the Dekhan, with instructions to resume the lands and root out Sivaji and his Mahrattas.

Shaista Khan, however, met with disaster. He captured the Mahratta fortress of Poona, but could not find Sivaji. One night he was drinking wine with his officers when Sivaji and his Mahrattas broke into the pavilion, and fell upon the intoxicated guests with drawn swords. The confusion was horrible. Some were killed, when the ladies of the zenana rushed in and put out the lights. Shaista Khan escaped with the loss of three fingers, but many of his officers were left bleeding on the floor. Meanwhile, swarms of Mahrattas were plundering the camp, and the Moghul soldiers were flying in a panic. Suddenly the enemy disappeared in the darkness, and presently the Mahrattas were to be seen in the distance, climbing a hill with their booty, and lighting up the whole country round with flaming torches.

Whilst Aurangzeb was smarting at the news, tidings reached him of another disaster. Sivaji and his Mahrattas had broken into the Moghul port of Surat, and plundered the town, whilst the Nawab of Surat shut himself up in the fort, and no one ventured to beat off the marauders, except the Christian Kafirs, as they were called, at the English and Dutch factories. On this occasion an Englishman named Smith was carried off prisoner to the Mahratta camp outside the town, where the illustrious Sivaji was torturing the native householders to surrender their hidden hoards, and occasionally cutting off hands and legs as an efficacious method of inducing them to comply with his demands. Now and then a head was cut off to encourage the others.

Aurangzeb stifled his rage and mortification at the news from Poona and Surat, and feigned a desire to make friends with Sivaji. He praised the Mahratta for courage and cleverness before all the grandees in the Durbar, and sent the Raja of Jeypore to persuade Sivaji to come to Delhi, and promised that the Mahratta should be appointed Viceroy of the Dekhan in the room of Shaista Khan. The "mountain rat," as Sivaji was called, fell into the trap. He went to Delhi with the full conviction that Aurangzeb would make him Viceroy. He was received in the magnificent hall of audience, but placed so low down on the platform that he knew he had been duped. Accordingly, he shouted out that the Padishah had broken his word, and that all the grandees who had been placed above him were cowards. He then left the platform and stalked out of the palace. How he got off with his life is a mystery to this day. It is said that he escaped from Delhi in an empty vegetable basket, and disguised himself as a Hindu beggar; but it is certain that he reached Poona in safety, and that Aurangzeb was ever afterwards afraid of attacking him.

At last Shah Jehan died at Agra, and it was whispered that he had been murdered at the instigation of Aurangzeb. There is certainly something suspicious about the death of the captive sovereign, for Aurangzeb issued proclamations forbidding his subjects from writing the history of his reign, as if to prevent any record of the parricide from being handed down to posterity. Accordingly, for some years little is known of the current of events in India, beyond stories of wars and disasters in Cabul, and plots within the palace, which seem to have hindered Aurangzeb in the accomplishment of his ambitious designs for the establishment of Islam as the universal faith throughout all India.

Aurangzeb made one more effort to entrap Sivaji. He sent Shah Alam, his eldest son next to the imprisoned Mahmud, to command the Moghul army in the Dekhan, with orders to sham a rebellion. Nothing was more natural in Moghul times than for the eldest son of the Padishah to rebel against his father; and all the Muhammadan generals joined in the rebellion, as well as the Rajputs under the Raja of Jeypore. But Sivaji was on his guard, and suspected that Aurangzeb was playing his old game of craft. Accordingly he professed to throw himself heart and soul into the cause of the rebels, but refused to leave his stronghold in the mountains. He pledged himself to keep order in the Dekhan, whilst Shah Alam waged war against his father in Hindustan. So far the sham rebellion was a failure. An imperial army appeared upon the scene, and Shah Alam was obliged to sham a surrender. The rebel officers were put to death or sent into banishment, whilst the Raja of Jeypore is said to have been poisoned. Henceforth, however, Shah Alam was powerless to rebel, although every crown prince had done so since the days of Akbar, for neither Moghul nor Rajput would have ever trusted him again.

About the twentieth year of the reign of Aurangzeb, the Moghul empire was thrown into a ferment. Aurangzeb had begun to work out his scheme for the conversion of the Hindus to the religion of the Koran. A great Hindu pagoda was burnt down near Delhi. Another magnificent pagoda at Muttra, whose gilded domes could be seen from Agra, was turned into a mosque. The Viceroys of provinces were commanded to destroy all pagodas and idols in their respective jurisdictions in like manner. The celebration of Hindu festivals was strictly forbidden; and religious mendicants, who had flourished in all parts of India from a remote antiquity, were driven out of Hindustan. No Hindus were allowed to serve the Moghul government in any capacity, unless they turned Muhammadans; and stories are told of Brahmans, who renounced the worship of idols and accepted the religion of the Koran, being specially appointed to high posts and commands.

Most of the Hindus appear to have submitted to their fate. On one occasion, however, the city of Delhi was threatened by a mob of fanatics. An old woman, who pretended to exercise supernatural powers, called on the people to dethrone the Padishah as the enemy of the gods. The bulk of the Moghul army was away in Cabul, and a body of horsemen which was sent against the rioters was defeated and scattered. Aurangzeb, however, was a match for the prophetess. He raised another body of horsemen, and fastened holy texts and magical devices to the manes of their horses; and the fanatics were so frightened that they fled at the first charge, and many were cut to pieces, whilst the popular belief in the old lady was shattered for ever.

Henceforth Aurangzeb was regarded as a demon and sorcerer, against whom it was useless to contend. At the same time those Hindus who abandoned their national faith, and accepted the creed of Islam, were often the most active in persecuting their fellow-countrymen, and in filling their private coffers with the spoils of idolatry. Apostacy from Hinduism was the highest virtue in the eyes of Aurangzeb; it covered a multitude of sins, and was a certain way of securing wealth and honour.

But Aurangzeb took one step which threatened to shake the empire to its foundations. From the days of the early Caliphs it had been a fundamental law of Islam that if a people were brought under Muhammadan dominion, but refused to embrace the Muhammadan religion, they must pay a poll tax known as Jezya, or otherwise forfeit their lives and property. Under this rule the Hindus had paid the Jezya to the early Muhammadan conquerors of Hindustan; but the tax had been abolished by Akbar, as contrary to the principles of toleration laid down by Chenghiz Khan, and no such tax had been levied by Jehanghir or Shah Jehan.

Aurangzeb reversed the policy of his predecessors, and ordered the Jezya to be levied from all who refused to become Muhammadans. The amount was not heavy; about half-a-crown a month for merchants, a shilling a month for artisans, and sixpence a month for poor people; but, small or great, it drove the Hindus into rebellion. Men who had looked helplessly on whilst pagodas were destroyed and idols carried away, began to revolt against the appeal to their pockets. Little is known of these insurrections, beyond the fact that they broke out in different quarters of the empire. The Sikhs rebelled in the Punjab, and the more timid inhabitants of Bengal took up arms in the same cause; and it would seem that the Hindus only wanted a national leader to enable them to throw off the yoke of the Muhammadans, whom they outnumbered twenty or thirty-fold.

One formidable rising broke out in the city of Delhi. A vast mob of Hindus blocked up the way to the mosque, and there were no means for dispersing them. At last Aurangzeb ordered the elephants to charge, and numbers were trampled to death. The massacre had its effect. The Hindus yielded to their destiny and paid the Jezya, although they did not cease to complain of the heaviness of the burden.

But Aurangzeb was mad enough to attempt to compel the princes and people of Rajputana to pay the Jezya; and it is a marvel how nearly he succeeded in carrying out his object.

In Jeypore the tax was actually collected by the officers of the Moghul; but the Raja was dead, and his rightful heir was a prisoner in the hands of Aurangzeb, and consequently no opposition was raised.

In Jodhpore the case was different. The Raja was dead but his widow was regent, and for a long time she resolutely refused to permit the Jezya to be levied. At last a compromise was effected. The Jezya was not levied from her subjects, but redeemed by a cession of territory.

The Rana of Oodeypore alone bore the brunt of the storm. He was deaf to all the demands and threats of Aurangzeb. The Moghul might invade his territories, capture his cities, and carry away his harvests; but he and his subjects would fly to the recesses of the Aravulli mountains, as their fathers had done before them, and fight on until the bitter end.

Aurangzeb, puffed up with oriental pride, resolved to crush the refractory Rana, as Darius and Xerxes thought to crush the Greeks in days of old. Four overwhelming armies, under the command of the Padishah and three of his sons, were brought up from the extremities of the empire to blockade and starve out the Rana. But neither the Great Moghul nor the princes of the blood could prevail against the stubborn obstinacy of the Rana. The rocks were his ramparts, and no one but a Bheel or a goat could have forced the interminable defiles. For years the strength of the Moghul was frittered away before the Aravulli mountains, and the Rana of Oodeypore was as far off as ever.

Suddenly Aurangzeb was thrown into a panic by the rebellion of his favourite son Akbar. The prince had been worked upon by the regent princess of Jodhpore, who tempted him to revolt against Aurangzeb, as Aurangzeb had revolted against

Shah Jehan, and sent an army of fifty thousand Rajputs to support him. For a long time the Padishah refused to believe that Akbar had turned against him, but at last his eyes were opened, and he saved himself by a craft which never failed him. He sent artful letters to Akbar, praising him for having betrayed the Rajputs; and he took care that the letters should fall into the hands of the Rajputs. The Jodhpore general at once concluded that Akbar was a traitor, and his rebellion a sham, like that of Shah Alam; and all his Rajputs went back that very night to tell the story at Jodhpore. At early dawn Akbar saw that his allies had vanished, and fled for his life. After endless adventures and hair-breadth escapes he at last found a refuge in the fortresses of the Mahrattas.

Aurangzeb was deeply moved by the rebellion of Akbar. Occasionally he mistrusted his other sons, and had imprisoned Mahmud for life in the fortress of Gwalior; but Akbar was the youngest of his acknowledged sons, and as dear to him as Absalom was to David. Rebellion, however, was an unpardonable sin, and Aurangzeb was forced to patch up a peace with the Rana, and to turn his whole strength against the Mahrattas and compel them, if possible, to surrender the rebel Akbar. It will suffice to say that Aurangzeb was thwarted; that the Mahrattas defied him in the mountains of the Konkan, and that Akbar eventually escaped to Persia, where he died in exile.

Aurangzeb retired from Rajputana about 1682; he died in 1707. During the intervening period of a quarter of a century he never returned to Delhi. He was warned by the fate of his father, Shah Jehan, not to expose himself to a rebellion of his sons by shutting himself up in the palace; and he spent the remainder of his days in camp, wandering to and fro with his army, like his Moghul ancestors, Chenghiz Khan and Timour.

The splendour of the camp life of Aurangzeb was remembered for generations after his death. It resembled the pageant march of Jehanghir from his palace at Ajmere to the first halting-place, as seen and described by Sir Thomas Roe; but it was rendered more imposing by a long array of cannon, elephants loaded with treasures, waggons piled up with records and accounts, and camels carrying drinking water from the river Ganges. The approach of Aurangzeb was heralded on all occasions by clouds of incense, but whether it was only intended to perfume the imperial camp, or was a relic of the old worship of the Padishah, is a question which must be left to conjecture.

But although Aurangzeb was more or less foiled by the Rajputs and Mahrattas, he extended the Moghul empire further south than any of his predecessors. Sivaji died about 1680, and within a few years after his death Aurangzeb conquered the Muhammadan Sultans of Bijapore and Golkonda, and his generals conquered the Hindu Carnatic between the Kistna and the Coleroon rivers, and compelled many of the Rajas of the Peninsula to pay tribute. At the same time he came in contact with the English settlements. Bombay was beyond his reach, as it was surrounded by the Mahratta country; but the name of Aurangzeb was a household word at Surat, Madras, and Calcutta, and he was regarded in Europe as the greatest Asiatic sovereign next to the Shah of Persia or Emperor of China.

Aurangzeb had always been curious about European nations. He had ascended the throne in 1658, the very year that Oliver Cromwell died, and he lived to the year 1707, being the second year of the reign of Queen Anne. Shortly after his accession to the throne he fell foul of his tutor in public Durbar for having told him that Holland was a great empire; that England was larger than France; and that the King of France was a Raja of the second class; whereas he had heard on competent authority, doubtless from Bernier, or other Frenchmen who lived at Delhi, that the King of France was the greatest sovereign in Europe.

There was, however, a serious misunderstanding between Aurangzeb and the English, which led to a lamentable war. The East India Company had obtained a royal charter from successive sovereigns of England, granting them the sole right of trading with the East Indies; but it was impossible to prevent interlopers from interfering in this trade, and these interlopers were often downright pirates, who plundered the ships of the Moghul going on pilgrimage to Mecca, and more than once ill-treated some lady pilgrims that belonged to the Padishah's zenana. Aurangzeb was naturally furious at the insult, and wreaked his wrath upon the East India Company, but after much mischief had been done on both sides, there were explanations and concessions, and during the latter years of the reign the English had very little reason to complain of the Moghul.

One grievance is typical of the times. The English exported large quantities of saltpetre from Patna, and drove a roaring trade during the civil war in England between Charles and his parliament, and the war in Europe between William of Orange and Louis the Fourteenth. But the Sultan of Turkey complained that much of the saltpetre was used for the slaughter of Muhammadans, and Aurangzeb, who was a Sunni like the Sultan, prohibited all further exportations from his territories.

Gemelli, the Italian traveller, had an audience with

Aurangzeb in 1695, and describes him as of a low stature, with a large nose, slender in body, and stooping with age. He walked leaning on a staff forked at the top, yet endorsed petitions without spectacles, and showed, by his cheerful smiling countenance, that he was pleased with doing business in the Durbar. His beard was white, and his complexion olive coloured.

The Christian Sultana, the favourite of Aurangzeb, came to a sad end. She had a son, whom the Greeks would have called Cambyses;[1] and she persuaded Aurangzeb to make him Sultan of the newly conquered territories of Bijapore and Golkonda. No sooner, however, was Aurangzeb dead than his three other sons went to war with each other, and two were defeated and slain, whilst Shah Alam, the survivor, ascended the throne under the name of Bahadur Shah. The poor Christian mother pleaded hard for Cambyses, but her tears and prayers were thrown away. Bahadur Shah was too good a Muhammadan to permit the son of a Christian mother to reign as Sultan over Muhammadan territories. Cambyses was defeated, captured, and murdered, and the fate of his mother is a mystery to this day.

---

[1] Our forefathers called him Cawn Bux, which is tolerably intelligible. Modern scholars, however, persist in writing it Kam Bakhsh, which is somewhat trying to English readers. Cambyses is less troublesome.

UPRISING OF THE MAHRATTAS.

VIII.—*Maha Rajas and Brahmans.*

1627 to 1748.

BEFORE Aurangzeb was Padishah, and when he was only Viceroy of the Moghul Dekhan, a new Hindu power was rising in the western Ghats, known as that of Sivaji the Mahratta. Something has already been told of Sivaji: his alliance with Aurangzeb before the rebellion of the princes, and his subsequent outbreak at Poona, plunder of Surat, and extraordinary adventures at Delhi. But Sivaji is the founder of the once famous Mahratta power, which shook the Moghul empire to its foundations, and threatened to overshadow the rise of British power in India until it was crushed by the wars at the beginning of the nineteenth century. Moreover, there are other incidents that will appear hereafter which render the tale of Sivaji and his Mahrattas one of the most interesting in Indian history.

Sivaji was born in 1627, the last year of the reign of Jehanghir, and he died in 1680, about the middle of the reign of Aurangzeb. Prior to this period little or nothing was known of the Mahrattas. They were an obscure race of hardy cultivators, occupying the mountains of the Konkan, between Goa and Surat, and spreading eastward over the plains of the Dekhan as far as Nagpore. The Mahrattas of the plains became peaceful subjects of the Sultans of the Dekhan, or of the Great Moghul, and for a long time had no history. But the Mahrattas of the Konkan maintained their independence in their natural fortresses, like the mountaineers of Wales before they were conquered by Edward the First. Occasionally they served as mercenaries in the Muhammadan armies, but many became freebooters and cattle-lifters, and were the terror of the neighbouring plains.

The Mahrattas of the Konkan were intelligent and active, like all mountaineers, but they were rude and ignorant. They claimed kinship with the Rajputs, but they were smaller in stature, with long arms, and had nothing of Rajput politeness or ideas of chivalry. They were superstitious in the extreme, especially in the worship of gods, cows, and Brahmans. They abstained from flesh meat, and lived chiefly on grain and vegetables, regarding milk, butter, and fruit as the luxuries of life. They were grasping and sordid to the last degree, but passionately fond of jewels and ornaments, and lavish in offerings to idols and pagodas.

The father of Sivaji was a Mahratta chief, or free lance, who possessed fortresses at Poona and Joonere, about seventy miles to the eastward of Bombay, as well as the lands round about. Sivaji was born in the fortress of Joonere, but the place was soon afterwards captured by the Moghul. Subsequently the father of Sivaji left the boy and his mother at Poona, and went away to the south and married another wife, and founded a new home amongst the Hindu Rajas of the Peninsula.

Sivaji was a brigand from his boyhood. At the age of

sixteen he was organising bands of followers and repairing mountain fortresses. He could not read or write, but is said to have been an excellent archer, marksman, and horseman. Above all, he was skilled in the use of those treacherous weapons which are peculiar to the Mahrattas—the crooked dagger hidden in the sleeve which was known as the "scorpion," and the steel curved blades which were ringed on to the fingers and known as "tigers' claws," being invisible when the hand was shut and terrible when the hand was open.

It was probably at this period that Sivaji organised the system of plunder, or chout, which is associated with his name. If the inhabitants of a district or village paid him chout, or one-fourth of the yearly land rent which was levied by their Suzerain, they were exempted from Mahratta plunder and devastation; but otherwise they were exposed to the constant inroads of the Mahratta marauders.

All this while Sivaji was most attentive to the worship of the gods, and most reverential towards Mahratta Brahmans. His military captains were taken from any caste, but all his civil officers were Mahratta Brahmans. In after years, when he became a Maha Raja, every post from the Ministers downwards was filled by Mahratta Brahmans.

At last the Sultan of Bijapore sent an army against Sivaji. The crafty Mahratta feigned to be in the utmost alarm. He implored forgiveness for his misdeeds, and promised to be a faithful vassal for the future. Accordingly, the Muhammadan general agreed to meet him without attendants and without arms. Sivaji was bent on murder. He worshipped his gods and received his mother's blessing, and went to the spot armed with the scorpion and the tigers' claws. The Muhammadan general was treacherously slaughtered, whilst the

Mahrattas attacked the camp, and the Bijapore soldiery fled in the wildest confusion.

It would be tedious to dwell on the further exploits of Sivaji. Every year, in the month of October, when the rainy season was over and the cool weather had begun, Sivaji and his Mahrattas set out in bodies of light horse, and ravaged the plains, and collected plunder and chout, until the end of the dry weather in the following June, when they returned to the mountains, and spent the rainy season under the cover of their fortresses. The Muhammadan generals occasionally took the field against them, but might just as well have made war on wasps or locusts, for whenever their heavy cavalry and elephants came within sight of the enemy, the Mahrattas on their active ponies were over the hills and far away.

Sivaji, however, never could recover the fortresses which had been captured by the Moghuls. Joonere, where he was born, was lost whilst he was a child; and Poona, further south, had been taken by Shaista Khan. Accordingly he fixed his head-quarters at Raighur, another hill fortress some distance to the south of Poona.

In 1674 Sivaji was enthroned at Raighur as Maha Raja of the Konkan, and three Englishmen from Bombay were present with gifts and congratulations. Sivaji had performed all the preliminary ceremonies of fasting and pilgrimage, and married a new wife in honour of the occasion. He took his seat upon the throne, surrounded by insignia of Hindu royalty—golden fishes' heads elevated on banners, and golden scales symbolical of justice. He was solemnly weighed in the Oriental fashion, which seems to have been common to Moghul and Hindu; and the silver and gold which balanced his weight in the opposite scale were given to the Brahmans as alms.

The three Englishmen had some trouble at Raighur.[1] They could not live on grain and vegetables, and no animals were slaughtered by the Mahrattas. At last they were supplied with half a goat a day by an old Muhammadan butcher who lived at the foot of the hill. The butcher was delighted with his new customers. Within a few days they had bought as much meat as he had previously sold in as many years, and he made a journey up the hill for the sole purpose of seeing the flesh-eaters. Indeed, no one in India, excepting Englishmen, ventured to eat roast joints. Muhammadans and Portuguese were content with small stews or curries, whilst the Mahrattas were horrified at the idea of eating any meat at all.

In 1675, the year after the enthronement of Sivaji, an English physician, named Fryer, went from Bombay to Joonere, to attend the Moghul governor of the town. He described the Mahrattas as a ragged lot, with their hair covering their ears. The Moghuls were more decent and respectable. The whole country from Bombay to Joonere was a desolation. The people were half-starved wretches, living on grass and herding in kennels, and were so harassed by marauding parties that they often fled from their miserable dwellings to hide themselves in caves and jungles. Moghuls and Mahrattas destroyed everything; they reaped the harvests, drove away cattle, carried off women and children into slavery, and burnt down the jungles in order to drive out the poor fugitives.

On reaching the town of Joonere, Dr. Fryer was received by the Nawab in Oriental state. The floor of the hall was

[1] This fortress, so celebrated in Mahratta history, is called Rairee by English writers in the last century.

spread with a cotton mattress on silver pedestals. The great man sat on a sort of throne at the further end, bolstered up with embroidered cushions. He was smoking a silver hookah with great pomp, for this is a sign of rank and dignity amongst Orientals. It is contrary to eastern etiquette for an inferior to smoke in the presence of a superior, or for a son to smoke in the presence of his father. The officers of the Nawab stood on his right hand. Before him lay his sword and buckler, whilst a page stood by with his bow and arrows. Fryer took off his shoes, made his salaam, and advanced to the left hand of the Nawab.

Dr. Fryer had been called in to attend one of the ladies of the zenana; accordingly the astrologers fixed a lucky day for seeing the patient, and the skill of the doctor was tested by placing a healthy damsel in a bed shut round with curtains. Fryer was allowed to feel the pulse of the pretended patient, and said that there was nothing the matter with her. This decision satisfied the bystanders that the English doctor was a paragon of science and skill.

Dr. Fryer then saw the real patient, and relieved her by bleeding. Next day another lady wanted to be bled. Fryer was led, not into a chamber, but into an open court with a curtain drawn across it, to enable the ladies of the zenana to have a peep at the English doctor. At that moment down came the curtain with a rush, and revealed a bevy of females in *dishabille.* None of the ladies, however, thought of running away, but they put their hands to their faces and peeped at the doctor through their fingers. Fryer saw some needlework and parings of fruit lying about, and concluded that working samplers and eating mangoes were favourite amusements in Oriental zenanas.

Dr. Fryer grew very intimate with the Nawab, and the

two discoursed together on the current topics of the day. The Nawab would not talk about trade; he knew nothing about it, and cared nothing. He strongly objected to any peace between the Moghul and the Mahrattas. So long as there was war both he and other Moghul generals could draw pay from the Imperial treasury for troops that only existed on paper, and receive presents from the Sultans of Bijapore and Golkonda. Indeed, for many years before the Sultans were conquered by Aurangzeb, they spent large sums in bribing the Moghul generals to keep at a distance, and in bribing Sivaji to keep the Moghuls employed. Meanwhile there was not a Sepoy in any of the armies that cared one jot about the causes of the war. The only question with the Sepoys was that of pay, which was called salt. So long as they got their salt, Hindus would serve the Moghul and Muhammadans would serve the Mahratta. Pay was often in arrears, and there were large deductions in the shape of commission to the paymasters, but loyalty to the salt was the ruling sentiment in Indian armies.

When Dr. Fryer had finished his attendance on the Nawab of the town, he was called away to attend on the Nawab of the fortress. This grandee was one of Aurangzeb's pets—a Brahman who had renounced the worship of idols and embraced the religion of the Koran. But the apostate was as grasping and avaricious as ever. Sivaji had always been anxious to recover the fortress of Joonere, because he was born there, and he offered an enormous bribe to the ex-Brahman to deliver up the place. The renegade accepted the money, and then sent a secret hint of what was done to the commander of the Moghul army in the field. The result was that seven thousand Mahrattas were sent to occupy the fortress, but were attacked by an ambuscade and slaughtered to a man.

Sivaji died about the year 1680. Before his death he was the terror of the Dekhan and Peninsula. In 1677 he marched through the Dekhan towards the coast of Coromandel, and founded the kingdom of Tanjore, in the Delta of the Coleroon and Cauvery rivers. On this occasion he passed through the neighbourhood of Madras, and was presented with English medicines by the gentlemen at Fort St. George.

Sivaji is the hero of the Mahrattas, and the founder of the dynasty of the Maha Rajas of the Konkan. He was succeeded by a son named Sambhaji, who lacked the genius of his father, and was betrayed by his own Minister into the hands of Aurangzeb. Sambhaji was offered his life if he would become a Muhammadan; but he replied that he would not abandon the gods of his fathers unless Aurangzeb gave him one of his daughters in marriage. The Great Moghul was stung by the insolence of the Mahratta, and Sambhaji was not only condemned to a horrible death, but his remains were thrown to the hunting dogs.

Sambhaji left an infant son, who was heir to the Mahratta throne, but the boy was taken prisoner by the Moghuls, and brought up in the zenana of Aurangzeb, under the name of Sahu Raja. After the death of Aurangzeb, in 1707, Sahu Raja was placed upon the throne of the Mahrattas as a vassal of the Great Moghul; not, however, at Raighur, which had been captured by Aurangzeb, but at Satara, still further south.

Sahu Raja was a very different prince from his father or grandfather. As a child he had been the spoiled favourite of the zenana, and he grew up to be a weak and effeminate Maha Raja, wasting his life in idle pleasures, and leaving the administration in the hands of the hereditary Brahman

Ministers and officials by whom he was surrounded. In his latter days he became imbecile, and dressed his dog in brocade and jewels, and placed the royal turban upon its head in the Durbar. His generals acquired large territories, and collected chout in remote provinces which had never been reached by Sivaji; but he was conscious of his dependence on the Brahmans, and used sometimes to boast that he had conquered all India and given it to the Brahmans.

Sahu Raja lived on till the year 1748. Meanwhile the sovereignty of the Mahrattas was transferred from the Maha Rajas to the Brahmans; in other words, from the house of Sivaji, who founded the Mahratta empire, to the hereditary Minister who was known as the Peishwa. So long as Sahu Raja was alive this revolution was carried on noiselessly, to prevent needless alarm; but no sooner was he dead than his successor was shut up as a State prisoner in the fortress of Satara, and the Peishwa removed the Mahratta court to Poona, the old ancestral home of the illustrious Sivaji. Henceforth the dynasty of Peishwas reigned at Poona, whilst the puppet Maha Rajas were State prisoners at Satara.

The Mahratta empire became greater under the Brahmans than ever it was under the Maha Rajas. The lieutenants of the Peishwa were the founders of the modern kingdoms of the Guicowars of Baroda, the Scindias of Gwalior, the Holkars of Indore, and the Bhonslas of Nagpore. They conquered Guzerat, Malwa, and large territories in the Dekhan, and collected chout from the Punjab to the Carnatic, and from Bengal to Mysore. They ceased to heed the Maha Rajas of Satara, but acknowledged the Peishwa as their rightful Suzerain, and were responsible to the court of Poona for all the revenue, plunder, and chout which they collected through their freebooting armies.

Whilst the Mahratta empire of the Peishwas was extending over India, the Muhammadan empire of the Moghuls was breaking to pieces. The successors of Aurangzeb reigned at Delhi, but they were shut up in the imperial palace, and no longer moved their camps through Hindustan and the Dekhan, as in the days of their illustrious ancestors. Their power had dwindled to a shadow, and the shadow was a bone of contention between rival Viziers and grandees, who plotted against each other, and often assassinated each other, without scruple or shame. Meanwhile the Viceroys threw off their dependence on the court of Delhi, and became independent princes, and converted their provinces into independent kingdoms. In this manner the Nawabs of Oude, Bengal, and the Carnatic, and the once famous Nizam of Hyderabad, became Sultans of India, excepting that they still retained the old name of Nawab, and professed to hold their territories under the authority of the Great Moghul.

Whilst the Moghul empire was breaking to pieces through internal disorders, it was exposed to the constant assaults and ravages of the Mahrattas, which could only be averted by the ignominious payment of chout. The result was that chout became an institution; and the Peishwas of Poona, with the wild audacity of Brahmans, began to collect chout in all parts of India as an inherent right; and whenever the right was disputed, they plundered, ravaged, burnt, and murdered without mercy or remorse.[1]

---

[1] Chout, or one fourth, was always a familiar idea with the people of India. In the administration of civil justice one fourth of every amount awarded by a judicial decree went to the judge as his perquisite. Sitting in judgment was thus a profitable employment, to say nothing of the bribes in the shape of presents which were always sent

In 1738—39 an overwhelming army of Persians, under Nadir Shah, invaded Hindustan. Nadir Shah was a brigand like Sivaji, but he became a great conqueror like Cyrus or Nebuchádnezzar, and ruled an empire which extended from the Euphrates to the Indus. He would have been a giant by the side of the Mahratta, for he had a noble presence, large eyes, a voice like thunder, and an aspect so terrible that men bent before him in fear and trembling.

The Moghul armies fled from Nadir Shah like sheep flying from a lion. He entered Delhi with the pride of a conqueror, and took up his abode in the palace, whilst some of his soldiers were on bivouac in different parts of the city. In the middle of the night there was a rising of the inhabitants, and many of the Persians were slaughtered. On the morrow Nadir Shah wreaked his revenge on Delhi. From eight o'clock in the morning until three o'clock in the afternoon there was nothing but sack, fire, and carnage, whilst Nadir Shah sat in a little mosque in the public square, exulting in his vengeance with the ferocity of a demon. At three o'clock the butchery was brought to a close, but the streets were choked with burning houses and bleeding bodies. In the end Nadir Shah carried away the treasures of Delhi and the empire, with all the priceless jewels of the Peacock's Throne.

The invasion of Nadir Shah was a death blow to the Moghul empire. The Peishwas of Poona threatened to become the Suzerains of India, but the Padishahs of Delhi dwindled into a pageant and a name.

---

to the judge or magistrate as propitiatory offerings. No wonder that the English merchants refused to apply to native courts for redress in their dealings with natives.

HISTORY OF BRITISH INDIA.

IX.—*Madras and Calcutta: The Black Hole and its Revenge.*

1600 to 1757.

THE East India Company was a hundred and fifty years old, and had established trading towns at Madras, Calcutta, and Bombay, before the British nation troubled itself about Padishah or Peishwa, Sultans or Rajas. Roe's mission to the Great Moghul made some stir in the reign of James the First, and stories of Hindu idolatries and Muhammadan tragedies were topics of discourse amongst the educated few. But Englishmen in India were busy with providing cotton goods and other Indian commodities for the home markets, and with selling scarlet cloth and cutlery to native merchants, and consequently took little heed of the current of events unless it threatened themselves. As for the Englishmen in England, they were too much distracted with their own politics and wars to concern themselves about the campaigns of Aurangzeb or the ravages of the Mahrattas.

Madras was the earliest territorial settlement which the English founded in India. It dates as far back as 1639, in the reigns of Shah Jehan and Charles the First, when Muhammadan Sultans were reigning in the Dekhan and Hindu Rajas were reigning in the Peninsula. A factory on the coast of Coromandel, far away to the south of the Moghul empire, was surrounded with walls and bastions, and mounted with cannon, and was pointed at as Fort St. George by every ship sailing up or down the Bay of Bengal. Within the fort were little streets of houses, occupied by Europeans. Outside the fort was a large native town, inhabited by a mixed population of Hindus, Armenians, and others; whilst round about were native villages of weavers, dyers, and other artisans, with mud huts and water tanks peeping through groves of trees and fences of cactus and prickly pear. The territory was very small—a strip of sand on a surf-bound shore, stretching six miles along the Bay and one mile inland.

For this strip of sea-board the English had agreed to pay a rent of 1200 pagodas a year, or nearly £600, to a little Hindu Raja. The Raja was conquered by the Sultan of Golkonda, and the Sultan was conquered by Aurangzeb; but the rent still remained the same, whilst the English Government at Madras raised a yearly revenue from customs and ground rents, which averaged about 40,000 pagodas, or nearly £20,000, irrespective of all profits of trade.

From the beginning of the eighteenth century the English paid the yearly rent to the Nawab of the Carnatic, who ruled all the country from the river Kistna southward to the Coleroon, and lived in Oriental luxury at the city of Arcot, about seventy miles to the westward of Madras. The Nawab of the Carnatic was in his turn dependent on the Nizam of Hyderabad—a still grander personage—who ruled the old territories of Bijapore and Golkonda, to the northward of the river Kistna.

In the time of Aurangzeb, the Nawab and the Nizam had been the most obedient servants of the Padishah; but ever since the invasion of Nadir Shah, in 1738-39, they had kept back the revenues of their provinces, and set up as independent princes. All this while, however, they were harassed by the Mahrattas and exposed to frequent demands for chout. Madras was tolerably safe from the Mahrattas, for the native powers had a wholesome dread of the cannon on Fort St. George.

But the war for the Austrian succession was raging in Europe, and in 1746, the year of Culloden, Madras was captured by the French, and the English inhabitants were carried away as prisoners of war to the French settlement at Pondicherry, about a hundred miles to the southward. Subsequently the English tried to capture Pondicherry, but failed. At last, in 1748, Madras was restored to the English under the treaty of Aix-la-Chapelle.

But, in spite of the peace between Great Britain and France in Europe, there was no peace in India. The English and French East India Companies were commercial rivals, burning to ruin each other. The Nawab of the Carnatic and the Nizam of Hyderabad were gathered to their fathers, and rival sons and kinsmen were fighting for the vacant thrones, regardless of the Suzerainty of the Great Moghul. The English at Madras and the French at Pondicherry took opposite sides, and fought against each other in the native armies, regardless of the treaty of Aix-la-Chapelle. The French got the better of the English, for Dupleix, the governor of Pondicherry, was a brilliant Frenchman, very different from the plodding traders at Fort St. George; and the Nawab of the Frenchman's choice was enthroned at Arcot, and his Nizam was enthroned at Hyderabad, whilst the English had no Nizam at all, and the Nawab of their choice was closely besieged by the French and Muhammadan armies in the remote town of Trichinopoly.

Robert Clive came to the rescue. He boldly marched a small detachment from Madras to Arcot, captured the city and fortress, and compelled the French and Muhammadans to raise the siege of Trichinopoly. The exploits of Clive and Lawrence are forgotten now, but they ended in the triumph of the English in the Carnatic and the enthronement of their Nawab at Arcot. Clive went to England a year or two afterwards, and was praised by William Pitt as "the heaven-born general," and rewarded with the commission of Colonel.

But Great Britain and France were soon weary of Indian wars. No one cared what Nawab reigned at Arcot, or what Nizam reigned at Hyderabad. The rival East India Companies were emptying their treasuries, whilst their servants in India were fighting one another in the armies of native princes, and all trade was at a standstill.

In 1755 a peace was signed at Pondicherry. The English Nawab was to reign at Arcot, and the French Nizam was to reign at Hyderabad; whilst Dupleix, the arch spirit of the war, was removed from the governorship of Pondicherry, and returned to France a ruined man.

Meanwhile Colonel Clive had been sent from England to Bombay to form an alliance with the Mahratta Peishwa at Poona, and drive the French out of Hyderabad. Clive, however, was met at Bombay by the news of the peace at Pondicherry. He joined an English fleet, commanded by Admiral Watson, in rooting out some dangerous pirates on the coast of Malabar, and then went to Madras. By this time another war between Great Britain and France was threatening to break out in Europe, which is known in history as the Seven Years' War; and Clive was once more hoping to engage in a campaign against the French, and to drive them out of India.

At this crisis terrible tidings arrived from Bengal. The English settlement at Calcutta had been captured and sacked by the Nawab of Bengal; the property of the East India Company had been scattered to the winds; and a hundred and twenty-three English prisoners had been suffocated to death in a barrack cell known as the Black Hole.

The English had settled at Calcutta, on the bank of the river Hughly, during the latter half of the reign of Aurangzeb. They rented three native villages, on the condition that they were neither to build fortifications or land cannon; but during the rebellion of the Bengalis against the persecutions of Aurangzeb they were permitted to build a wall round their factory, and it was henceforth known as Fort William. Outside the fort were the houses and gardens of the English inhabitants, together with a church and other buildings overlooking the factory. The native villages were still further away from the banks of the river, and were partly protected by a ditch, which the native inhabitants had begun to dig some years previously to keep out the Mahrattas.[1]

Traditions of the English in these early days still linger in Bengal. There was Dr. Gabriel Boughton, who cured the daughter of Shah Jehan after her dress had caught fire, and obtained from her imperial father permission for the English to settle in Bengal. After him was old Job Channock, the founder of Calcutta; and the neighbouring village of Barrackpore is called Channock by the natives to this day. Job

[1] The Mahratta ditch has disappeared for generations, but it is supposed to have run along the line of route now known as the Circular Road.

saved a Bengal widow from being burnt alive in a suttee, and then married her himself, and became half a Hindu, and sacrificed a cock every year to the goddess Durga. Next to him was a Dr. Hamilton, who went to Delhi with an English deputation early in the eighteenth century, and cured the Great Moghul of a painful disease; but the result was that the skilful doctor was not allowed to return to Calcutta, until he pretended that all his medicines were exhausted, and that he must go to England to procure a fresh supply. Meanwhile the English at Calcutta passed their days in pleasant monotony—busy all the forenoon, sleeping all the afternoon, and spending their evenings in boating, shooting or fishing, and then paying visits to one another.

The English thought themselves as secure at Calcutta as at any port in Great Britain. Never, since the Hindu rebellion against Aurangzeb, had any enemy appeared against Calcutta. The Nawab had demanded subsidies from time to time, but was always appeased by money and presents. The Mahrattas ravaged Bengal, defeated the Nawab, and blockaded his capital at Murshedabad, about 120 miles to the northward of Calcutta; they took possession of Orissa, and compelled the Nawab to pay chout for the remainder of his territories;[1] but they were never seen at Calcutta, and never approached the Mahratta ditch. There was no fear of the French, for the Nawab had forbidden all wars between the English and French within his territories. Two or three hundred soldiers were kept at Calcutta; not, however, so much for the defence of the settlement as for the protection of the English boats that plied between Calcutta and Patna.

---

[1] Bengal includes the three provinces of Bengal proper, Behar, and Orissa; but all are comprehended under the general name of Bengal.

The old Nawab of Bengal died at Murshedabad, in April, 1756. He was succeeded by a grandson, a young man of twenty, named Suraj-ud-daula, better known to the English soldiers as "Sir Roger Dowler." But the young Nawab had many rivals, and he suspected that one of them was harboured by the English at Calcutta. He was also told that the English were planting cannon on the river side, and were going to make war on the French, contrary to his late grandfather's orders; whilst his imagination was fired by stories of the vast wealth of the English at Calcutta, as fabulous as those of the palace of Aladdin. The result was that on the 16th of June the Nawab appeared in the outskirts of Calcutta with an army of 50,000 men.

The English knew that the Nawab was coming, but seem to have lost their heads. They ought to have demolished the houses and other buildings outside Fort William, and cleared away the rubbish; they might then have held out within the factory walls, and have kept the enemy in constant alarm with shells by day and sallies by night. The English, however, tried to save their houses by placing outposts outside the town; and the enemy drove in the outposts; and the Christian inhabitants flocked into the factory, whilst the enemy opened fire under cover of the buildings. The fighting lasted from Wednesday till Saturday, and then the women were carried to the ships, whilst Mr. Drake, the governor of Calcutta, and some other men of standing, made their escape in like manner.

On Sunday morning, the 20th of June, there was more fighting; but the garrison lost heart at seeing the ships moving away down the river. The rains had begun with their accustomed fury. The English soldiers broke into the arrack stores and got helplessly drunk. A flag of truce was held out; but the Nawab's soldiery were swarming over the walls, and the factory, with all its warehouses, workshops, and offices, was soon in the hands of the Muhammadans.

The Nawab was puffed up with the pride of victory, but exasperated at the smallness of the booty. He had only found fifty thousand rupees in the English treasury, whilst much of the merchandise was embezzled or destroyed by his own soldiery. Night was coming on, and the prisoners, to the number of a hundred and forty-six, were driven by clubs and swords into the Black Hole—a chamber which was less than twenty feet square, and had only two little gratings at the entrance to let in fresh air.

The Black Hole had been built for refractory soldiers, and probably never held more than four or five prisoners at a time. To cram in a hundred and forty-six human beings was death by torture. The night was sultry and stifling, and but for the rain severy soul in the place would have perished of heat apoplexy. Large bribes were offered to the jailers for deliverance; but the Nawab was asleep, and no one dared to wake him, or to remove the prisoners without his orders. Then followed cries for water, and one or two good Samaritans brought water-skins to the gratings, but the wretched victims fought like madmen for the water, whilst the native guards brought lighted torches, in order to gloat over their sufferings. It is needless to dwell on the horrors of the night. Next morning twenty-three were dragged out alive—the remainder had perished of heat and suffocation.

The news of this catastrophe of the 20th of June did not reach Madras until the following August. An avenging force, under Clive and Watson, left Madras the following October, but had to beat against the north-east monsoon. On the 1st of January, 1757, the expedition reached Calcutta, and recovered the place after very little fighting; whilst a force was sent up the river and captured the Muhammadan town of Hughly.

The Nawab took the field with his army of rabble soldiery, but was in mortal fear of Clive. He never dreamed that the English would return to Bengal, and the fall of Calcutta and Hughly filled him with painful surprise. Worst of all, he had enemies and traitors in his camp, and knew not whom to trust; and he moved about uneasily with his troops, swearing that he was the friend of the English, and promising to restore all the goods and money that had been carried away from Calcutta. But he was constantly changing his mind. He refused to let Clive capture the French settlement at Chandernagore, hard by the town of Hughly; then he yielded under pressure, but shortly afterwards withdrew his permission. Meanwhile he was secretly sending letters to the French at Hyderabad, imploring them to come to Bengal and help him to drive out the English.

Clive was exasperated at all this craft and lying. He was not over anxious to punish the Nawab, for he must have known that the Black Hole disaster was partly the result of an accident. He was willing to be friends with the Nawab provided that it was possible to trust him, but he wanted a restitution of the plundered property, and he was burning to drive out the French. He captured Chandernagore on his own responsibility, and the French governor and other refugees were entertained by the Nawab, and some were enrolled in his service.

When Clive discovered that the Nawab was enlisting Frenchmen and making overtures to the French at Hyderabad, he resolved to take the bull by the horns. He turned the tables against the Nawab by coming to a secret understanding with the traitors in his camp, and especially with a Muhammadan general named Meer Jaffier. A treaty was arranged, under which Meer Jaffier pledged himself to join Clive with a division of the army and to grant all that the English required, provided that he was made Nawab of Bengal in the room of Suraj-ud-daula. When this was concluded, Clive took the field with his small force, and advanced to Plassy, within thirty miles of Murshedabad, and there waited to be joined by Meer Jaffier.

The Nawab had already marched to Plassy, as if on his way to Calcutta, with 50,000 foot, 18,000 horse, and fifty pieces of cannon, accompanied by forty French refugees from Chandernagore. Clive had only 1000 Europeans, 2000 Sepoys, and nine or ten pieces of artillery. After some hesitation Clive resolved on battle. Then followed a cloud of smoke and dust. Meer Jaffier held aloof from the action, and made no effort to join Clive; and none of the Nawab's troops fought with any spirit, except the forty Frenchmen. The Nawab kept in his tent, and was beside himself with terror. At last he fled from the field with his favourite wives and jewels, and was seen no more by Europeans, whilst his army fled in all directions, leaving Clive in the virtual possession of Bengal. Ten days afterwards the Nawab was betrayed to Meer Jaffier, and barbarously murdered.

Clive forgave Meer Jaffier's inaction, and enthroned him at Murshedabad as Nawab of Bengal. A treaty was concluded, under which Meer Jaffier agreed to pay a million sterling to the East India Company, and three-quarters of a million as restitution money to the inhabitants of Calcutta, natives as well as Europeans. He also granted everything for which the English had been petitioning the Great Moghul ever since their first settlement in India, and above all the inestimable privilege of carrying every commodity duty free through every part of his dominions.

Meer Jaffier lavished immense sums on Clive and his officers and soldiers, as well as on different members of the little local government at Calcutta; but this money was taken from the public treasury of the Nawab. Clive refused to receive any private presents from Meer Jaffier, and never seems to have known of the treasures which were hidden away in the zenana of the palace, and were said to have amounted to several millions sterling. Meer Jaffier complained that the public money was exhausted by the donations and restitutions, whilst he was sharing the hidden hoards with the very few natives who were in the secret. What Meer Jaffier did with the money will appear hereafter; but two of his fortunate partners entered the service of Clive as writers on about thirty shillings a week; and ten years afterwards one of them died leaving a million and a quarter sterling, whilst the other spent ninety thousand pounds sterling on his mother's funeral alone.

But Clive was tempted to commit one act which sullies his name. A Hindu, named Omichund, had been the medium of communication between Clive and Meer Jaffier and the other traitors. When the secret treaty was being concluded, Omichund threatened to reveal the plot to the Nawab, unless a clause was inserted in the treaty granting him a sum equal to three hundred thousand pounds sterling. Clive met this rascality in Oriental fashion. A sham treaty was drawn up containing the desired clause, in order to keep Omichund quiet; and Clive not only signed the treaty, but, finding that Admiral Watson had some scruples in the matter, he forged Watson's signature. At the same time a real treaty without the clause was signed by all parties. After the victory at Plassy Omichund was told that he had been duped by a sham treaty, and is said to have gone out of his mind. But the action of Clive, although it did not put a penny in his pocket, and only checkmated a consummate villain, has been condemned to this day as a stain upon his character as an English gentleman.

All this while the people of Calcutta were overpowered with joy; such joy as rarely happens once in a lifetime. They had been humiliated to the dust and stripped of all their possessions, but Clive had avenged the insult to the English name and raised them from poverty to riches. Boats from Murshedabad arrived at Calcutta loaded with rupees and bullion to the value of nearly a million sterling, and other boats were known to be coming with additional cargoes of precious metal. For the moment Calcutta was elevated to the seventh heaven of felicity. Enemies greeted one another like friends and brothers. The sack of Calcutta and tragedy of the Black Hole passed away like hideous dreams; and Robert Clive, the victor at Plassy and saviour of the English in India, was glorified as the national hero from Bengal to the British Isles.[1]

---

[1] Bombay has not been mentioned in the foregoing chapter. It was ceded by the Portuguese to the English in 1661, but did not play a part in history until the administration of Warren Hastings. The story is told in Chapter XI.

X.—*Clive and the Merchant Empire of Bengal.*

1725 to 67.

ROBERT CLIVE was a Shropshire man, born in 1725, of the middle class. In his boyhood he was wild and headstrong; passionate and fond of fighting; climbing a church-steeple to astonish his native town; and forming other boys into a lawless band, demanding apples and halfpence from the shopkeepers on the condition of sparing their windows. Nothing could be done with him, and in his eighteenth year he was shipped off to Madras, as Macaulay says, to make a fortune or to die of fever.

At nineteen Clive landed at Madras as a writer in the service of the East India Company, and was placed in the secretary's office as a clerk; but the drudgery of the desk could not tame him, and he was as wayward and stubborn as ever. He offended the secretary, and was ordered by the governor to apologise, which he did; but when the secretary tried to smooth matters by inviting him to dinner, he replied that he had only been ordered to apologise, and not to dine. Twice he fought a duel at Madras. Twice, also, he tried to shoot himself, but missed fire each time.

In 1746, when Clive was twenty-one, he was carried to Pondicherry with the other English prisoners, but managed to escape from the town disguised as a Muhammadan. He then asked and obtained a commission as ensign in the Company's service, and threw himself heart and soul into the war with the French. He marched to Arcot through such a storm of rain and lightning that the native garrison thought him a demon or sorcerer, and fled in a panic at his approach. He held Arcot against overwhelming odds, and foiled the enemy in every possible way, until he was the idol of the Sepoys, and even the Mahrattas glorified his genius and valour.

Colonel Clive was scarcely thirty-two years of age when he won the battle of Plassy. He was the same in Bengal as he had been in Shropshire, and secured a fortune for life from Meer Jaffier much in the same way as he had secured apples and halfpence in his boyhood. But the discipline of a soldier's life had made a man of him; by forcing him to obey it had fitted him for command. Although absolute master of the destinies of Bengal, he acted as became a servant of the East India Company. The Shropshire boy might have seized the sovereignty of Bengal, and become another Sivaji; but the trained soldier left Meer Jaffier to reign after his own fashion; and had the new Nawab been fitted for his post, Clive would have been content to uphold the Company's trade in Bengal in its new position and privileges without interfering in the Muhammadan government.

But Meer Jaffier was tyrannical and incapable. He turned out the Hindu officials, who governed towns and districts, and tried to place his own Muhammadan kinsmen and dependents in their room. At this crisis the Mahrattas came and demanded arrears of chout, whilst the eldest son of the Padishah, known as the Shahzada, appeared on the frontier, supported by the Nawab of Oude and a large army, and declared that he had been appointed Viceroy of Bengal by his imperial father. Meanwhile the disaffected Hindu officials were either breaking out in open revolt, or secretly intriguing with the invaders.

Meer Jaffier was utterly unable to cope with these difficulties. He might have been a tolerable general when he was a younger man, but he had grown old and self-indulgent. He stupified himself with opium, or idled away his time in the company of singing and dancing girls. He appeared in public loaded with pearls and precious stones, whilst his rabble army was clamouring for pay. He was entirely dependent upon Clive, and there was no one but Clive and his European soldiers to keep the peace in Bengal, or defend the country from Mahratta or Muhammadan invaders.

The courtiers at Murshedabad held Meer Jaffier in such contempt that they called him "Clive's Jackass." One day a courtier was rebuked by the Nawab for having offended Clive by permitting his servants to fight those of the English Colonel. "Me offend the Colonel?" he cried, with a sneer; "why, I never rise in the morning without making a salaam to his Jackass." The whole court was convulsed with secret laughter, whilst the Nawab was perhaps the only Muhammadan in Murshedabad who did not understand the sarcasm.

The Mahrattas were drawn away from Bengal by an Afghan invasion; whilst Clive routed the armies of the Shahzada and Nawab of Oude, and compelled them to retire. Clive, however, was convinced that nothing could save Bengal from future invasions and revolts but a standing army of 2000 European soldiers and a corresponding force of drilled Sepoys. The difficulty was to find the money. The

East India Company could not maintain a standing army out of the profits of their trade, and Meer Jaffier could not maintain one so long as he was left to squander the revenues of the country on jewels and dancing girls, and possibly on secret presents to English officials at Calcutta to secure their interest and support.

Meanwhile the Moghul court at Delhi was anxious to obtain money from Bengal. In the days of Aurangzeb at least a million sterling had been sent every year from Bengal to Delhi; but ever since the invasion of Nadir Shah there had been a stoppage of the supplies. Accordingly, the Vizier at Delhi secretly offered the government of Bengal to Clive, provided that the great English Colonel would engage to send a share of the revenue to the imperial treasury at Delhi.[1] Clive could not accept such an offer for himself after having secured a splendid private fortune from Meer Jaffier, and he would not accept it in behalf of the East India Company, for the Directors had offended him.

In the end, Clive threw over the East India Company, and wrote direct to the great William Pitt, who was at this time at the head of the English Ministry. He proposed that the British nation should accept the sovereignty of Bengal from the Padishah at Delhi; pay a yearly rent of half a million sterling to Delhi as the imperial share of the revenue; devote another half-million to the maintenance of a standing army in Bengal; and keep the surplus, which he estimated at two millions sterling, towards paying off the national debt, or doing something else for the benefit of the nation.

Pitt, however, was engaged in his memorable struggle

---

[1] In the technical language of Moghul forms, Clive was offered the "Dewanny" of Bengal. See *Short History of India.*

for the rights of Parliament against the growing pretensions of the Crown. Accordingly, he declined the proposals of Clive on the ground that the sovereignty of Bengal would render the British Crown all powerful, and endanger the liberties of the people of England.

In 1760 Colonel Clive returned to England, leaving the English merchants at Calcutta to do the best they could with the small means at their disposal for protecting the English settlements and factories in Bengal. In 1761 the war with France, which had been raging in Southern India ever since 1757, was brought to a triumphant close by the victories of Sir Eyre Coote and capture of Pondicherry. But the Moghul empire was breaking to pieces. New principalities were springing up in different parts of India, chiefly on a basis of plunder and blackmail. At last in 1761, the very year in which the English captured Pondicherry, the Mahrattas were defeated by the Afghans in the battle of Painput, in the neighbourhood of Delhi, near the very spot where the Kauravas were slaughtered by the Pandavas in the great war of the Maha Bharata. The defeat was followed by a massacre of Mahratta prisoners by the victorious Afghans, which paralysed the Mahratta rulers, and was followed by weeping and wailing throughout the Mahratta country. The reigning Peishwa is said to have died of a broken heart, and his successor at Poona was so harassed by his domestic enemies that for nearly ten years little or nothing was heard of the exploits of the Mahrattas.

Meanwhile the Nawab Meer Jaffier had become a dead weight on the little English community at Calcutta, as insupportable as the old man of the sea on the shoulders of Sindbad the sailor. At last they threw off the burden by a *coup d'état*. In 1761, Meer Jaffier was deposed by the English merchants, and his son-in-law, Meer Cossim, was set up in his room without the slightest opposition or disturbance. Meer Jaffier yielded to his fate with a patience and resignation worthy of the animal after whom he had been nick-named; but he was wise enough to leave Murshedabad, where he would certainly have been murdered by his successor, and to remove with his family and treasures to Calcutta, where he took up his abode under the protection of the English, who had first set him up and then supplanted him.

This revolution was hailed with great satisfaction by the English, but proved anything but an unmixed blessing. At first Meer Cossim was most submissive to the English. He granted all that the English required of him; he confirmed all the privileges which had been conceded by Meer Jaffier, including the exclusive right of transporting their goods throughout his territories duty free; and he engaged to provide a yearly subsidy for the maintenance of a permanent European force for the protection of Bengal. But all this while he meant mischief. Craftily and quietly he cut off all connection with the English. He avoided all money disputes, which had created so much ill-feeling between the English and Meer Jaffier, by making over three large districts to the Company, and leaving the English to govern the inhabitants and collect the revenue as they pleased, in lieu of paying the money direct out of his own treasury.

Meer Cossim then left Murshedabad, which was only 120 miles from Calcutta, and fixed his capital at Monghyr, which was more than 300 miles. He reduced his expenditure to a minimum by cutting down costly establishments which had been only maintained for pomp and show, and discharging the bulk of his rabble soldiery. He then busied himself at Monghyr in the creation of a new army of picked men, drilled in the English fashion; whilst he began to cast cannon and manufacture muskets, as if preparing for war.

Meer Cossim was unquestionably a Muhammadan general of energy and capacity; and possibly he might have reigned in peace with his English neighbours, but for one of those misunderstandings which seem to be the work of some demon of mischief, and which soon created a deadly quarrel between the two parties.

The East India Company had always persisted in paying its servants in India the smallest possible salaries, and that without any pensions on retirement. It however permitted its servants to engage in private traffic, so long as they did not interfere in the trade between India and Europe. Accordingly civil and military servants speculated in the traffic with different ports in the Eastern seas, and by such means were often enabled to return to England with considerable fortunes.

Before the victory at Plassy the Company's servants in Bengal had never dreamed of engaging in the retail trade carried on by the native dealers in the towns and villages up country. When, however, Meer Jaffier was enthroned at Murshedabad, he granted them, as already stated, the privilege of carrying commodities to all parts of his dominions, free from the duties which were otherwise collected by the Nawab's officers on all highways and rivers. Accordingly the English at Calcutta began to traffic in the products of the country, such as salt, betel nut, tobacco, oil, rice, sugar and opium; and as they paid no duty, they undersold the native dealers and soon monopolised the whole trade. Indeed, the native dealers would have been ruined, but in self-defence they began to buy permits, known as dustucks, from the Company's servants, which bore the

Company's seal, and sufficed to exempt them from the payment of duties at the different toll-houses.

Meer Jaffier had quietly submitted to these transactions. He had deemed it better to sacrifice the inland duties rather than quarrel with the English. The down-trodden Hindus of Bengal were afraid to raise their voices against the English. They were helpless and effeminate, and a very different race from the independent Rajput or active Mahratta. Moreover they had been oppressed for generations by the Zemindars, who farmed the land revenue, and were for the most part Muhammadans of Persian extraction, having no fellow feeling or sympathy for Bengali idolators.

Meer Cossim was a Nawab of a very different stamp from Meer Jaffier. He complained bitterly that the native dealers were deprived of their livelihood, and that he himself was robbed of the transit duties, in order to fill the pockets of the English at Calcutta; and the Bengali dealers readily joined in the clamour when they found that the Nawab was on their side. In reply the English quoted the treaty, and certainly the terms of the treaty were in their favour, and they naturally refused to surrender a privilege under which the youngest servant of the Company might clear a thousand a year by the sale of dustucks alone.

Meer Cossim checkmated the English by abolishing the transit duties altogether, and thus placed the native dealer on the same level as the English merchant. The profits of the servants of the Company vanished in a moment, and they were furious at the loss. The question was discussed by the Governor and Council at Calcutta. The majority argued that Meer Cossim had violated the treaty, since the privilege was no longer of value to the English; whilst the minority argued on the opposite side, that the Nawab had a sovereign right to grant a boon to his subjects which the English had no right to dispute. But one-sided interpretations of the treaty only exasperated the Nawab, who was already smarting under the pretensions of the English; whilst arguments, based on the inherent rights of sovereignty, were scoffed at by men who had placed the Nawab upon the throne, and could depose him at their pleasure.

In 1763 the English at Calcutta determined to send two of their number, Messrs. Amyatt and Hay, as a deputation to Monghyr to settle matters with the Nawab. Meer Cossim replied that there was nothing to settle; he had abolished the duties, and could not listen to any deputation. When, however, Amyatt and Hay reached Monghyr, they were fêted and feasted in oriental fashion, but kept under close surveillance so as to prevent their intriguing with disaffected grandees. At this crisis a boat arrived from Calcutta, loaded with goods and fire-arms for the English factory at Patna, about 100 miles further up the river. Meer Cossim was suspicious and alarmed. He kept the boat at Monghyr; he permitted Amyatt to return down the river to Calcutta, but he detained Hay at Monghyr as a hostage.

Then followed one of the saddest tragedies in history. The Englishmen at Patna were cut off from all communication with the English capital at Calcutta by the Nawab's army at Monghyr. Accordingly they thought to secure their safety at Patna by taking possession of the town. They captured Patna by surprise, whilst the native garrison fled in a panic; but within a few hours the English soldiers got drunk, and the native garrison returned and recovered the place.

Meer Cossim regarded the attack on Patna as the

beginning of a war. His forces took the English factory by storm, and sent all the English residents to Monghyr as prisoners of war. Another English factory at Cossimbazar, near Murshedabad, suffered the same fate as the factory at Patna. Meanwhile Meer Cossim sent orders to his officers throughout his dominions to slaughter the English wherever they could be found; and Mr. Amyatt was murdered on his way to Calcutta, and his head was cut off, and sent in triumph to the Nawab at Monghyr.

The Governor and Council at Calcutta were maddened by the tidings. They proclaimed Meer Jaffier Nawab of Bengal in the room of Meer Cossim, and sent an avenging army up the river. Murshedabad was captured after some hard fighting; for the drilled troops of Meer Cossim fought better than any native force which the English had hitherto encountered in India. Meer Cossim was alarmed at the loss of Murshedabad, and retreated from Monghyr to Patna, taking all his prisoners with him, to the number of 150 English souls.

At Patna Meer Cossim was aroused by worse tidings. The English army had advanced from Murshedabad and captured Monghyr. In his wrath Meer Cossim ordered the slaughter of his English prisoners. They had been lodged in a large Muhammadan mansion built round a square court, like a college quadrangle. Three of them, including Mr. Hay, were ordered to come out and were cut to pieces outside the buildings. The Sepoys, commanded by a European deserter, known as Sombre, or Sumru, climbed to the roof of the buildings and fired upon the English prisoners who had congregated in the centre court. Those who escaped the volley sought shelter in the buildings, but were quickly followed by the Sepoys, and a fearful slaughter ensued. The

English, driven to desperation, fought with brickbats, bottles, and articles of furniture. The Sepoys were struck with admiration, and refused to fire on unarmed men; but Sombre struck down the ringleaders, and compelled the Sepoys to carry on the work of slaughter until every Englishman was dead or dying. The remains were then thrown into a well in the courtyard.[1]

The massacre of Patna sealed the doom of Meer Cossim. The avenging army of the English advanced against the blood-stained city, and took it by storm. But Meer Cossim had vanished. He had fled into Oude with his family and treasures, but was soon despoiled of his wealth by the Nawab, and perished a few years afterwards in miserable exile.

All this while the Directors of the East India Company in England were alternately alarmed and delighted at the revolutions in Bengal. In those days it was often six months before a letter from Calcutta could reach London, and another six months before an answer could reach Calcutta. Consequently the dispatches from the old India House in Leadenhall Street were alternately filled with reproaches and rejoicings. The Directors were very angry at the dethronement of Meer Jaffier. They were delighted at the new arrangements with Meer Cossim. Next they were extremely wrath with their servants for having engaged in the inland trade; but considered, with strange inconsistency, that the Company ought to have shared in the profits. Finally, whilst they were chuckling over the abolition of the transit duties by Meer Cossim, they were horror-stricken by the massacre at Patna.

---

[1] The story of Sombre and his subsequent adventures will be told further on.

But news of a still more portentous character was reaching England. The puppet Padishah at Delhi had been murdered by his Vizier, and the exiled Shahzada had been proclaimed Padishah under the name of Shah Alam; and Shah Alam had appointed the Nawab of Oude to be his Vizier, and the two were marching a large army towards Bengal with the view of wresting the territory from Meer Jaffier and the English.

In this desperate state of affairs all eyes were directed to Clive. By this time the famous Colonel was an Irish peer, in the full enjoyment of a magnificent fortune, and less than forty years of age. Nevertheless he accepted the post of Governor of Bengal, and went out to India with the full determination of settling the government on a lasting basis, without adding a guinea to his private means beyond the salary awarded to him by the East India Company.

Lord Clive reached India in 1765, and found at Madras that his work was already cut out for him. Sir Hector Monro had inflicted a crushing defeat on the Padishah and his Nawab Vizier at Buxar, and the Padishah was a suppliant in the English camp, whilst the Nawab Vizier had fled into exile, leaving the whole of his vast territory of Oude at the absolute disposal of the English. To crown all, Meer Jaffier was dead, and the only legitimate heir to the vacant throne was an infant grandson aged six, exactly the kind of baby Nawab that Clive wanted to impose upon Bengalis, French, and Dutch, whilst he settled the government of Bengal after his own fashion but under the cover of the Nawab's name.

On landing at Calcutta, however, Lord Clive found that the Governor and Council had done their best to thwart him. They were preparing to send an English force to the other end of Hindustan, to place the young Padishah on the throne at

Delhi; and they had agreed to make over the whole of Oude to the new government, as the beginning of a restored Moghul empire. In Bengal they had done worse. They had concluded a corrupt bargain with a grandee of Murshedabad, named Muhammad Reza Khan. The infant grandson had been set aside as too young for money dealings. An illegitimate son of Meer Jaffier, aged twenty, was placed on the throne of Murshedabad, under the guardianship of Muhammad Reza Khan; whilst the Governor and Council helped themselves to £200,000 out of the public treasury.

Lord Clive was furious at these transactions. "It was downright madness," he said, "to send an English force from Calcutta to Delhi." As regards the bargaining at Murshedabad, he declared that the whites had joined the blacks in plundering the public treasury. He was twitted with having received a present from Meer Jaffier, but he replied that he had earned the money by his victory at Plassy, whereas the Calcutta Governor and Council had rendered no service whatever.

Lord Clive was unable to punish the delinquents, but he settled the affairs of Bengal on the basis which he had suggested to William Pitt six or seven years previously. He procured from the young Padishah, Shah Alam, a formal grant of all the revenues of Bengal, and engaged to pay him in return a yearly tribute of a quarter of a million sterling. He then took over the revenues of Bengal in favour of the East India Company, devoting half a million to the support of the puppet Nawab and his native officials, half a million to the maintenance of a standing army, and a quarter of a million to the Padishah, retaining the surplus for the pockets of the English shareholders. The Nawab was powerless to resist this transfer of the revenues; and Lord Clive assured the Court of Directors that the young man would be as much a cypher in the future government of Bengal as if he had been an infant of six, as at first proposed.

Lord Clive was anxious to keep the Padishah in Bengal, to play the part of a pageant Suzerain; but Shah Alam was vexed at not being conducted to Delhi, and refused to live in Bengal. Accordingly Lord Clive restored Oude territory to the Nawab Vizier, with the exception of certain territories round Allahabad, which were reserved for the Padishah; and he arranged for the Padishah to live at Allahabad, under the protection of the Nawab Vizier. In return, the Nawab Vizier paid the English half a million sterling towards the expenses of the recent war.

On this occasion the Nawab Vizier of Oude tried to secure the friendship and support of Lord Clive by making him a present of £100,000. Such presents were in accordance with Oriental usage, but had been strictly prohibited by the East India Company; and it was the violation of this law by the Governor and Council in their money dealings at Murshedabad which had excited the wrath of Lord Clive. Accordingly the offer was declined with thanks.

Lord Clive returned to England in 1767, but his latter years were embittered by his enemies. He died in 1774 at the age of forty-nine, leaving a name which will be for ever bound up with the history of the British Empire in India.

The career of Sombre, the miscreant who butchered the English at Patna, at the command of Meer Cossim, is one of those stories of real life which are stranger than fiction. Sombre was a morose Franco-German, named Walter Reinhardt, who had deserted more than once from the English to the French and back again. He had re-enlisted in an English regiment under the name of Somers, but was nicknamed

Sombre on account of his evil expression. Then he had again deserted his colours, and entered the service of Nawab Meer Cossim, who gave him the command of a brigade of Sepoys; and from this time he was known to the natives by the name of Sumru, being a Hinduised form of Sombre.

After the massacre of Patna, Sombre fled into Oude with Meer Cossim, and entered the service of the Nawab Vizier. After the battle of Buxar the English demanded his surrender, but the Nawab Vizier refused to give him up on the ground that he was a refugee. The Nawab Vizier, however, was only anxious to maintain his public character as a protector of refugees; but privately he offered to procure the assassination of Sombre if some English gentleman would be present as eye-witness of the execution. This offer was of course refused; and Sombre escaped from Oude with a battalion of Sepoys and a body of European outcasts, the scum of different nations, and after a variety of adventures entered the service of the Delhi government, and secured the valuable district of Sirdhana, in the neighbourhood of Murat, for the support of his troops.

Thus the villain, who murdered the English at Patna, rose to wealth and influence, and was virtually the prince of Sirdhana. He died in 1778, leaving a widow, who had been originally a slave girl, but was henceforth known as the Begum Sombre. This lady outlived her husband for more than half a century, and not only governed the territory of Sirdhana and collected the revenues, but often appeared at the head of her troops, and took an active part in the old wars. Begum Sombre professed the Catholic religion, and built a handsome church at Sirdhana.

XI.—*Poverty and Famine: Deeds and Misdeeds of Warren Hastings.*

1768 to 1785.

FOR a brief period Lord Clive's political system was lauded to the skies as the perfection of mercantile wisdom. No sovereign was dethroned; no country was annexed; no people were brought under the English yoke. Consequently there was nothing to alarm the sensibilities of the English nation, or the jealousies of their French or Dutch rivals. A Nawab was still reigning at Murshedabad, under the guardianship of Muhammad Reza Khan; and the native officials were left in sole charge of the civil government.

For a while the English rigidly abstained from all interference with the country government. They took over the revenues, and protected Bengal from revolt and invasion, not, however, for the benefit of the people, but to swell the profits of the East India Company; whilst the people of Bengal were so ignorant and slavish that they raised no complaint whatever, except that the English had no regard for the poor, and would not deliver them from their hereditary oppressors.

But native rule, protected by the English, became worse than native rule kept in check by the possibility of rebellions.

The young Nawab was an imbecile, and his guardian was intent upon making a fortune; whilst there was robbery and oppression amongst native officials of every grade. The revenues of Bengal began to diminish so rapidly that it was feared they might slip away altogether. Meanwhile, Bengal was drained of its wealth. There was no longer a stream of silver flowing from England to India for the purchase of Indian cottons, silks, and muslins; but the surplus revenues of Bengal, and the surreptitious gains of the Company's servants, were flowing in the opposite direction, from India to England.

The Directors of the East India Company stormed and raved at their servants in Bengal, but to no effect. In 1770-71 Bengal was desolated by a famine, which carried off a fourth of the population; and it was currently reported that Englishmen at Calcutta had joined Muhammad Reza Khan in hoarding up rice and selling it at fabulous prices to the starving Bengalis. True or false, it was evident that another Clive was wanted at Calcutta, and in 1772 the East India Company appointed Mr. Warren Hastings to be Governor of Bengal.

Warren Hastings was a little man with a resolute cast of features, indomitable energy and courteous manners. He was born in 1732, seven years later than Clive, and was always a good boy and fond of his book. At ten years of age he went to Westminster School, and William Cowper and Elijah Impey were amongst his schoolfellows. He never climbed a church steeple or fought other boys, like Robert Clive; but at fourteen years of age he was first in the examination for the foundation, and was distinguished for swimming and boating.

In 1750, when Warren Hastings was nearly eighteen years

of age, he landed at Calcutta as a writer in the service of the East India Company; and after the battle of Plassy, in 1757, he was sent to Murshedabad to reside as an agent for the Company at the Court of Meer Jaffier. In 1761 he was a member of the Council at Calcutta, where he stood up for the sovereign rights of the Nawab, Meer Cossim. He went to England in 1764, where he drew up a plan for cultivating Persian literature at Oxford, and became acquainted with Dr. Johnson. In 1769 he returned to India as member of Council at Madras; and it was during this voyage out that he fell in love with Mrs. Imhoff, the "elegant Marian," who eventually became Mrs. Hastings. In 1772 he went to Calcutta as Governor of Bengal.

By this time Clive's political system was broken up by events. The young Padishah, Shah Alam, had run away to Delhi with the Mahrattas, and was placed on the throne of the great Moghul, and thereby forfeited the tribute he had received from the English, and the territory which he had received from the Nawab Vizier of Oude. Muhammad Reza Khan was arrested for embezzlement, and brought to Calcutta for trial, and eventually acquitted. But native rule was at an end in Bengal. The collection of the revenue was entrusted to European servants of the Company. The seat of government was transferred to Calcutta, and the Nawab was left at Murshedabad with nothing to do, whilst the yearly allowance to the family was reduced from half a million to £160,000.

About this time there were secret dealings between Warren Hastings and the Nawab Vizier of Oude. It will be remembered that the Nawab Vizier owed the restoration of his dominions to the policy of Lord Clive, and tried to buy the friendship of the hero of Plassy by presenting him with a douceur of £100,000, which was declined with thanks.

The Nawab Vizier was now anxious for the help of a brigade of the Company's troops to enable him to subdue a warlike tribe on his western frontier, known as the Rohilla Afghans, and at the same time to recover the territories which had been abandoned by the young Padishah, when he ran away to Delhi with the Mahrattas.

Accordingly, in 1773, there was a secret meeting between Warren Hastings and the Nawab Vizier at Benares. The services of a brigade and its European officers were made over to the Nawab Vizier, and the territories round Allahabad were restored to him, and the Nawab Vizier agreed to maintain the troops, and to pay over nearly a million sterling to the Calcutta treasury. At the same time there is reason to suspect that Warren Hastings accepted the £100,000 that had been refused by Lord Clive, and this would account for the secrecy that he observed in concluding the bargain.

The after results of the dealings between Warren Hastings and the Nawab Vizier were calamitous. The Rohillas were conquered by the Company's forces, but plundered by the cowardly soldiers of the Nawab Vizier, and all the blame was thrown upon Hastings. Meanwhile Hastings appointed an English servant of the Company, named Middleton, to reside at Lucknow as a confidential medium for carrying on personal dealings with the Nawab Vizier; and the consequence was that there were more secrets and more suspicions.

Warren Hastings had rendered great service to the Company by relieving its finances; but he had difficulties of his own. He was surrounded with parasites, whom he was obliged to gratify with government contracts and other lucrative jobs, lest they should turn against him. Suddenly there was a change in the government of Bengal which rendered further secrecy impossible.

The indignation of the Parliament and people of England had been roused to fever heat by the mismanagement of the Company's affairs in India. Whilst Englishmen were returning from Bengal with enormous fortunes, reports were rife of the sufferings of the natives and wrongs of deposed Nawabs. The merits of Warren Hastings were as yet unchallenged in England; but it was resolved to introduce new blood into the Calcutta Council by the appointment of three members from England, who should not be servants of the East India Company, but should be selected by the English Ministers.

Accordingly Warren Hastings was appointed Governor-General of all the English possessions in India, including Bengal, and only one other servant of the East India Company, a Mr. Barwell, was nominated to a seat in the Council. Three independent members were sent out from England, who had no previous knowledge of India; their names were General Clavering, Major Monson, and Mr. Philip Francis. The new Governor-General and Council were vested with the control of all transactions of the English with native princes, whether at Calcutta, Madras, or Bombay.

Warren Hastings was President of the Council, but he had only one vote as an ordinary member, unless the votes were equal on both sides, when he had a casting vote as President. But so long as the three new members voted together they would always be in a majority of three to two.

The three members from England landed at Calcutta in 1774, and the prestige of Warren Hastings was soon threatened by the new triumvirate. To make matters worse a new Supreme Court of Justice was established at Calcutta, with new Judges sent out from England by the English Ministers, and consequently as independent of the East India Company as the three new members of Council. At first the new

Judges of the Supreme Court were inclined to co-operate with the new members of Council; but the Chief Justice was Sir Elijah Impey, the school-fellow of Warren Hastings at Westminster; and without going nicely into details it will soon be seen that Hastings managed to win over Impey to his own side.

Philip Francis was the moving spirit of the new triumvirate in the Council. He was the cleverest of the three, and is believed to be the author of the "Letters of Junius." From the very first Francis suspected that Hastings was a corrupt man. At the same time he seems to have been bent on ruining Hastings in the hope of supplanting him in the post of Governor-General.

The triumvirate began by condemning the Rohilla war, and calling for all the correspondence between Hastings and Middleton. Hastings produced extracts which he declared to be official, but kept back the letters on the plea that they were private and confidential. The triumvirate refused to accept this explanation, and Middleton was recalled from Lucknow, and a Mr. Bristow was appointed in his room.

Shortly afterwards the Nawab Vizier died, and was succeeded by his son. But the mother and mother-in-law of the new Nawab Vizier, popularly known as the two Begums, claimed all the money in the public treasury, amounting to two or three millions sterling, as having been given to them by the deceased Nawab Vizier. The claim of the two ladies on the public money was perhaps ridiculous; but the new Nawab Vizier brought it forward as an excuse for not paying his father's debts to the Company. Hastings was of opinion that the Nawab Vizier was bound to pay his father's debts, but that the English had nothing to do with the claim of the two Begums. Philip Francis, however, insisted upon interfering, and the money was made over to the two Begums, less a quarter of a million which was paid to the Bengal government towards the liquidation of the debt, and the Begums were secured in the possession of their treasures by a British guarantee.

By this time every native in Calcutta thought that Warren Hastings had lost his authority, and that Philip Francis was the rising man. Accordingly a host of native informers began to bring charges of bribery and corruption against Hastings, which were greedily taken up by Philip Francis and his confederates. Amongst others, a wealthy Brahman of bad character, named Nuncomar, accused Hastings of having received a bribe from a member of the Nawab's family at Murshedabad, in return for an appointment as manager of the Nawab's household; and another bribe from Muhammad Reza Khan for having connived at his embezzlements.

There is no doubt that Nuncomar was a villain. It was known that he had forged letters and seals, and carried on a treasonable correspondence with the French; and consequently no reliance could be placed upon his accusations unless they were proved by undeniable evidence from other quarters. Hastings, however, stood upon his dignity, and refused to answer charges brought against him by such a miscreant, or to be tried by his own members of Council.

Accordingly Philip Francis persisted in believing that Hastings was guilty, and would probably have gone further; but Nuncomar was suddenly arrested on a charge of forgery, and brought to trial in the Supreme Court before Sir Elijah Impey and a jury of Englishmen. In those days forgery was a capital offence under English law, but had never been treated as such in India. Nevertheless Nuncomar was found guilty by the jury, and sentenced to death by the judge; and he was publicly hanged at Calcutta, to the bewilderment of the natives, who could not understand why a man should be put to death for forgery, or why a Brahman should be executed whatever might have been his crime. From that moment, however, no more charges were brought against Hastings in India. Even Francis was paralysed for a while, whilst Hastings recovered his *prestige*, although he was still in the minority at Council.

About this time there were troubles in Western India. The English at Bombay were about to play a part in history, and the Mahratta powers were also appearing on the scene; and it will be necessary to leave Bengal for awhile and glance at the progress on the other side of India.

As far back as 1661, the little island of Bombay had been given to Great Britain as part of the dowry of Catherine of Portugal, on her marriage with Charles the Second. Subsequently it was transferred to the East India Company, and proved a most desirable acquisition. The island was easily fortified against the Mahrattas of the Konkan, whilst the harbour was one of the finest in the world, and a safe refuge for all ships from the Persian Gulf, the Red Sea, and the coast of Mozambique. Above all, the English at Bombay were altogether independent of the Moghul, and were thus not only free from all interference, but were able to offer an asylum to the English at Surat in time of trouble.

For nearly a century the trade with Bombay suffered heavy losses from the pirate fleets which scoured the Indian Ocean, and found a secure retreat in fortified creeks and harbours off the coast of Malabar. These pirates have long since disappeared, but from the earliest period on record down to the middle of the eighteenth century, they were the pest and terror of the Indian seas. For many years, however, the East India Company maintained a large naval force for the protection of merchant ships; and the destruction of Gheria in 1756 by Colonel Clive and Admiral Watson struck a blow at the piratical system from which it never recovered.

Meanwhile the Mahrattas had captured several of the Portuguese fortresses on the coast of the Konkan, and amongst others, a little island named Salsette, and a little promontory named Bassein, which more or less commanded the entrance to Bombay harbour.

The English had long coveted possession of these two strongholds, and the Court of Directors in London had repeatedly pressed the matter on the attention of the Bombay Governor and Council; but the Mahrattas were so proud of having wrested the places from a European nation like the Portuguese that they would not part with them for any money that could be offered. Under these circumstances the Bombay government sent an English merchant to reside at Poona, ostensibly for the purpose of maintaining friendly relations with the Peishwa, but mainly to seize any opportunity that might offer for obtaining possession of Salsette and Bassein.

At last there was a catastrophe at Poona. In 1773 a Peishwa was murdered, and an uncle, named Ragoba, succeeded to the throne. The Muhammadan Nizam of Hyderabad marched an army towards Poona to take advantage of the distractions. A Muhammadan adventurer, named Hyder Ali, who had dethroned the Raja of Mysore, and founded a new Muhammadan kingdom in the Western Peninsula, advanced another army with the same intent. Ragoba took the field, and gained some successes; but in his absence from Poona, an infant was brought forward as a posthumous son of the murdered Peishwa, and placed upon the throne under a Council of Regency.

Ragoba was thus suddenly deprived of his sovereign authority. In this extremity he applied to Bombay, and offered to cede Salsette and Bassein, provided the English helped him to recover the throne. In 1775 an English force took the field, and captured Salsette and Bassein, and was fast restoring the fortunes of Ragoba, when the war was suddenly stopped by the orders of the Governor-General and Council at Calcutta.[1]

Both Hastings and Francis agreed in condemning the Mahratta war; but Hastings wished to push it to a speedy conclusion, whilst Francis was bent on stopping it at once, and Francis had the majority. Accordingly a treaty was patched up with the Mahrattas, in which Ragoba was thrown over; and the Regency at Poona ceded Salsette, but obstinately refused to give up Bassein. Subsequently the Court of Directors in England expressed their full approval of the treaty with Ragoba, but denounced the treaty with the Regency at Poona. At the same time Colonel Monson died at Calcutta; and Hastings, supported by Barwell, and his own casting vote as President, was enabled to carry his measures in spite of the opposition of Francis and Clavering.

The period in question, 1778—82, was one of sore peril for British interests all over the world. Great Britain was at war with her revolted colonies in North America. France had espoused the American cause; and a French agent had

[1] The relative claims of Ragoba and the infant are involved in some obscurity. It subsequently transpired that Ragoba was the murderer of the deceased Peishwa; but this was not known to the English at Bombay when they agreed to help Ragoba, whilst it was generally believed that the infant was a supposititious child.

reached Poona, and was stirring up the Mahrattas with the hope of being supported by an army from France. Warren Hastings sent a force under General Goddard to march across India from Bengal to the Mahratta country. Before, however, Goddard reached the theatre of war, the English at Bombay had sent a force to Poona to place Ragoba on the throne of the Peishwas. This expedition from Bombay proved a failure; it was surrounded by a host of Mahrattas under Mahadaji Scindia, and compelled to surrender at discretion under what is known as the Convention of Wurgaum.

Warren Hastings and his Council repudiated the Convention and renewed the war, not so much to conquer the Mahrattas as to defeat the designs of France. The services of Warren Hastings throughout this Mahratta war are beyond all question; his energies never flagged, whilst his resources were inexhaustible. At one time the Muhammadan powers secretly confederated with the Mahratta powers against the English. Hyder Ali desolated the Carnatic up to the walls of Fort St. George; but an expedition was sent from Bengal to Madras, under the veteran general, Sir Eyre Coote, and drove back the invading army. The Mahrattas of Nagpore advanced into Orissa and threatened to invade Bengal, but were induced to retire without fighting. The Nizam of Hyderabad, who was said to have been the prime mover in the secret confederation, deemed it advisable to remain at home and do nothing.

The foremost power amongst the Mahrattas at this period was Mahadaji Scindia of Gwalior. This restless and ambitious prince had taken the young Padishah, Shah Alam, under his wing at Delhi, and at the same time was establishing a commanding influence over the Council of Regency at

Poona. At last his famous fortress at Gwalior was stormed by an English force under Captain Popham—an exploit worthy of Clive which electrified half India. Accordingly Mahadaji Scindia was compelled to come to terms. Peace was concluded with the Mahrattas; and although the English restored all the territories they had conquered, the war had raised the British government to the highest rank amongst the powers of India.

Meanwhile Warren Hastings had triumphed, not only over the French and Mahrattas, but over his domestic enemies at Calcutta. General Clavering made an unsuccessful attempt to seize the post of Governor-General, but died shortly afterwards. Philip Francis, after fighting a duel with Hastings, in which he was wounded, returned to Europe disappointed of all his hopes, but burning to be revenged on his successful rival.

But from the moment that Warren Hastings was delivered from the surveillance of the independent members of Council he was as domineering and almost as unscrupulous as in the earlier days of his government. Before the Mahratta war was over there was a pressing want of money in Bengal. Hastings demanded an extraordinary subsidy from the Raja of Benares, who was a feudatory of the East India Company; and the Raja had not only the temerity to refuse payment, but stirred up an insurrection at Benares, in which four companies of British sepoys were cut to pieces, and Hastings narrowly escaped with his life. The Raja was ultimately seized with a panic, and fled into exile; but the arbitrary action of Hastings, however worthy of an Oriental despot, was almost universally condemned in England.

Warren Hastings had dealings with the new Nawab Vizier of Oude, which involved him in still greater obloquy. A heavy debt was due from this potentate to the East India Company, and could not be paid because the state treasures at Lucknow had been made over to the two Begums. There was another secret meeting at Bėnares, at which Hastings acknowledges having received a present of £100,000. Hastings was told that the Begums were implicated in the rebellion of the Raja of Benares, and he was induced to withdraw the British guarantee which had been given to the two Begums, and to leave the Nawab Vizier to recover the state treasures in any way he pleased. The result was that the servants of the Begums were subjected to imprisonment and torture to compel the ladies to surrender their hoards; and Warren Hastings has been charged with complicity in the crime, although it is difficult to believe that he would knowingly countenance actual torture.

The present of a hundred thousand pounds must have bothered Warren Hastings. After some hesitation he reported having received the money to the Court of Directors, and requested permission to keep it. The Directors refused, and Hastings considered himself to be an ill-used man; a circumstance which confirms the suspicion that he had received a like sum at his previous interview with the deceased Nawab Vizier, but kept the matter a profound secret in his own bosom.

Warren Hastings returned to England in 1785 at the age of fifty-three. His capacity as an administrator has never been doubted, whilst the public services he rendered to the East India Company and the British nation may serve to overshadow his faults, although it is difficult to extenuate them. The part he played in the Rohilla war, his treatment of the Raja of Benares, and his complicity in the cruelties practised by the Nawab Vizier of Oude on the servants of the two Begums, naturally exposed him to the condemnation of Englishmen, and led to his famous trial at Westminster Hall. But the lines of his old schoolfellow, William Cowper, may still be borne in mind:—

> "Hastings! I knew thee young, and of a mind,
> While young, humane, conversable and kind,
> Nor can I well believe thee, gentle then,
> Now grown a villain, and the worst of men."

The people of Bengal never associated the name of Warren Hastings with cruelty or oppression. In their eyes he was the great English Sultan, who delivered them from the oppressions of their own fellow countrymen, and his name was celebrated in Bengali songs which still linger in the memory of living men. To this day it is difficult for those who are familiar with the events of his career as the first Governor-General of India to avoid some degree of sympathy for the sorrows that embittered the evening of his life.

Warren Hastings lived for more than thirty years after his return to England, and was destined to see the East India Company become the paramount power over Muhammadan and Mahratta. He died in 1818 at the advanced age of eighty-five.

The administration of Warren Hastings is an era in the history of British India. As already seen, it is marked by important changes in the government of the East India Company. Up to this date no one but the servants of the Company had any share in the government of India; and Madras, Calcutta and Bombay were independent of each other. The Governor of each Presidency was picked out of the merchant service of the Company, and was assisted by a Council consisting of the book-keeper, the warehouse-keeper, and the collector of customs, who was also a justice of the peace in the native quarter. But the chief of every factory up country was regarded as an extraordinary member of Council; and on important occasions, such as the breach with Meer Cossim in 1763, all the extraordinary members were summoned to the Presidency town to take a part in the consultations.

The English Parliament and Ministry reconstituted this Council in Bengal by the appointment of three new members from England, and took away the independence of Madras and Bombay by the appointment of a Governor-General in Council, with supreme authority over all the English settlements in India. But the main object of the English Ministry was to put a stop to all wars in India, and those of Warren Hastings showed that further changes were necessary in the constitution. Accordingly a Board of Control, consisting of six members of the Privy Council, was instituted to control the affairs of the East India Company in England; and Lord Cornwallis, who was altogether independent of the Company, was appointed Governor-General of India, whilst the members of Council in Bengal were once more selected from the servants of the Company.

XII.—*Cornwallis, Shore, and Wellesley.*

1786 to 1805.

THE wars of Warren Hastings were followed by a lull. Great Britain was at peace with France and America, and the East India Company was at peace in India. But the Muhammadan dominion which had been founded by Hyder Ali in Mysore was still a terror to the Carnatic. Hyder Ali was dead, and in 1784, his son and successor Tippoo Sultan had been coaxed into a treaty with the English, known as the treaty of Mangalore; but there was nothing to prevent a renewal of the war; and in 1789 Tippoo broke the peace by a wanton attack on an ally of the East India Company. The war which followed is almost forgotten now. Lord Cornwallis, who was Governor-General from 1786 to 1793, persuaded the Peishwa and the Nizam to join the English in subduing a common enemy, and compelled Tippoo to purchase a peace by the cession of half his territories and a payment of three millions sterling.

Lord Cornwallis next tried to maintain a permanent peace in India by a balance of power. He invited the Nizam and the Peishwa to enter into a confederacy, under which no one of the three powers should engage in a war without the consent of the other two. But the Nizam and the Peishwa were quarrelling over the Mahratta claims to chout; and the Nizam wanted the protection of the English against the Mahrattas, whilst the Peishwa protested against any interference on the part of the English, and Lord Cornwallis was obliged to leave them to settle their quarrels their own way.

In 1793 Sir John Shore, one of the Company's servants in Bengal, succeeded Lord Cornwallis as Governor-General. He was specially selected on the recommendation of Lord Cornwallis to carry out certain changes in the revenue system of Bengal, which will be described in a future chapter. By this time the Mahrattas were preparing to make war upon the Nizam, and Shore declined to interfere. The consequence was that for a brief interval all the Mahratta feudatories were arrayed against the Nizam under the banners of the Peishwa; and in 1795 the Nizam was utterly routed in the battle of Kurdla, and would probably have been swept away altogether, but at this juncture the Mahrattas took to quarrelling amongst themselves, and thus enabled the Nizam to recover slowly from the blow.

"Declining to interfere" has always been a favourite policy with the English people, but has sometimes been detrimental to British interests. When the English refused to protect the Nizam, he naturally sought the alliance of the French, and entertained French officers at Hyderabad, who drilled and disciplined battalions of Sepoys. By this time Great Britain was at war with France. The French king had perished by the guillotine, and the Reign of Terror had been established in Paris; and the French officers at Hyderabad were carrying the colours of the French Republic and wearing the cap of liberty on their buttons. Daulat Rao Scindia, the successor of Mahadaji, maintained a similar French army in Hindustan; whilst Tippoo Sultan of Mysore was enlisting

French soldiers and renewing his old intrigues with the French authorities.

Such was the state of affairs in 1798, when Lord Wellesley landed at Calcutta as Governor-General in succession to Shore. Within three weeks he found that war with Tippoo was inevitable. The French governor of Mauritius had issued a manifesto announcing that Tippoo had formed an alliance with the French Republic, and was about to join in the war against the English; whilst a hundred Frenchmen appeared in Mysore and proclaimed a Republic, planted a tree of liberty, and hailed the Sultan as "Citizen Tippoo." To crown all, news arrived that Napoleon was conquering Egypt and contemplated the conquest of India.

Tippoo was invited to explain, but procrastinated and prevaricated. Meanwhile Lord Wellesley prepared for war, and was ably seconded by his younger brother, Colonel Arthur Wellesley, afterwards Duke of Wellington. He called on the Nizam to join in the war, and engaged to protect him against the Mahrattas, but required him to dismiss his French officers and disband his French battalions. The last operation was carried out without firing a shot. As soon as it was announced at Hyderabad, the French Sepoys broke out in mutiny for arrears of pay, and threatened their own officers. The English authorities interfered, and took the French officers under their protection, whilst the French Sepoys, to the number of eleven or twelve thousand, were quieted by being paid up and dispersed within a few hours.

The war against Tippoo was short and decisive. He was environed by the English armies of Madras and Bombay, but continued to hold out in his fortified capital at Seringapatam. At last the English prepared to take the place by storm. General David Baird, who had suffered three years' horrible captivity in Seringapatam, volunteered to lead the storming party. Two columns entered the breach, and then wheeled right and left; and after a terrible slaughter the British flag waved over Seringapatam. The dead body of Tippoo was found in a gateway, and was buried in the mausoleum of his father with all the honours of a military funeral.

The fall of Tippoo was hailed as a relief throughout the greater part of India. His cruel persecutions of the Hindus and his barbarous treatment of his English prisoners had steeled all hearts against him, irrespective of his alliance with the French. A portion of the newly conquered territories was divided between the English and the Nizam. The remainder was formed into a Hindu kingdom, and an infant representative of the family, which had been supplanted by Hyder Ali, was literally taken from a hovel and placed upon the throne of Mysore.

The downfall of Tippoo was followed by the downfall of the Nawab of the Carnatic. The Nawab had never been able to defend his territories from invasion, and consequently was useless as an ally, and he had sealed his doom by carrying on a treacherous correspondence with Tippoo. Accordingly he was reduced to the condition of a pensioner, like the Nawab of Bengal; and his territories were brought under British administration, and incorporated with the Madras Presidency.

The Mahratta powers were now the only remaining obstacle to the establishment of a permanent peace in India. The Nizam of Hyderabad was driven to accept the English alliance as his only protection against the Mahrattas. He ceded the territories he had acquired after the Mysore war for the support of a Subsidiary Force of drilled battalions of Sepoys, commanded by British officers, for the maintenance of the public peace; and he was pledged to engage in no war or negotiation whatever without the knowledge and consent of the British government. But the Mahratta powers had as yet no enemy to fear; they were unconquered and independent; and they could not be expected to accept the Suzerainty of the British government, in preference to that of their own Peishwa, until they had been compelled by circumstances to apply for British protection.

The Mahratta empire was distributed between the Peishwa of Poona, and his four lieutenants or feudatories; namely, the Guicowar of Baroda, Scindia of Gwalior, Holkar of Indore, and the Raja of Nagpore; but in order to realise their geographical position it may be as well to take a bird's eye view of the whole country to the southward of the Himalaya mountains.

The first great belt or zone, known as Hindustan, stretches from the Punjab eastward to Bengal, and is bounded on the south by the Nerbudda river. In 1801-2 the whole western quarter was held by the Mahrattas. The Guicowar of Baroda possessed a great part of Guzerat, but in 1801 he was driven to accept the Suzerainty of the East India Company on the same terms as the Nizam. With this exception Daulat Rao Scindia was paramount in Hindustan. He had taken Shah Alam, the Padishah of Delhi, under his protection, and collected the revenues between the Punjab and Oude in the name of the Great Moghul. At the same time there was a war for the succession in Holkar's principality of Indore on the Nerbudda river; and Scindia attempted to arbitrate the matter by his sole authority. The influence of Scindia was not confined to Hindustan, but stretched over a great part of the Dekhan, for he professed to take the Peishwa of Poona under his protection, and was consequently paramount in the Mahratta empire.

The Dekhan, or second great zone between the Nerbudda and Kistna rivers, was divided between the Mahrattas and the Muhammadans. The western Dekhan was held by the Peishwa of Poona; the northern Dekhan by the Raja of Berar and Nagpore; whilst the region south of Nagpore and east of the Peishwa formed the Muhammadan dominion of the Nizam of Hÿderabad.

The Peninsula, or third zone, was quiet. The East India Company was paramount over Mysore in the west and the Carnatic in the east; and every Hindu Raja to the south of the Kistna acknowledged the British government as its Suzerain.

All the Mahratta feudatories owed allegiance to the Brahman Peishwa, as the Suzerain of the Mahratta empire; but the Peishwa was himself half crushed by the preponderating influence of Daulat Rao Scindia. Indeed, it is not too much to say that at this crisis Daulat Rao Scindia was a more terrible personage in the eyes of the English than Tippoo Sultan had ever been. He was not only paramount at Delhi and Poona, but he had formed an army of Sepoy battalions under a French general named Perron; and he empowered Perron to collect the revenues of the Doab, or region between the Jumna and the Ganges, for the maintenance of his force. Thus a French kingdom was already existing in embryo in the neighbourhood of Delhi; and if Scindia had allied with France against the English, Napoleon might have landed a French army in Scindia's dominions, joined Perron, and reigned at Delhi in the name of the Great Moghul.

To make matters worse for Lord Wellesley, Hindustan was threatened by an invasion of the Afghans, and there was no one to oppose them. Nadir Shah had carried off the wealth of India only sixty years before, and there was nothing to prevent the Afghans from doing the same. Fortunately the Afghans were divided amongst themselves, and fighting one another, as they always seem to have been doing, and consequently the scare passed away.

In 1802, by a stroke of good fortune, the Peishwa was induced to accept British Suzerainty. He had lost the protection of Scindia, who had gone to Indore to place one of the sons of the deceased Holkar on the throne. At this crisis an illegitimate member of the Holkar family, named Jeswant Rao, suddenly appeared at Poona with an army of brigands, and utterly routed the forces of the Peishwa.

This defeat filled the Peishwa with wild alarm. He fled towards Bombay, and yielded to the terms of Lord Wellesley on the condition of being restored to his throne at Poona. A treaty was concluded at Bassein on the last day of the year 1802, and territories were ceded for the support of a Subsidiary Force like that maintained by the Nizam; and in 1803 the Peishwa was conducted to Poona by Colonel Arthur Wellesley and placed upon the throne of his fathers, whilst Jeswant Rao Holkar returned to Indore and took possession of the kingdom.

Scindia was much troubled at the treaty of Bassein, which placed the Suzerain of the Mahratta empire in subordination to the East India Company. He hastened to the Dekhan to form a confederation of Mahratta princes against the English, but was only joined by the Raja of Nagpore; for the Guicowar of Baroda had been already driven by a civil war to accept the Suzerainty of the English, whilst Jeswant Rao Holkar refused to leave Indore. Scindia and the Nagpore Raja were however troubled and uncertain, but at last assumed a hostile front; and Colonel Wellesley brought matters to a crisis by the glorious victory at Assaye, followed by that at Argaum. By the end of 1803 both Scindia and the Nagpore Raja yielded to their fate and accepted British Suzerainty.

Meanwhile General Lake had engaged in a victorious campaign in Hindustan, and won the battles of Alighur, Delhi, and Laswari, which broke up the French battalions for ever, and placed the East India Company in possession of the North-west Provinces. At Delhi General Lake had an audience with the Padishah, Shah Alam, and found him old, blind, and poor. Accordingly Shah Alam was again taken under British protection, as he had been in the days of Clive, and maintained at Delhi on a liberal pension.

The year 1804 saw Lord Wellesley at the pinnacle of his greatness. The British government had become the paramount power in India in the room of the Great Moghul, and above all was the sole and acknowledged arbiter of peace and war. At the same time it had acquired sufficient territories for the maintenance of the public peace of India for all time to come. The Rajput princes gladly tendered their submission to British Suzerainty in return for protection against the Mahrattas, and treaties were being concluded accordingly, when a mishap threw the whole scheme of British imperial rule into confusion.

Jeswant Rao Holkar, who had usurped the throne of Indore, was a Mahratta of the stamp of Sivaji. He scorned the new system of drilled battalions of Sepoys, and boasted that so long as the home of the Mahrattas was in the saddle, they had set at nought the most skilful operations of regular armies. During the campaigns of Wellesley and Lake he had collected plunder and chout from the Rajput princes as the inherent right of the Mahrattas; but when the wars were over he doubted whether the English would respect this sacred right, and he was bothered by orders from General Lake to leave off plundering British allies and return to Indore. Accordingly he tried brag and swagger, and threatened to burn, sack, and slaughter hundreds of thousands, unless the English permitted him to collect chout, and guaranteed his possession of Indore.

The English were willing to leave Jeswant Rao alone, provided that he kept within the hereditary territories of the Holkar family. But as Jeswant Rao still continued to ravage Rajputana, General Lake marched an army against him, and forced him to retreat southward towards Indore. But the hot season began, and Lake returned to cantonments, leaving Colonel Monson in command of a strong brigade to hold Holkar in check.

Colonel Monson followed Jeswant Rao into Indore territory, when the Mahratta suddenly turned round with fresh reinforcements, and a train of artillery. At the same time there was treachery in Monson's camp, and he was alarmed by false rumours, and induced to retreat northwards towards Agra. At this moment the rains began with their usual violence, and the retreat of Monson became a rout; and Hindustan was convulsed by the news that a British army had been cut to pieces by Jeswant Rao Holkar, and that Scindia and other native princes were joining in the attempt to throw off British supremacy.

Such were the disasters that clouded the latter months of Lord Wellesley's administration. Colonel Wellesley was unable to move owing to a famine that desolated the Dekhan; whilst Jeswant Rao had been joined by the Raja of Bhurtpore, and had gone off to Delhi in the hope of capturing the Moghul capital, and assuming the sovereignty of Hindustan in the name of the Padishah.

But Jeswant Rao was beaten off from Delhi by a small force under Colonel Ochterlony. General Lake took the field, but wasted several weeks in vainly endeavouring to storm the vast mud fortress of Bhurtpore. At last the Raja of Bhurtpore grew frightened, and returned to the British alliance, whilst Lake chased Holkar into the Punjab, and compelled him to make his submission.

Meanwhile the Parliament and people of England had fallen into a panic. They had been dazzled by the brilliant successes of Lord Wellesley, and now they were dazed by the retreat of Monson, and what appeared to be a general uprising of the Mahratta people. Accordingly Lord Cornwallis was again sent out to India as Governor-General to undo all that Lord Wellesley had built up; to restore conquered territories, cancel the new treaties, and drift back as far as possible into the old policy of non-intervention.

The administration of Lord Wellesley is associated with the names of several distinguished men, who familiarly revered him as the "glorious little man." There was Arthur Wellesley, afterwards the hero of the Peninsula and Waterloo; General Lord Lake, the conqueror of Hindustan; General Ochterlony, who had fought against Hyder Ali under Sir Eyre Coote, and who successfully defended Delhi against Jeswant Rao Holkar; and Sir John Malcolm, who is best known by his missions to Persia, but who also took an active part in all the leading events of the time—the disbandment of the French battalions at Hyderabad, the capture of Seringapatam, the restoration of the Peishwa to Poona, and the negotiations with Daulat Rao Scindia and the Raja of Nagpore after Assaye and Argaum. There was also Sir Thomas Monro, who rendered himself illustrious by his familiarity with the old Hindu systems of revenue and land tenures.

To these should be added Mountstuart Elphinstone, Butterworth Bayley, Charles Metcalfe, the Stracheys, and many others, whose names will for ever live in the history of British India.

Lord Wellesley left India in 1805, a disappointed and baffled man; but he lived long enough to see his policy justified by events, whilst another generation arose that respected his genius, and acknowledged the value of his services to India. He died in 1842, at the advanced age of eighty-two.

XIII.—*Perplexities of Indian Politics.*

1805 to 44.

LORD CORNWALLIS died before he had been ten weeks in India, and was succeeded by Sir George Barlow, a servant of the Company, who had been a member of Council under Lord Wellesley. The consequence was that Lord Wellesley's policy was only half reversed. The Nizam, the Peishwa, and the Guicowar were required to keep their treaties, which prevented them from engaging in any wars or negotiations without the consent of the Governor-General. Scindia lost all his influence at Delhi, and all his territory to the northward of the river Jumna; whilst he was prevented by the treaty of Bassein from any open interference in the affairs of the Peishwa. But the East India Company withdrew British protection from the Rajputs; and Scindia and Holkar were left to plunder Rajputana, and were only bound over to respect the territories of the East India Company and its allies.

Under such circumstances lawlessness and anarchy soon began to prevail in Central India and Rajputana. Scindia and Holkar were unable to support their overgrown armies out of the revenues of their diminished territories. They had no power to disband their soldiers, and no money to discharge arrears of pay. They were thus compelled to collect plunder and chout wherever they dared. The victories of Arthur Wellesley and Lord Lake had taught them caution, but in Rajputana they could do as they pleased; and other predatory leaders, notably an Afghan named Ameer Khan, soon began to follow their example.

A single story will serve to illustrate the condition of Rajputana. Sir George Barlow was succeeded by Lord Minto in 1807. At this time the Rajas of Jeypore and Jodhpore were fighting for the hand of a daughter of the Rana of Oodeypore; and nearly every chieftain in Rajputana took a part in the war. Ameer Khan the Afghan fought sometimes on one side and sometimes on the other, for with him it was a mere question of pay. Meanwhile the Mahrattas under Scindia and Holkar were not slow in ravaging the country.

Under these desperate circumstances the Rana implored the British government to interfere. He offered to cede half his territories to the East India Company in return for British protection; and both Jeypore and Jodhpore, whilst fighting for the hand of the princess, besought the Governor-General to put an end to the war. But nothing could be done. Indeed the British nation was engaged in a deadly struggle against France and Napoleon, and Lord Minto was engaged in expeditions against the French in the Mauritius and the Dutch in Java, and had but little inducement to remedy the woes of Rajputana. At last the Rana bought the protection of Ameer Khan by the cession of a quarter of his dominions; and the barbarous Afghan forced the wretched father to stop the war by the murder of his daughter. The princess drank a cup of poison and sacrificed her young life to save her country. Then followed a lull, but every chieftain in Rajputana was horrified at the crime.

Meanwhile the East India Company was threatened by an enemy from the northward. A Rajput tribe from the neighbourhood of Cashmere, known as the Ghorkas, had conquered the valley of Nipal in the southern slopes of the Himalayas, and begun to commit aggressions on their neighbours with the view of extending the Ghorka empire. They appropriated districts and villages on the British side of the frontier, and threatened to subdue the whole region from the Himalayas to the Ganges. Protests and remonstrances were thrown away on these arrogant conquerors; and in 1814 Lord Moira, afterwards Marquis of Hastings, who succeeded Lord Minto as Governor-General, was forced to declare war in defence of British territories.

The Nipal war lasted two years. The British forces had to cut through the forests of the Terai at the foot of the Himalayas, and to drag cannon up the precipitous heights, and thread their way along narrow shelves or through dangerous ravines. At first they met with disasters, but the gallant Ochterlony turned the fortunes of war. One by one he captured the mountain fortresses of the Ghorkas, and at last marched his army within fifty miles of the capital at Khatmandu. Then the Ghorkas came to terms and signed a treaty of peace; and from that day to this, with the exception of a brief interval of unrest in the first Afghan war, the Ghorka rulers have been on friendly terms with the British government.

But the disasters of the first Ghorka campaign awoke wild hopes amongst the Mahrattas. The Peishwa carried on secret intrigues with his old feudatories. The Guicowar of Baroda held aloof; he had sent his Brahman Minister on a mission to Poona to settle the Peishwa's claims to chout; but the Baroda Minister was murdered by assassins near Poona at the instigation of the Peishwa. Daulat Rao Scindia of Gwalior prepared to join the Peishwa, and secretly invited the Ghorkas to confederate with the Mahrattas against British supremacy. Holkar of Indore was powerless to help the Peishwa. Jeswant Rao Holkar had killed himself with drinking cherry brandy; and his widow had adopted an infant, and tried to carry on the government as Regent mother; but Ameer Khan, the Afghan, interfered in the conduct of the affairs, and appropriated very much of the revenue and territory. The Raja of Nagpore did nothing, but awaited the course of events.

Meanwhile organised gangs of robbers, known as Pindharies, were beginning to be a terror to the whole country. These scoundrels were the scum of India. Originally they had been camp followers of the Mahratta armies; plunderers of the dead and wounded; brigands and burglars of the lowest type. After the victories of Wellesley and Lake, they confined their operations to Rajputana and Central India; but as the fear of the British died out, they extended their ravages like the Mahratta horsemen in the days of Sivaji; and at last their flying hosts swept through the Dekhan and plundered hundreds of British villages on the coast of Coromandel, and returned in safety to their remote haunts in the hills and jungles within the territories of Scindia and Holkar. The horrors committed by these callous ruffians are beyond all telling. They subjected their victims to such cruel torture and outrage, that whole families destroyed themselves rather than fall into their clutches.

Lord Hastings was bent upon the extirpation of the

Pindharies, but they were secretly protected by Scindia and Holkar, and Lord Hastings was anxious to avoid any collision with the Mahrattas. In 1817 he brought up the armies of Madras and Bengal, and suddenly environed the homes of the Pindharies, and broke up the robber gangs for ever, before it was possible for the Mahratta powers to throw any obstructions in the way. Many of the Pindharies were slain in action; others fled to the jungles and were devoured by wild beasts, or put to death by neighbouring villagers in revenge for former cruelties; but the survivors surrendered to the English, and were granted lands for cultivation on the condition that they rigidly abstained from all marauding raids for the future. The result was that the Pindharies were soon absorbed in the rural population, and within a generation the memory of their atrocities began to die out of the land.

Whilst the British forces were in pursuit of the Pindharies, the Peishwa at Poona broke out in open war. He attacked the British cantonment in the neighbourhood of Poona with overwhelming forces, but to his shame and surprise was repulsed and routed by the European soldiers. In revenge he burnt down the British Residency, and the valuable library of Mr. Mountstuart Elphinstone, the British Resident, was destroyed in the flames.

At this crisis, a force, which had been sent in pursuit of the Pindharies, was recalled to Poona, and the Peishwa took fright and fled during the night with the bulk of his army. For months he was followed through hills and jungles by a British detachment, and at last surrendered to Sir John Malcolm. His territories were taken over by the East India Company, and eventually incorporated with the Bombay Presidency; but he himself was permitted to spend the remainder of his days at Bithoor, near Cawnpore, on a pension of £80,000 per annum.

Throughout these operations not one of the four great Mahratta feudatories joined the Peishwa. The Guicowar of Baroda was beyond his influence. Scindia was confounded at seeing Lord Hastings take the field in person, and he abandoned the Peishwa to his fate, and vowed to be faithful to the British government for the future. Ameer Khan disbanded his army, and withdrew from all interference with Indore; and in return was guaranteed in the possession of the territories he had acquired, and his successors are known to this day as the Nawabs of Touk.

But Holkar's territory of Indore was in sore peril. The infant Raja and the Regent mother were delivered from Ameer Khan only to fall into the hands of the standing army of Holkar, and the army had been bought over by the Peishwa. The Regent mother offered to surrender to the English, but was murdered by the soldiery. But the army of Holkar was routed and scattered by Sir John Malcolm in the once famous battle of Mehidpore; and the government of Indore was settled by placing the infant Raja under the joint guardianship of a Mahratta Minister and the British Resident at Indore.

The Raja of Nagpore waited until all chance of success was over. He then suddenly declared for the Peishwa, and attacked the British cantonment near the city of Nagpore; but his overwhelming forces were beaten back by a little army of Sepoys led by British officers. He then expressed his sorrow, and would have been forgiven, but he still sent secret messages to the flying Peishwa, whilst it was discovered that he had been guilty of the murder of his predecessor. He managed, however, to escape from Nagpore, and eventually died in exile.

Nagpore was thus left at the disposal of the British government, but Lord Hastings refused to annex it to the Company's dominions. An infant grandson of a deceased Raja was placed upon the throne under the guardianship of Mr. Richard Jenkins, the British Resident at Nagpore; and Mr. Jenkins conducted the administration during the minority with the help of Native officials.

Lord Hastings had strengthened the British empire and secured the permanent peace of India, but his wars and conquests were contrary to the instincts of the British nation. No people in the world are more tenacious than the English of the sanctity of their own territories, but no people are less inclined to extend their empire at the expense of others. The extinction of the Pindharies was hailed as a relief, like the downfall of Tippoo, because it delivered the people of India from a load of anxiety and terror. But the Suzerainty of the East India Company over the Native States of India was regarded with suspicion and distrust. The people of England could only be taught by after experiences that the exercise of such a Suzerainty was necessary for the maintenance of the public peace in India; and for a long time a rigid rule was laid down that there was to be no interference whatever in the internal affairs of any Native principality, unless the necessity was proved beyond all question.

As a matter of fact, however, British officers were often obliged to interfere to save a principality from absolute ruin. Amongst the Rajput States especially treasuries were often empty; the revenues had been mortgaged to bankers and others for years to come; no further loans could be obtained except under the British guarantee; whilst money was urgently required to discharge arrears of pay due to mercenary armies as a necessary preliminary to the disbandment of the soldiery.

Political officers, who were posted at Native courts to keep up friendly relations, were often entreated by a Native ruler to secure a loan, or the peaceful disbandment of an army of Arabs or other foreign mercenaries, or the reduction of expenditure in the teeth of interested courtiers and officials, or the recovery of Crown lands from the usurpations or encroachments of hereditary nobles. Again, the recognition of the British government was necessary on the succession of a new ruler to prevent civil wars between different claimants for the throne; and it was often necessary on the appointment of a Minister or Regent to protect the incumbent from the plots and intrigues of unscrupulous rivals.

But whilst Native princes were often grateful to the British government, they sometimes chafed under their treaty obligations. They had been delivered from the harassing demands of the Mahrattas, but their hands were tied in other directions, for they could no longer take up arms against one another, or form leagues against the British Suzerainty, or encourage rebels in neighbouring States, or publicly commit acts which are regarded by civilised nations as crimes. But every Native ruler was held to his allegiance, especially in early days, by the conviction that whilst the East India Company might be pledged to protect the State, it might at any moment dethrone a disaffected ruler and set up a more accommodating member of the family in his room.

The degree of British interference in the affairs of a Native principality has always been a vexed question; but instead of arguing the point it may be as well to tell a few stories of cases that actually occurred in a past generation, as illustrative of the difficulties which have occasionally compelled the British government to fulfil its duties as Suzerain.

The Raja of Jeypore in Rajputana died in 1818, leaving an infant son and two queens. The infant was placed upon the throne, but there was a dispute as to which of the queens should act as Regent during the minority; and the first queen, although of higher rank, was set aside in favour of the mother of the infant.

The next question was the appointment of a Minister to conduct the administration. The Thakurs, or hereditary nobles, elected one of their own body to the post, in the hope of thereby securing themselves in the possession of the lands which they had appropriated during the troubles from the royal demesnes. The appointment of this Minister was recognised by the British government, and consequently he was supported by the British authorities in Rajputana; and he so far performed his duty to the State as to insist upon a restitution of the usurped lands.

Meanwhile the Regent mother was anxious to appoint her paramour to the post of Minister, and she bought over the Thakurs by engaging to permit them to keep the estates they had wrongfully acquired. Then followed the war of factions, accompanied by plots, murders, and mutinies in the army, until it was evident that Jeypore was drifting into anarchy and ruin.

All these evils might have been stopped at any moment by the interference of the British government in the shape of an armed force, but it was restrained by its own avowed policy from attempting anything of the kind. At last the British government reluctantly tried to secure the public peace in Jeypore by permitting the Regent mother to appoint her favourite to the post of Minister, whilst the man whom it had previously supported was obliged to retire to his estate in the country. But the old war of faction was soon renewed, and for sixteen years the government was in confusion, the revenues were squandered, whilst the British government was unable or unwilling to interfere.

At last the Regent mother died, but her favourite continued in the post of Minister. The infant Raja attained his majority, but was confined and then murdered by the Minister, who thereupon placed an infant son of his victim on the throne in the hope of prolonging his monopoly of power. But the Minister found that public opinion was against him, and offered to resign his power into the hands of the British government. Two British officers were sent to Jeypore to investigate the circumstances, and one was murdered in the public streets, whilst the other narrowly escaped with his life; and it was discovered that the attack had been directly instigated by the Minister.

The direct interference of the British government as Suzerain of India had now become a positive duty. The Minister was imprisoned for life. Six Thakurs were selected to form a Council of Regency during the minority of the Raja; and a British officer was appointed to reside at Jeypore as Political Agent of the Governor-General, to superintend the working of the administration as President of the Council of Regency.

The infant prince grew up to be the educated and enlightened Maha Raja of Jeypore, who died in 1880, universally regretted by his own subjects as well as by the British government. From the time he attained his majority he devoted himself to improving his country, and promoting the well-being of his people. In the present day his capital of Jeypore is the most advanced city in Rajputana. He died without heirs, natural or adopted; and a successor has been chosen by the Thakurs, and placed upon the throne, with the approval of the British government.

The principality of Bhurtpore furnishes another instance of the beneficial action of the Suzerain to remedy internal disorders when they are beyond the control of the individual State. Bhurtpore was originally a predatory principality, which had been founded in the seventeenth century, or perhaps earlier, by a tribe of low caste emigrants from the Punjab, known as Jhats, and possibly akin to the ancient Getæ. In the eighteenth century their strength lay in huge fortresses of mud, of which the stronghold at Bhurtpore, near Agra, that held out against Lord Lake, is an existing type.

A Raja of Bhurtpore died in 1825, and the British government recognised the succession of an infant son, under the guardianship of an uncle. A cousin of the infant bought over the Bhurtpore army, put the infant in prison, and murdered the guardian uncle. Accordingly the British government interfered as the Suzerain of India. Lord Combermere advanced against Bhurtpore, and mined its huge mud walls with gunpowder. Then followed a terrific explosion, in which the British troops rushed in and captured the fortress. The usurper was confined as a state prisoner, and the infant Raja was restored to the throne under the guardianship of a Political Agent and a Council of Regency.

Another case for interference arose at Gwalior, the principality of Scindia. Daulat Rao, the bugbear of Lord Wellesley at the beginning of the century, died peacefully in 1827, leaving no son, real or adopted. On his death-bed, however, he requested the British Resident at Gwalior to settle the future government of his State. Accordingly his widow was permitted to adopt a son, and govern the country during the minority as Regent mother. But when the Raja attained his majority, the lady refused to lay down her authority, and Lord William Bentinck, who was Governor-General at the time, was reluctant to interfere. At last a civil war broke out, and part of the army sided with the Raja and the remainder followed the Regent mother. The war, however, was stopped at the outset by the interference of the British government, and the Regent mother retired from the scene, whilst the Raja ascended the throne under the name of Jankoji Rao Scindia.

Jankoji Rao died in 1843, leaving no son in his turn, real or adopted. He left a widow, but she was only a girl of twelve; however, she was allowed to adopt a boy, but was obviously too young to fill the post of Regent mother.

Lord Ellenborough had recently arrived in India as Governor-General, and he was opposed to the formation of a Council of Regency. He was alarmed at the overgrown army of Gwalior, which swallowed up the revenues of the State, and was becoming turbulent and disaffected; and he proposed that the individual who had served as Minister under Jankoji Rao should serve as Regent during the minority, and appears to have already contemplated large reductions in the Gwalior army.

But the Mahratta girl of twelve managed to outwit the great Lord Ellenborough. Girl-like, she was bent upon appointing the "Keeper of the State Jewels" to be Regent at Gwalior. At this crisis the Regent in power over-reached himself by betrothing his little niece to the boy Raja, in the hope of thereby strengthening his authority; and the Mahratta girl dismissed him from his post on her sole authority, and appointed the "Keeper" to be Regent in his room.

The fiasco was amusing to the lookers on, but exasperating

to Lord Ellenborough. The new Regent distributed largesses amongst the Gwalior soldiery, and bought them over to his side. Disturbances broke out, and fifty or sixty people were killed. Accordingly, Lord Ellenborough ordered the British army to advance to Gwalior under the command of Sir Hugh Gough. Then followed the British victories at Maharajpore and Punniar. The dangerous army of Scindia was reduced in numbers, and a Subsidiary Force, under the command of British officers, was formed in its room under the name of the Gwalior Contingent. Six nobles were selected to form a Council of Regency during the minority, under the direction of the British Resident at Gwalior.

The infant prince grew up to be Maha Raja Jyaji Rao Scindia, who still occupies the throne of Gwalior, and has proved himself to be one of the most enlightened rulers amongst the Mahratta feudatories.

XIV.—*Native Life in Villages and Towns.*

POLITICAL life in India, and the revolutions of a past age, have been told in previous chapters. Domestic and social life of the Natives in general may now be brought under review; the phases which have existed from a remote antiquity, and the modifications which have taken place under the influence of British rule.

The better classes of Natives of India are quiet and orderly, inclined to gravity and sometimes to haughtiness, but otherwise well-behaved, polite and kindly, taking life as it comes, but rather overweeningly fond of money. The lower classes in towns, especially coolies, boatmen, hackney carriage drivers, palanquin bearers, are a noisy, active, obtrusive people, confusing in all they do and say, and especially clamorous as regards fees and fares. The population of the villages, especially those remote from Europeans, are ignorant, credulous, and to all appearance timid and submissive; but they will often be found independent and even turbulent where their interests as a community are threatened, although they may be indifferent as regards individual acts of wrong or oppression that only affect a single family or household, and do not concern the village, tribe or caste, to which they may belong.

Domestic life in families is altogether different from that which prevails in England. In Europe there is an independence amongst the individual members of a family which has no existence in India, excepting where it is beginning to develope under the influences of English education. In England, as a rule, boys and girls may be interested in the marriages of their elders, but they are never troubled about their own. Amongst the sons, marriage rarely becomes a matter of consideration, until the young man has at least attained his majority, which in England is not until he is twenty-one. In noble or wealthy houses the marriage of the eldest son may be of family importance because of the respect for primogeniture; but still much is left to the force of circumstances and his own inclinations. Younger sons, however, take their own chance in life, and generally choose their own profession, trade, or occupation; consequently their marriages depend upon themselves, and not upon their parents or guardians. Daughters mingle freely in society at the discretion of their parents; and as they grow up to womanhood they may or may not receive the addresses of one or other of the opposite sex. In all cases, up to the age of twenty-one, the marriage of the daughter is legally contingent on the consent of her parents or guardians; and after that age such consent is considered as morally necessary. In a word, the marriage of a daughter is supposed to turn upon the state of her affections, controlled more or less by the suitability of the match as regards age, rank and fortune, and the approval of the parents or guardians.

In Hindu families, from the highest to the lowest, there is no element of chance or uncertainty in the matter. The marriage of sons and daughters, whilst still boys and girls, is the religious and paramount duty of parents; and is thus a constant source of anxiety to parents, and to parents alone, from the day that the infants become children. The marriage must be within the same caste and occupation as the parents on either side; and the question of relative wealth is of comparatively small importance provided other conditions are observed. Last and not least, when a proposed marriage has been found eligible in other respects, it is deemed indispensable, in accordance with the universal belief of the people of India, that the horoscopes of the boy and girl should be compared by astrologers, to ascertain whether the union is likely to be happy as regards the compatibility of temper or fortune, as foretold by the appearance of the planets at the respective births of bridegroom and bride. Indeed, as already stated, in treating of the marriage of Rama, this belief in astrology is probably the reason why Hindu children are married at an early age, before their affections can be seriously engaged, or they are capable of selecting their own partners.

Whilst Hindu boys and girls are married as children, they do not live together as man and wife until the bride is about twelve, and the bridegroom is sixteen or older; and then they do not attempt to set up independent housekeeping as in England, but invariably live in the household of the parents or natural guardians of the boy husband. This arrangement is often followed by something like domestic tyranny on the part of the mother of the bridegroom towards her son's wife. The mother is supreme mistress in every Hindu household, and the daughters-in-law are bound to obey her, and to fulfil every household duty that may be assigned to her, and to bear reproof and scolding, not only without cavil, but without even an unpleasant word. The boy husband is always reluctant to interfere, and will beg his wife to submit to her fate, rather than attempt to remonstrate with his mother. Filial duty towards both parents is always paramount in Hindu households, and sons are bound to pay as much respect to their mothers as to their fathers, and to be almost as subservient as the daughter-in-law.

But the women of India, like women in other countries, have peculiar ways of carrying out their own sweet will, without having recourse to disrespectful language, or violating the decorum of the family. They can refuse to eat, or they can fall into fits, or otherwise alarm the household, and compel some alleviation of their wrongs. Moreover, the unpleasantness shown by a mother towards a daughter-in-law is generally remedied by the birth of a grandchild, which softens the heart of the elder lady towards the young wife and her babe. Indeed, there is no reason for believing that marriages are unhappier in India than in any other country, excepting as regards the inferiority of the progeny; for it appears to be an established fact that the children of youthful parents do not possess the same physical strength and endurance, or the same independence and self-reliance in mind or character, as the children of parents of maturer years.

The Hindus as a rule only marry one wife, and no respectable man, excepting a Raja, will follow the example of the Muhammadans in taking more than one partner. But it is a recognised institution, sanctified by religion and custom, that every Hindu should be the father of a son; because a son alone can perform the Sraddha, or solemn feasting of the dead, which is supposed to be necessary to relieve the soul from the pains of purgatory. This duty is of paramount importance in every family, and was performed by the sons of Dasaratha as told in the legend of Rama. Accordingly, in the event of there being no offspring, or only a family of daughters, a husband was accustomed to take a second wife, in the hope of becoming the father of a son; or, in the event of further disappointment, to adopt the infant son of some near kinsman, to be his heir and representative, and perform the Sraddha after his decease. The custom of taking a second wife, whilst the first is alive, is dying out of India, or at any rate is no longer a matter of course as it was down to a generation or two ago. It is either carried out in secrecy, as if from a sense of shame, or a son is adopted as being more gratifying to the feelings of all concerned.

Hindus are very fond and proud of their children; and those who are well off will deck them in fine clothes and ornaments, especially on festival occasions, which sometimes leads to kidnapping and murder, especially in the case of little girls. As soon as boys are old enough, and their parents are not too poor, they are sent to school to learn to read, write and cipher. Until a recent period a school for the better class was kept by a Brahman in the colonnade of some temple; and in many cases such school had been carried on from father to son for many generations as a hereditary institution. Schoolmasters of a lower class taught the poorer children in their mud huts, or beneath the shade of trees, and were content with a fee of one anna, or three halfpence a month, and perhaps a little daily dole of betel, tobacco, or grain. In all cases the boys were taught to draw letters and figures on the sand with their fingers, or to chalk them on the floor, and after a while were raised to the dignity of writing on palm leaves; and on such occasions every little boy marched to school every morning with a bundle of leaves cleanly cut in oblong form under his arm, an earthen ink-pot in his hand, a reed pen behind his ear, and a little fried rice tied up in the corner of his cloth in case he should feel hungry during school hours.

During the last thirty years education in India has made an extraordinary advance under the national system introduced by the British government. Every school of any pretensions receives a grant in aid according to the yearly results of its teaching, and is brought under government revision; and a *furore* for English education has been setting in, which promises to convert the wealthier classes into an English-speaking people. At the same time the Native languages are by no means neglected, but Sanskrit is taught to the better classes, whilst much is being done to promote a better knowledge of the vernaculars amongst the masses. Moreover, higher schools and colleges have been established in the principal towns, and have been brought under the superintendence of Universities; and young Natives of superior intelligence and industry are competing for University degrees as certificates of fitness for higher and more responsible duties in law, medicine, trade, engineering and public employment, which have hitherto been only entrusted to educated Englishmen.

Under such circumstances the slate and pencil have superseded the writing on the sand and floor, and palm leaves are fast disappearing from general use, excepting for bazaar and household accounts, and other minor purposes, whilst English pens and paper are almost as much in vogue in India as in England.

But still infant marriages continue to be the rule in spite of the extension of education; and boys are often married to little girls whilst at school or college, after the old fashion which has prevailed from a remote antiquity. Girls, as a rule, are not educated, but are only taught in small numbers, or in more advanced families. Still there is reason to believe that in the course of years, when education and enlightenment have leavened the masses of both sexes, and astrology begins to yield to the higher claims of the rising generation to have a voice in their own marriages, infant unions will cease to be the rule, and young men and women will not enter into the bonds of wedlock until they are old enough to undertake the responsibilities of fathers and mothers, and to become the parents of a vigorous and energetic offspring.

The virtues of the Hindus are more domestic than political. As supporters of their poorer kinsfolk, in general charity and almsgiving, and in public benefactions, they will compare favourably with European countries. To this day no poor laws are necessary in India, and every son holds himself responsible for his father's debts. It may thus be predicted that with the spread of education, and the diminution of infant marriages, which in themselves are fatal to political development, and a closer association with Europeans in public life and private enterprises, the Hindus will in the long run be fitted for that representative form of government which opens up a larger field for the exercise of the moral and intellectual energies, and is conducive to the welfare, not only of the family, the caste or the village, but of the people at large.

The Hindus are distributed into village communities, each being complete in itself. The village or parish is not a mere collection of huts or cottages, but includes a certain area of cultivated or culturable land, as well as common land for pasturage. The bulk of the inhabitants of a village are Ryots—a term which is applied to cultivators who pay rent for their farms, as distinct from Zemindars, who pay rent to the government for their estates. Some of these Ryots are hereditary proprietors or joint proprietors of the village lands, subject only to the payment of rent; whilst others are immigrants who have taken over lands for cultivation, and whose rights are only defined by law or usage.

Every village has or had its own hereditary officials and artisans, which vary in different parts of India. Thus there is a village head man, an accountant, and a watchman; a Brahman priest, schoolmaster, genealogist and astrologer; and often there is a hereditary carpenter, potter, tailor, barber, washerman, and the like. Some of these are paid by yearly fees in grain or money, or by being allowed to cultivate bits of land rent free, or by other perquisites difficult to specify.

Every village community was thus a little republic self-contained; and so long as it paid the yearly rent of its lands to the ruling power for the time being, and met occasional demands for supplies of grain, carriage, cattle or forced labour, it was left to manage its own affairs. Under harsh rulers the villages may have been oppressed by heavy exactions and forced contributions and subsidies; and they must have suffered severely from invaders and marauders; but otherwise the villagers and village officials lived on in the same hereditary grooves, which are the peculiar feature of old Hindu life. Each village community conducted its own business, and administered justice after a primitive fashion, in which crimes against the person or property were mixed up with breaches of caste and violations of Brahmanical laws, or offences such as witchcraft and sorcery. Knotty points were referred to punchayets, or councils of five arbitrators; or to trials by ordeal, and other superstitious practices which are passing away under British administration and regular codes of law. All that is practically useful in these village organisations has been preserved, and even fostered, under British rule; but many of their functions are at an end, like those of the Saxon hundreds and tythings, courts leet, and such like; or have passed into the hands of policemen, magistrates and sessions judges. Questions such as landmarks, village boundaries, and local usages may still be referred to village authorities; but the village tribunals have long ceased to be engines for enforcing Brahmanical observances or caste laws.

Village life in India is rude and primitive, like its ancient institutions, but is not without its charms. The cottages are huts of mud or clay, thatched with straw, half hidden by clumps of bamboos, plantains, or cocoa nuts. The Ryots are to be seen cultivating their fields, or tending cows, goats, or buffaloes. The women cook the family meals, sweep floors, husk rice, make cakes, or spin cotton; whilst swarms of naked children ara making mud pies or playing old-fashioned games. There are trees casting a refreshing shade, under which village magnates smoke and gossip, and religious mendicants pass to and fro; public tanks where the villagers bathe and pray; and little temples where they make their offerings and worship the gods. Yet every household has an individual life. At sunrise every one is astir; at sunset the labours of the day are over, and there is busy conversation everywhere. There is talk about the bullocks, the cows, and the crops; births, deaths, and marriages; ploughing, sowing, and harvesting. But money is the burden of every conversation; rupees, annas and pice; the rental of the fields, the interest due to money-lenders, the cost of presents and feasts, and the loss or profits on every transaction in the farm or household. It is only at rare intervals that public news reaches an Indian village, or the slightest interest is shown in any change of law or administration, or any revolution in the current of affairs outside the village bounds.

When the East India Company first came into possession

of Bengal, the village communities in that quarter had been nearly obliterated by the oppressions of the Muhammadans and the persecutions of Aurangzeb. The villages had lost much of their individual life by being grouped into districts under the charge of different Zemindars, who were held responsible to the Nawab for the collection of the revenue from the Ryots within their several jurisdictions. These Zemindars were removable at the pleasure of the Nawab, but it is possible that they exercised certain hereditary and proprietary rights over the lands or farms within their districts or estates. They were often imprisoned and cruelly used by the Nawab, whenever there was any falling off in the collections; and they in their turn coerced the Ryots, and subjected them to numerous exactions under a variety of pretences, such as the birth of a son, or the marriage of a son or daughter of the Zemindar, or to provide for some payment, fine or subsidy demanded by the Nawab. The villagers had no redress, for the Zemindars were supreme in their districts. It was of course possible to petition the Nawab against a tyrannical Zemindar, but any complaints exposed them more than ever to the oppression of the Zemindar, who was always ready to throw the blame upon the Ryots for any falling off in the collections.

After Lord Clive obtained possession of Bengal, there was, as already seen, an alarming diminution in the revenue. Warren Hastings endeavoured to remedy the evil by abolishing the Native government, and dealing direct with the Zemindars. He treated them only as revenue collectors, and leased the districts for a term of five years to the highest bidders, giving the preference to existing Zemindars. The plan, however, proved a failure. There was too much competition for the post of Zemindar, and many offered larger rents than they could afford to pay, in the hope of being enabled to realise larger rentals from the Ryots. The consequence was that there were many defaulters, and leases of the districts were often put up for resale. Then followed more confusion and disorder, and doubtless more pressure was brought to bear upon the Ryots, checked only by the fear that the Ryots might be driven to throw up their holdings, and seek a livelihood elsewhere.

Efforts were made to correct these evils by investigating registers of land, and vernacular records; but these documents were untrustworthy. Many had been more or less altered or falsified, whilst others had been destroyed during the revolution which accompanied the fall of Meer Cossim. Mr. Shore, who was a member of Lord Cornwallis's government, proposed that provisional leases should be granted for ten years, during which further investigations should be made; but very much time and money had been already wasted on similar inquiries without any satisfactory result.

At last Lord Cornwallis, who succeeded Warren Hastings as Governor-General between the years 1786 and 1793, got rid of the difficulty by proposing that the existing rentals paid by Zemindars should hold good for ever; and that the Zemindars should be left to deal with the Ryots, and thus become the real proprietors of their respective districts, as much so as the proprietors of landed estates in England, so long as they paid their yearly rental to government.

Meanwhile some remarkable discoveries were made as regards the working of the village system in the Madras Presidency. It will be remembered that whilst the Muhammadans had established their rule in Hindustan and the Dekhan as far back as the days of the Normans and Plantagenets, the Peninsula remained unconquered under Hindu rule. The old Hindu empire of Vijayanagar, or Narsinga, extended over the whole of India to the south of the Kistna river; and thus Hindu institutions, such as village communities, retained their ancient integrity.

In 1565, being the ninth year of the reign of Akbar, the Hindu empire of Vijayanagar was overthrown by a confederacy of the Muhammadan Sultans of the Dekhan, in the once famous battle of Talikota. Ram Raja, the last sovereign of the Hindu dynasty, was slain on the field, and the ancient metropolis of Vijayanagar was sacked and depopulated, until nothing remained but the ruined palaces and temples of stone and granite, which still testify to its magnificence in days of old.

The Hindu empire was dismembered; the provinces became kingdoms, and the local governors became Rajas, and thus the Hindu administration continued to be carried on as under imperial rule. The Peninsula was exposed to occasional invasions of the Muhammadans, but it was not until the end of the seventeenth century that the Carnatic was brought under the rule of a Muhammadan Nawab, and not until the latter half of the eighteenth century that the Muhammadan rule of Hyder Ali was established in Mysore.

Under the old Hindu *régime* the village records were singularly complete, and comprised registers of the public revenue, and of all transfers of land between individuals. These had been neglected or ignored by the Muhammadan rulers, and even their use was interdicted in Mysore. But in the province of Canara, on the coast of Malabar, Sir Thomas Monro discovered that the registers had been kept for centuries, and were replaced by fresh copies whenever they were worn out; and that these records sufficed to prove that many of the Ryots were the real owners of the land, subject to the payment of a yearly rent to the existing ruler.

In the present day these details are of small interest, excepting for the light they throw on old Hindu history; but they serve to explain the Ryotwarry settlement in the Madras Presidency, under which the British government deals direct with the Ryots, and the Village settlement in Bombay and the North-West Provinces, under which the British government deals with the joint village proprietors.

Hindu life in towns differs from that in villages only in exhibiting a greater display of wealth, better streets, finer houses, more enlightenment and knowledge, and more association with Europeans and western civilisation. The Hindu from a remote village enters a European capital with fear and awe, as something strange and wonderful, and also impure and dangerous. Sometimes he will not eat within the town, but will fast until his return to the suburbs. But railways and telegraphs have done much to break up this credulity and superstition; and whilst schoolmasters are instructing the rising generation, steam and electricity are carrying on the work of education by driving out the childish ideas of the rural population.

In olden time the great towns of India were distinguished by the emulation of wealthy Hindus in the celebration of religious festivals, as well as in the magnificence and prodigality of entertainments at marriages, and the funeral feasts known as Sraddhas. But the superstitious element in these ceremonials is already dying out, and but for the credulity and influence of Hindu women would probably disappear altogether. But ancient grandams, trembling mothers, and anxious wives are terrified lest any evil should befall husbands or children, in consequence of any neglect of gods or

Brahmans; whilst the tyranny of custom is kept alive by children and dependents, who look forward to the festival time as a general merrymaking; as well as by the rivalry between families and households, which opposes every reduction in the expenditure, whether as regards the presents to be given away, the number of guests to be invited, or the money to be distributed amongst Brahmans and the outside poor.

The cruel rites and observances which belonged to some of the old Hindu religions have already disappeared from India. Widows are no longer condemned to burn themselves alive, or otherwise sacrifice themselves, on the death of their husbands. Children are no longer thrown into a river amongst the alligators, as propitiatory offerings to the wrathful deities. Religious devotees no longer swing themselves upon hooks, or publicly perform other revolting ceremonies as atonements for sin. But Western civilisation does not always promote the happiness of Hindu families. It is not enough to cast away the malpractices of paganism unless the rising generation of Hindus are delivered from the dangerous excesses which intoxicate and destroy, and but too often render civilisation itself a doubtful blessing.

But good and evil are ever mingled together in human progress. Hindu elders may mourn over the decay of the old restraints of religion and caste, which forced the rising generation to remain moral against their will; which kept the boy in the strict grooves of law and custom by the terrors of expulsion or excommunication; and doomed the widow to the funeral pile in order that she might escape the shame and temptations of enforced celibacy. But freedom of will is necessary to the regeneration of the Hindus. Without it they are little better than children, fearing the rod and yearning for sweetmeats and applause. But when they cease to live under the restraints of children after they are grown up to be men and women, and cease to marry whilst they are as yet only boys and girls, they may hope to play a part in the future well-being of their country, to take a share in the representative government of India, and become the fathers and mothers of a great nation.

Mention has been made of the old Hindu empire of Vijayanagar, which flourished in India during the wars of the White and Red Roses, and was dismembered in the sixteenth century during the reign of Akbar. A few traditions of this forgotten empire have been preserved by the Muhammadan historian Ferishta, who was born within four or five years of the battle of Talikota; and they may be retold in the present place as authentic relics of Hindu history, and as illustrations of Hindu life in courts and palaces, as compared with that in villages and towns.

When the Muhammadans conquered the Dekhan, Krishna Rai, Maha Raja of Vijayanagar, was Sovereign, or Suzerain over the whole Peninsula. He was a Hindu warrior, who fought and reigned like Sennacherib or Nebuchadnezzar. He was an incarnation of pride, like "Kehama, the Destroyer," as pictured by Southey. He hated the Muhammadan Sultan as a barbarian and intruder, but he was in no hurry to measure swords with the invaders.

In those days the whole of the Dekhan to the northward of the Peninsula was governed by one Sultan, who reigned at Koolburga, which is now a railway station between Bombay and Madras. The Sultan was as scornful as the Maha Raja, but for a long time was equally shy of measuring swords with the Hindus.

One day the Sultan of the Dekhan had been drinking wine, and hearing flattering songs in his palace at Koolburga, and his heart swelled within him, and instead of paying the musicians in silver and gold, he gave them an order on the treasury of Vijayanagar, and ordered his Minister to affix the royal seal.

Krishna Rai could hardly believe his eyes when he read the draft, ordering him, the greatest prince in India, to pay the beggarly musicians who had been performing before a Muhammadan Sultan. The messenger was at once placed upon a donkey, and led through the streets of Vijayanagar with every mark of contempt. Then the Maha Raja called together all his horse, foot, and elephants, and marched with a mighty host to punish the Sultan. He captured a fortress on the frontier, and slaughtered every man, woman, and child within the place, excepting one soldier, who escaped to tell the story to the Sultan. Having achieved this triumph, Krishna Rai took fright and went back to Vijayanagar, wondering and worrying as to what the Sultan would do.

The Maha Raja was not left long in doubt. No sooner had the Sultan heard of the disaster than he went to the public mosque at Koolburga, and swore upon the Koran that he would never sheathe his sword until he had slain a hundred thousand idolators. He invaded the territories of his Hindu neighbour with a great host of Muhammadans, and slaughtered young and old without pity. In vain the Brahmans harangued the Hindu soldiery, and denounced the Muhammadans as the destroyers of temples and murderers of cows; the armies of Vijayanagar could not face the Muhammadan, and Krishna Rai was compelled to sue for peace. The Sultan was also weary of the war, and granted peace on the condition that Krishna Rai paid the musicians, and the haughty Maha Raja had no alternative but to comply.

Years passed away. Krishna Rai was gathered to his fathers, and another Maha Raja, named Deva Rai, sat upon the throne of Vijayanagar. About this time a Brahman came to the Hindu court, and told Deva Rai that a Hindu goldsmith in the Dekhan had a daughter who was the most beautiful damsel ever seen, and that she had never been married after the manner of Hindu girls; for when her parents wished to betroth her to a boy of her own caste she persuaded them to put off the ceremony.

Deva Rai was smitten with this description. He sent the Brahman with rich presents for the parents of the damsel, and a golden necklace of betrothal to throw over her shoulders; for if she once wore the necklace she could not refuse to become his bride. The goldsmith and his wife rejoiced over the good fortune of their daughter, and the Brahman tried to throw the necklace, but the damsel drew back her head and refused to marry the Maha Raja. Her parents asked why she declined such great honour; and she replied that if she once entered the palace at Vijayanagar she would never see them again. Moreover, she had dreamed that she was to become a Muhammadan, and to marry a Sultan.

Deva Rai was furious at the loss of so beautiful a bride. He sent an army into the Dekhan to bring her away from the Sultan's territory; but her parents were frightened at the approach of the troops, and fled into the jungle, taking their daughter with them.

The Sultan was now angry in his turn. His territory had been violated by Deva Rai, and he was resolved to avenge the insult. He invaded the Peninsula, devastating and

P

slaughtering after the old fashion; and he refused to come to terms unless Deva Rai gave him a daughter of his own in marriage.

The Maha Raja was sorely troubled at the idea of giving his daughter to a Muhammadan bridegroom, but he was compelled to yield. The marriage was celebrated with the utmost magnificence, as if to cover his humiliation. The Muhammadan army lay encamped at a distance of four miles from the city of Vijayanagar; and the road between the two was lined on either side like a street with shops and shows, and all who came were feasted and fêted for forty days. The marriage rites were performed in the palace within the city, and carpets were laid along the street from end to end, and then the Sultan carried away his bride to the camp.

When the honeymoon was over, the bridegroom and his bride returned to the city in grand procession to pay a visit to the Maha Raja. Banners were flying, music was playing, and beautiful children were scattering flowers of gold and silver. After three days the happy pair went back to the camp, but the visit was unpropitious. The Maha Raja accompanied his son-in-law only half way, and then returned to his palace; and the Sultan was so exasperated with his father-in-law for not going the whole way that he secretly burned to be revenged.

After this the Sultan returned with his bride to his own city, and sent for the goldsmith's daughter who had caused the war. The damsel was very beautiful, but the Sultan did not care to make her his second wife, and accordingly gave her in marriage to his son, and the dream of the damsel was fulfilled in due course.

But the Sultan did not die just yet. After he had been married ten years he again invaded the Peninsula, and made war upon Deva Rai; but his army was smitten by a pestilence, and he was compelled to return to the Dekhan.

Then Deva Rai in his turn resolved on revenge. He invaded the Dekhan with a host of Hindus, and cut off the heads of thousands of Muhammadans and built them into a tower. He then burnt down mosques and shrines, and slaughtered the villagers like sheep. At last the Muhammadans recovered heart, and drove the Hindus out of the Dekhan; and then invaded the Peninsula, and slew Hindu women and children without mercy.

Deva Rai was very downhearted at his defeat. He called together a great council of Brahmans and Kshatriyas, and begged them to tell him truly why the Hindus were always beaten by the Muhammadans. The Brahmans said that it was the will of God, and had been foretold in their sacred books. The Kshatriyas said that the Muhammadans had better horsemen and archers.

Accordingly Deva Rai took many Muhammadans into his pay, and built a mosque for them, where they could pray to God and their Prophet after their own fashion. But the Muhammadans would not bow their heads to an idolatrous Maha Raja; and Deva Rai knew not what to do. At last he placed a Koran over his throne, and when the Muhammadans prostrated themselves before the sacred book the Hindus thought that they were paying their homage to the Maha Raja.

But Deva Rai's mercenaries could make no head against his enemies, and he yielded to his fate, and henceforth paid tribute to the Sultan of the Dekhan.

Many years afterwards Deva Rai died, and the Minister set up an infant as a puppet, and governed the empire in his name. Three infants reigned in succession, and were each murdered in turn, whilst the Minister continued to be the real head of affairs.

Ram Raja was the son of the Minister. When he was a boy he was married to a granddaughter of Deva Rai, and when he was grown up he was proclaimed Maha Raja of Vijayanagar. Subsequently his pride and insolence drove the Hindu nobles into rebellion. He marched an army against the rebels, leaving his treasury in charge of a trusted slave. But the slave grew mad at the sight of the gold, and began to intrigue with a half-witted prince of the dethroned dynasty, and agreed to place the imbecile on the throne as Maha Raja on the condition that he himself was appointed to the post of Minister.

This arrangement was carried out, and accepted by the nobles, and Ram Raja was forced to abdicate the throne of Vijayanagar and retire to his estates. But the new Maha Raja murdered his Minister, and aggravated the nobles by his mad proceedings. In sheer desperation they rallied round Ram Raja; and then the imbecile Maha Raja invited the Sultan of the Dekhan to come to his assistance, and actually paid homage to the Sultan in the city of Vijayanagar.

Ram Rai and the nobles were aghast at this national humiliation. They pledged themselves to be obedient to the mad Maha Raja, if he would only get rid of the Sultan; and the Maha Raja was so delighted at their submission that he paid the Sultan vast sums out of the public treasury to induce him to go away.

No sooner had the Sultan returned to his own territories than Ram Rai and the nobles advanced to the Hindu capital to dethrone the madman. The Maha Raja knew that he had been deceived, and was frantic with rage. He put out the eyes of the royal elephants and horses, and cut off their tails. He tried to destroy the jewels in the treasury by crushing them with mill-stones. At last he heard his enemies breaking down the palace gates, and fell upon his sword and perished upon the spot.

Ram Rai ascended the throne of Vijayanagar in triumph. He had nothing to fear from the Muhammadans. The old empire of the Dekhan was broken up into five kingdoms, and the five Sultans were fighting against one another. Ram Raja, however, took the part of some Sultans against the others, and entered the Dekhan in order to fight side by side with his Muhammadan allies. But his Hindu soldiery committed horrible sacrilege; they stabled their horses in mosques, and performed pagan rites in Muhammadan shrines. At last all the Sultans forgot their quarrels and banded together against the common foe. Ram Rai was defeated and slain in the battle of Talikota, and the empire was dismembered into a number of petty kingdoms, but the temples and palaces of Vijayanagar remain unto this day.

XV.—*Sikhs, Afghans, and Burmese.*

Ante 1856.

DURING the thirty or forty years which followed the departure of Lord Wellesley from India the name of Runjeet Singh was a household word to Natives as well as to Europeans. He was known as King of the Sikhs, the Lion of Lahore, the Maha Raja of the Punjab; but he always styled himself the Commander-in-Chief of the Sikh army of the Khalsa, the brotherhood of God and the Guru Govind.

Runjeet Singh was a distinguished man, but his appearance was mean. He was a short and shrivelled warrior with only one eye, and a countenance deeply pitted with the small-pox; and neither cloth of gold, nor a profusion of jewels, nor the pomp of elephants and armies, could make him look like a hero. He could neither read nor write, and his knowledge of European affairs was a mixture of truth and fable; but there was a resolute rascality about the mouth, and a roguish twinkle in his single eye, which always impressed strangers. His life and career resembled that of Herod, King of the Jews, but he was not quite so bloodthirsty. He would order hands and feet to be cut off without mercy, but he shrunk from executions in cold blood. He professed the utmost zeal for God and the Guru, but was as shameless and dissolute in private life as any of the twelve Cæsars.

The Sikhs were a religious brotherhood formed by Nanuk Guru in the fourteenth century, but held together by a military enthusiasm like that of Cromwell's Ironsides. Their religion was a combination of Brahmanism and Muhammadanism, involving a belief in one God, and devotion to their living prophet or Guru. In the seventeenth century large reforms were carried out by Guru Govind, who was priest, prince, and teacher; but the Sikh leaders were cruelly persecuted by Aurangzeb, and their followers degenerated into guerilla bands of zealots and freebooters. In the eighteenth century they were conquered by the Afghans, and the Punjab became a province of the Afghan empire.

There has always been a marked contrast, as well as a bitter enmity, between Sikhs and Afghans. The Sikhs are wiry men, with unshorn locks and flowing beards, occasionally brigands, but otherwise brave and enthusiastic, and soldiers by birth and bearing. The Afghans are Muhammadans, stout and burly, with black eyes, and long black hair hanging down in curls. Their features are Jewish, and they have traditions of being descended from King Saul. They are good-natured to look at, and put on an air of geniality and politeness; but at heart they are treacherous and savage, and will commit robbery or murder without the slightest sense of shame. "Never trust a cobra or an Afghan" is a proverb which has long been current throughout Hindustan.

At the very beginning of the nineteenth century, when Runjeet Singh was about twenty years of age, he was appointed Viceroy of the Punjab under the Afghan *régime*. But the Afghans were fighting one another, and Runjeet Singh seized the moment for reviving the Sikh army of the Khalsa, and stirring up its enthusiasm against the Afghans. The result was that Runjeet Singh threw off the Afghan supremacy and compelled every Sikh chieftain to submit to his authority; and thus in course of time he became the sovereign of the Punjab, and extended his empire over Cashmere and Peshawar.

Runjeet Singh was soon feared by all his neighbours as a conquering power; and he might have invaded Hindustan, and become one of the conquerors of India, but his career was stopped by the British government. He was wise enough to yield to circumstances, and to consent that the river Sutlej should be the boundary between the two states; and from that day the two powers kept up a friendly alliance based upon mutual interests. The British government was anxious to maintain Runjeet Singh as a barrier against all invasions from the north-west; and Runjeet Singh was anxious to give the English no pretence for interfering in his territories. The two powers were thus on speaking terms as next-door neighbours, and very friendly when they met; but Runjeet Singh was jealous of any intrusion upon his dominions, and deaf to all suggestions for opening up a trade on the river Indus, which was a favourite scheme of the East India Company in the olden time.

About 1826 there was a lull in Afghan affairs. Shah Shuja, the reigning Ameer, was driven out of Cabul by Dost Muhammad Khan, and fled through the Punjab towards Hindustan. On his way he was stopped by Runjeet Singh, and robbed of the famous diamond, known as the Koh-i-Nur, or "Mountain of Light," which had been carried away from Delhi by Nadir Shah. On reaching British territory Shah Shuja found an asylum, and lived for some years as a pensioner of the East India Company.

Dost Muhammad Khan consolidated his power as Ameer of Cabul, but he could not recover Peshawar from Runjeet Singh. About this time a rivalry was springing up between Great Britain and Russia in Central Asia. Russia was advancing southwards towards the river Oxus, and Great Britain was seeking to extend her influence north-westwards towards the same river, but the Punjab and Cabul stood in the way.

The East India Company was already in alliance with Runjeet Singh, and was desirous of forming an alliance with Dost Muhammad Khan; but the Dost would not give his alliance for nothing, and accordingly begged the Governor-General, Lord Auckland, to persuade Runjeet Singh to restore Peshawar. Lord Auckland, however, refused to do anything of the kind, as such a request would only give mortal offence to Runjeet Singh.

Accordingly Dost Muhammad Khan began to lend an ear to Russia, and went so far as to receive a Russian agent at Cabul. Thereupon Lord Auckland declared war against him, and prepared to restore Shah Shuja to the throne of Cabul, and thus establish a friendly power on the southern bank of the Oxus in the room of Dost Muhammad Khan.

The British invasion of Afghanistan began in 1838. A tripartite alliance was formed between the British government, Runjeet Singh, and Shah Shuja, against Dost Muhammad Khan; but Runjeet Singh refused to let the invading army march through the Punjab, and it was accordingly obliged to take a circuitous route through Scinde to Quetta, and thence to Candahar.

The Afghan campaign was a triumphant success. In 1839 Candahar was captured and occupied by a force under General Nott, assisted by Major (now Sir Henry) Rawlinson.

Ghuzni was taken by storm, and the British army reached Cabul, and formed a cantonment near the city. Shah Shuja was placed on the throne of Cabul, and was supposed to govern the country under the advice of Sir William Macnaghten, the English Minister and Envoy, who became the virtual ruler of Afghanistan. Dost Muhammad Khan fled from Cabul, but afterwards surrendered to Macnaghten, and was conducted as a prisoner to Calcutta, but treated on his arrival as the guest of the Governor-General.

The British occupation of Afghanistan was found, however, to be an expensive affair. Many influential nobles or Sirdars were bought over by pensions, whilst the hill tribes were kept quiet by subsidies, and all the money thus expended in behalf of Shah Shuja was advanced from the British treasury. Later on these money grants were reduced or withdrawn, and then the tide of disaffection began to turn against the English. The hill tribes broke out in rebellion, and the whole country was ready to rise against British supremacy.

Meanwhile Runjeet Singh died at Lahore, and the Punjab was disturbed by plots and assassinations. His son and successor was afraid of the army of the Khalsa, and turned to the British government for help and protection. He opened the Punjab to troops passing between British territory and Cabul, and prayed the British government to interfere and suppress the disorders of the Khalsa.

In October, 1841, Sir Robert Sale left Cabul with a brigade to open up the communication with the Punjab through the Khyber Pass, but he was stopped at Jellahabad and compelled to stand a siege. In November there was an insurrection at Cabul, and Sir Alexander Barnes, who was about to succeed Macnaghten as Minister and Envoy, was murdered by the mob. Then followed a series of disasters. Shah

Shuja was helpless and incapable. Macnaghten began to negotiate with the rebel leaders for the safe withdrawal of the British army, but was treacherously slaughtered. The army began to retreat from Cabul, and made its way to the Khyber Pass; but the winter had set in, the snow was falling, the hill tribes poured a murderous fire from both sides of the pass, and the whole of the army was either destroyed by successive volleys from the heights above, or perished in the snows, and only a single survivor escaped to Jellahabad.

In 1842 Lord Auckland was succeeded by Lord Ellenborough as Governor-General of India; and General Pollock marched an army through the Punjab, and relieved Sir Robert Sale at Jellahabad; and then drove the Afghan mountaineers from the heights which overlooked the Khyber Pass, and went triumphantly on to Cabul. All this while General Nott held his own at Candahar, and finally joined General Pollock at Cabul. The British government was satisfied by the re-establishment of its *prestige*, and resolved to withdraw from all further interference in Afghan affairs. Accordingly the whole force returned to Hindustan, carrying with them the gates of Somnath from the tomb of Mahmud of Ghuzni, as told in a previous chapter.

Thus ended the first Afghan war of 1839—42. Shah Shuja was murdered at Cabul, and Dost Muhammad Khan returned to Afghanistan, and was restored to his throne.

All this while the British government was alarmed at the course of events in the Punjab. Ever since the death of Runjeet Singh, in 1839, the whole country was disturbed; whilst the capital at Lahore was distracted by plots and assassinations, during which one ruler succeeded another with frightful rapidity. In 1843 two plots exploded at the same moment; the Maha Raja was murdered at the instigation of the Minister, whilst the Minister was murdered at the instigation of the Maha Raja.

Amidst the general confusion an infant son of Runjeet Singh was placed upon the throne under the name of Duleep Singh. His mother was Regent, and appointed her paramour to be Minister. The new government was absolutely at the mercy of the army of the Khalsa. Runjeet Singh had kept the army in hand by his iron will and the terror of his name, and by keeping the soldiery constantly on the move; but under his weak and worthless successors the army had become demoralised and unruly. It was controlled by committees of five, known as punchayets, who were elected from the ranks; and nothing could be done by the officers of the army, nor by the government at Lahore, without the consent of these punchayets; whilst the soldiery were perpetually clamouring for largesses and increase of pay.

At last matters reached a climax. The army of the Khalsa threatened to sack Lahore. The Regent mother, the Minister, and the Commander-in-Chief were alike in terror of their lives; and in November, 1845, they were driven in sheer desperation to try and save themselves by sending the Sikh army of 60,000 men and 150 guns across the river Sutlej for the plunder of Hindustan.

Lord Ellenborough had been succeeded by Sir Henry Hardinge as Governor-General of India in 1844. Before his departure he had foreseen that the Sikh army would, sooner or later, attempt the invasion of Hindustan; and this was the main reason why he had declared war upon Gwalior, and insisted on disbanding the overgrown army of Scindia, which might have made common cause with the invaders. His successor, Sir Henry Hardinge, was equally watchful of the progress of events in the Punjab, but was taken somewhat by surprise by the news that the Sikhs had crossed the Sutlej. Sir John Littler held the frontier fortress of Ferozepore with 10,000 troops and 31 guns, and might have been environed by the Sikhs; but he was relieved by the speedy arrival of the main army under Sir Henry Hardinge, the Governor-General, and Sir Hugh Gough, the Commander-in-Chief. Then followed the battles of Moodkee, Ferozeshahar and Aliwal; and in February, 1846, the crowning victory at Sobraon brought the war to a close.

The Punjab was now at the entire disposal of the British government, but it was difficult to know what to do. The existing Sikh government was corrupt, oppressive and depraved; and unless it was protected by British bayonets, it was liable to be upset at any moment by a successful plot or rebellion. To annex the country, even after a conquest, was opposed to British instincts, unless the measure was found absolutely necessary for the maintenance of the public peace. Accordingly, Sir Henry, now Lord Hardinge, contented himself with disbanding the greater part of the army of the Khalsa, and leaving the civil government, as he found it, in the hands of the Regent mother and her Minister, aided by the counsel of Major Henry Lawrence, who was appointed British Resident at Lahore.

On one point, however, Lord Hardinge was inexorable. He was willing to leave the government of the Punjab in the hands of existing rulers, but he would not fortify it with a British army in the shape of a Subsidiary Force, lest the British government should be rendered responsible for the maintenance of oppression and misrule. He was willing to keep a British force in the Punjab until the end of 1846, but he declared that on that date every British soldier and Sepoy must return to British territory.

But no human power could save the Sikh government from destruction. The Minister was convicted of stirring up a rebellion in Cashmere, and was removed from his post. The Regent mother was furious at this proceeding, and began to plot in secret with the enemies of the British government. The Sikh nobles, known as Sirdars, assured the British authorities that the disbanded army of the Khalsa would start into new life, and restore the old anarchy and disorder, the moment that the British force was withdrawn from the Punjab. Accordingly, the Regent mother was replaced by a Council of Regency, consisting of six Sikh Sirdars, under the direction of the British Resident; and thus, having done his best to prevent oppression on the part of the Sikh administration, Lord Hardinge consented to keep a British army in the Punjab until the infant Maha Raja, Duleep Singh, attained his majority.

In 1848 Lord Hardinge left India, and was succeeded by Lord Dalhousie as Governor-General. All this while the spirit of the Khalsa—the old fire of the brotherhood of faith in God and the Guru—was smouldering in the hearts not only of the disbanded soldiery, but of many of the Sikh Sirdars.

Shortly after the departure of Lord Hardinge a single spark set the Punjab in a flame. The Sikh governor of the province of Multan, named Mulraj, was offended with the Council of Regency on account of some money demand, and offered to resign his post. The offer was accepted, and another Sikh governor was sent to take the place of Mulraj, and was accompanied by two English officers, Mr. Vans Agnew and Lieutenant Anderson. The two Englishmen were treacherously murdered at the instigation of Mulraj, who thereupon hoisted the standard of rebellion over the fortress of Multan. An English force and a Sikh force were sent against the rebels, but the Sikhs suddenly went over to the enemy, and proclaimed a religious war against the English. Unfortunately the movements of the British army were delayed by the hot weather, and before the return of the cold season the paltry outbreak at Multan had culminated in a general rising against British Suzerainty.

In October, 1848, Sir Hugh, now Lord Gough, took the field. In January, 1849, he fought an indecisive battle at Chilianwallah, in which the English lost 2400 officers and men; and the tidings created so much alarm and indignation in England that Sir Charles Napier was sent out to India to take the post of Commander-in-Chief in the room of Gough. But there was no telegraphic communication in those days, and before Napier could reach India, Multan was captured by General Whish, and Lord Gough gained the crowning victory at Guzerat, which decided the fate of the Punjab.

Lord Dalhousie annexed the Punjab to the British empire, and brought it under British administration; and eventually Mr. John Lawrence was appointed Chief Commissioner, the same who afterwards became Governor-General of India, and was elevated to the peerage under the title of Lord Lawrence. Within a few years the Punjab underwent a transformation under British rule, which would have seemed impossible in the days of Runjeet Singh. It was traversed by roads and canals, and opened out to Western civilisation; whilst the disbanded soldiers of the Khalsa became peaceful cultivators, or enlisted under British banners, and proved their loyalty and devotion in 1857 at the storming of Delhi. To this day the administration of the Punjab is regarded as one of the greatest triumphs of British rule in India.

A year or two after the final conquest of the Punjab the attention of the British government was drawn to a very different quarter, namely, the remote region to the eastward of the Bay of Bengal, known by the general name of Burma. This territory runs southward from Bengal and Assam, as far as the kingdom of Siam in the Malacca peninsula; whilst it stretches inland up the valley of the Irrawaddy, as far as the frontiers of China.

The people of Burma are a Mongolian race, with high cheek-bones and wide mouths, but many have regular features and fair complexions. They have no infant marriages or system of castes, whilst their ideas and institutions are governed by the moral rules of Buddhism. The laity are taught that the practice of virtue, goodness, and loving-kindness will secure a higher state of happiness in a future life, or rather in a future transmigration of the soul. The priests or monks go still further, and devote themselves to lives of celibacy and contemplation, in the hope of delivering the soul from the pains and miseries of endless transmigrations, and entering into a state of everlasting rest or annihilation, known as Nirvana.

The Burmese are far more independent and self-reliant than the Hindus, and to all appearance, are a far happier people. The young people mingle in society as freely as the English. They indulge in singing and dancing as national performances, in which every young woman plays her part; and there is constant competition between different towns and villages, or between different quarters of the same town. The young men are given to boat-racing, playing at ball, games of chance, and fun and frolic of every description.

Every evening in Burma is known as "courting time," because the lads of the village go out in their gayest attire to pay their visits to the lasses, and this is a regular institution in Burma. The young people are orderly and well-behaved on such occasions, although the talk may be carried on with much mirth and laughter. The young lady of the house is the hostess. Whenever she wishes to give an evening, she places a lamp in her window as an open invitation, without which ordinary acquaintances would scarcely think of intruding. Such social gatherings are naturally popular with all the young people throughout Burma, but when they have chosen their partners for life and are regularly married, courting time is over for them, and left to the rising generation.

The religious worship of the Burmese differs widely from that of the Hindus. In India the temples are as gloomy as tombs, and the Brahmans are sombre and often greedy for money. In Burma the temples are gay and attractive; decorated with flags, flowers, pictures, gilding, and wax tapers; and crowded on festival occasions with throngs of men and women, boys and girls, in their best attire. Buddhist monks in yellow robes are to be found all over the country. They never ask for alms, and it is contrary to the rules of their order to receive or touch money. They mingle freely with all classes of the community, and are hospitably entertained wherever they go. In their respective villages they are the school-masters of the masses, and are supported by voluntary gifts of cooked food, which are freely bestowed upon them every morning. Indeed there is not a village in Burma that has not a monastery and a school.

By a strange fatality the history of Burma is one of the saddest in the world. In former times it was parcelled out amongst petty kings, who were always despotic, and often barbarous and cruel; and the country was so depopulated by wars and massacres that to this day a very large extent of fertile land is out of cultivation. About 1750 a Burmese adventurer, known as Alompra the hunter, raised an insurrection in Burma, and conquered one king after another, until he had created an empire, and founded a dynasty which is still reigning. But every one of his successors has been exposed to rebellion or revolution, and nearly every one has been murdered in his turn, with all his queens and children, to make way for a new rival, who is doomed to pass through the same bloody ordeal.

The kings of the house of Alompra have been arrogant and ignorant, regarding themselves as the greatest potentates in the world, and all outside princes as barbarians. English envoys have been sent to their court, and have been shown palaces and barges covered with gilding and decorated with looking-glasses; or been dazzled with displays of sovereign pomp, gaudily caparisoned elephants, fantastic soldiery, and obsequious ceremonial.

In 1824, Lord Amherst, who succeeded Lord Hastings as Governor-General of India, was forced into a war with Burma. The Burmese demanded the surrender of some political refugees, who had found an asylum in British territory; and when they found they could not get what they wanted they seized an island belonging to the English, and committed other aggressions, threatening to conquer Bengal unless the Governor-General complied with their demands.

Accordingly a British expedition was sent by sea to Rangoon, and advanced up the river Irrawaddy to the neighbourhood of the capital at Ava; and then the king became alarmed, and agreed to any terms which would satisfy the English. Accordingly, the British army was withdrawn from Burma, but two provinces on the coast known as Arakan and Tenasserim were taken over by the British government. At the same time the territory of Assam, to the eastward of Bengal, fell into the possession of the English, and has since then become famous for the production of tea.

The war of 1824—26 kept the Burmese quiet for awhile; but in 1841—42 there were restless movements, and rumours of coming war both in Burma and Nepal. These hostile demonstrations were attributable to the English disasters in Cabul, and rapidly died out when the British government recovered its *prestige*.

In 1851 some English sea captains were harshly treated by the Burmese authorities at Rangoon. Redress was demanded from the Burmese government, but an English envoy was treated with insult, and an English frigate was fired upon by the Burmese soldiery. In 1852 Lord Dalhousie sent another expedition to Rangoon, and before the end of the year the war was brought to a close by the annexation of Pegu, including the important port of Rangoon.

Major, afterwards General Sir Arthur Phayre, was the first Commissioner of Pegu, and in 1862 he was appointed Chief Commissioner of the whole of British Burma, including Arakan and Tenasserim. The success of British administration under Sir Arthur Phayre, General Albert Fytche, and their successors, was as marked in British Burma as in the Punjab; and Rangoon, from a small town with ten thousand inhabitants, has become a city with a population of more than a hundred thousand, and bids fair, whenever a trade is opened with Western China, to rival the great Indian capitals of Calcutta, Madras, and Bombay.

XVI.—*Sepoy Mutinies.*

1857 to 1858.

THE administration of Lord Dalhousie lasted from 1848 to 1856, and was the beginning of a new era in moral and material progress. Railways were laid down, and telegraph wires were hung from post to post throughout the length and breadth of India. These things are appreciated to-day, but a generation ago the credulous Hindus were whispering that the English were binding India in chains. Calcutta was lighted with gas, and the English were accused of magic and sorcery. Education was established on a national basis, and other bewildering measures were carried out which were to regenerate India.

Lord Dalhousie annexed the territories of Oude, Nagpore, and some other principalities; and British administration was introduced, in the hope that it would be attended with the same marked success as in the Punjab and Pegu. Since then, however, there has been a change of policy, and Native rulers have been encouraged to attempt similar reforms without changing the Native *régime.*

Lord Canning succeeded Lord Dalhousie in 1856, and at that time everything was quiet in India. But early in 1857 there was some uneasiness amongst the Sepoys in the Bengal army. In those days muskets were loaded at the muzzle with paper cartridges; and every soldier, European or Native, was obliged to bite off the end of his cartridge before loading. The Enfield rifle was introduced into the Bengal army, and was loaded with cartridges which required greasing; and the new cartridges were made in Calcutta, and greased with the fat of beef and pork, heedless of the fact that Hindus would be defiled in their own eyes by biting the one, whilst Muhammadans would be equally defiled by biting the other.

The result of such culpable carelessness was suddenly apparent at Barrackpore, a well known military cantonment about sixteen miles from Calcutta. A low caste Native asked a Brahman soldier for a drink of water out of his brass pot, but was refused on the ground that his lips would defile the pot. The man retorted that the lips of the Brahman were already defiled by biting cartridges greased with cow's fat. The taunt became the talk of the cantonment, and the Sepoys were startled at the idea that the British government was bent on destroying caste, and making the Sepoys eat beef until they were as strong as Europeans.

As a matter of fact the new cartridges had never been issued to the Sepoys at all; and had this been explained at once, and the Sepoys left to grease their own cartridges, the panic would have died out. But no explanation was offered, and the Sepoys at Barrackpore refused to receive the suspected cartridges; and the story spread from one military station to another; from Barrackpore to Allahabad, Cawnpore and Delhi, and finally to Meerut, which is forty miles beyond Delhi, and was at that time the largest cantonment in India, and the strongest as regards European soldiers.

At last the military authorities tried to explain away the mistake about the cartridges, and to promise that the new ones should never be issued; but the time for explanation had gone by, and the Sepoys refused to believe their commanding officers. Fresh stories got into circulation. The Sepoys were made to believe that the bones of cows and pigs had been ground to powder, and mingled with flour and butter, in order to destroy their religion and caste, and to compel them to become Christians. Under such circumstances the Sepoys became sullen and panic stricken; and nothing was wanting but a spark to set every cantonment in Northern India in a blaze.

There was some alarm at Calcutta lest there should be a mutinous rising at Barrackpore, and a regiment of European soldiers was brought from Burma to Bengal. But the presence of the European soldiers terrified the Sepoys more than ever, and they thought that their doom was sealed. There was an outbreak on the parade ground at Barrackpore. A Sepoy, named Mungal Pandy, fired a bullet at an English Adjutant, and other Sepoys attacked the Adjutant and his English Sergeant with the butt ends of their muskets; whilst not a man came forward to defend the two Englishmen. At last a Muhammadan orderly arrested Mungal Pandy, and the General commanding the station galloped up pistol in hand. The Sepoys fell back in terror, and the tumult was over; but Mungal Pandy was tried and executed, and the offending regiment was disbanded, and for a brief interval it was thought that the disaffection was over.

Alarming symptoms however appeared in other cantonments. At Lucknow, the capital of the newly annexed province of Oude, there was a mutiny amongst irregular levies, but it was promptly suppressed by Sir Henry Lawrence, who had been appointed Chief Commissioner. Next an attempt was made at Meerut, where the Europeans were exceptionally strong, to put the obedience of the Sepoys to the test. There were three Native regiments, two of infantry and one of cavalry; and the Sepoy cavalry was the one most suspected. On Wednesday, the 6th of May, the European force was drawn up on the open plain, consisting of a battalion of the 60th Rifles, a regiment of Dragoon Guards, two troops of horse artillery and a light field battery; sufficient to scatter four times the number of Sepoys. The regiment of Sepoy cavalry was paraded in the presence of this force, and cartridges were served out; not the greased abominations which had been manufactured at Calcutta, but the old cartridges which had been used by the Native army for generations. Eighty Sepoys stood out and refused to accept them; and the mutineers were arrested on the spot and tried by a court martial of Native officers, found guilty, and sentenced to various periods of imprisonment.

On Saturday, the 9th of May, the sentences were carried out. All the troops were under arms. The offenders were brought on parade, stripped of their uniforms, and placed in irons. They begged for mercy, but finding it hopeless they began to reproach their comrades for not striking a blow in their behalf, but not a Sepoy dared to stir. At last they were carried off, and placed in the jail under a Native guard.

Sunday, the 10th of May, 1857, was a sad day at Meerut. At five o'clock in the afternoon, when English ladies and gentlemen in the European quarter were preparing to go to church, there were cries of fire, volleys of musketry, frantic yells, a clatter of cavalry, and a bugle sounding an alarm. The three Sepoy regiments had suddenly resolved on mutiny. They had broken open the jail, and released all the prisoners; and were running about with arms in their hands, killing every European they met, and setting the English houses on fire. The European regiments turned out, but there was a strange delay when every moment was of vital importance; and meanwhile the Sepoys fled from Meerut, and were on their way to Delhi, and no attempt was made by the Europeans to pursue them.

Early next morning the mutinous Sepoys reached Delhi, and were soon joined by the Native regiments which were encamped on a rising ground about two miles from the city, known as the Ridge. There was only a small European force at Delhi, and the officers held out as long as they could in the hope that the Europeans at Meerut would come to their rescue. The mutinous Sepoys from Meerut had been joined by the insurgent rabble of Delhi, and the old Moghul capital was in revolt. The English ladies and children at the Ridge were sent to Flagstaff Tower, a small brick building at some distance off; but as the day began to close they were joined by the officers from the Ridge. No European soldiers came from Meerut, and one and all were compelled in the end to fly for their lives.

Meanwhile the mutiny had grown into a rebellion. The Sepoys broke into the palace and hailed the helpless old Moghul as their sovereign, and most of the so-called royal family of pensioners made common cause with the rebels. Every European found in the city or palace was cut down and murdered. The mob of rebels attempted to seize the English magazine in the heart of the city, but met with a signal disaster. Lieutenant Willoughby, the officer in charge, fired a train and blew the whole into the air, and hundreds of scoundrels, who were breaking in at the gate, were hurried into eternity in a moment of time.

The tidings of what happened at Meerut and Delhi spread an alarm throughout Hindustan. The greased cartridges at

Calcutta had created a mutiny at Barrackpore, but the incapacity of the military authorities at Meerut had turned the mutiny with a revolt at Delhi. At station after station the Bengal Sepoys followed the example set at Meerut, and displayed the same mixture of madness and terror. They broke out at twilight or midnight, murdered all they met, plundered all they could seize, and burnt down the houses; and then the bulk rushed off to Delhi to join the rebels, whilst not a few slunk off to their homes with their ill-gotten booty, and were heard of no more.

On the 30th of May there was an outbreak at Lucknow. Sir Henry Lawrence expected it, and was prepared. He had withdrawn the European community into the British Residency, and resolved to hold it until reinforcements could arrive. He was hemmed round with difficulties. The city extended four miles along the right bank of the river Goomti, and was teeming with a disaffected population of palace parasites, who had been reduced to poverty by the departure of the royal family to Calcutta. The British Residency stood between the city and the river. On the opposite side of the river was the Native cantonment, which was reached from the city by two bridges; and the first object of Sir Henry Lawrence had been to place a strong guard on the two bridges, so as to prevent communication between the mutinous Sepoys in the cantonment and the disaffected population in the city.

The Sepoys broke out in the Native cantonment at nine o'clock in the evening, killing, burning, and plundering according to their wont. They then rushed to the bridges, mad with excitement and an intoxicating drug, known as bang. But there they were received with a volley of grape, which cooled their ardour, and they beat a hasty retreat, hotly pursued by Sir Henry Lawrence. They were thus cut off from the cantonment as well as from the city, and had no alternative but to join the mass of rebels at Delhi.

But the whole province of Oude was soon in rebellion against British rule. The Talukdars, or rent collectors, answering to the Zemindars of Bengal, had lost under the new English revenue settlement many lands which they had usurped, and much of the power which they had previously exercised over the wretched Ryots; and they readily joined in a revolt which promised to bring back the old status. Even the Ryots, who had profited largely by the new revenue settlement, saw that their English protectors were at the mercy of rebels and brigands, and naturally fled for safety to the fortresses of their old masters. The result was that the handful of Europeans in the Residency at Lucknow was besieged by swarms of rebels of every description, and could only hold on and fight on against overwhelming odds, and wait anxiously for reinforcements which never seemed to arrive. Five weeks after the outbreak of the 30th of May, Sir Henry Lawrence received a mortal wound, but his dying counsel to those around him was "Never surrender!"

About this very time there was a horrible tragedy at Cawnpore, on the Ganges, about fifty-five miles from Lucknow. Six miles from Cawnpore was a palace which had been built by the dethroned Peishwa of Poona; and there the Brahman prince had lived to an extreme old age, in the indulgence of almost every vice that can degrade humanity, on a pension of £80,000 per annum from the East India Company. He died in 1853, and his pension lapsed to the Company. He had left no heirs, but was said to have adopted a young Mahratta Brahman, who was known as Nana Sahib. Of course the Mahratta applied for a continuance of the pension, and it was refused at once, especially as the Nana had inherited the private savings of the ex-Peishwa, amounting to half-a-million sterling.

It is a question to this day whether the Nana had really been adopted by the ex-Peishwa. The matter, however, is of no importance. Mahratta like, he brooded over his supposed wrongs until his head was half turned. He professed a warm friendship for the English, and liberally entertained British visitors at Bithoor; but he never wearied in telling his grievances to any one who chose to listen.

The military cantonment at Cawnpore was under the command of General Sir Hugh Wheeler. When the news arrived of the mutiny and revolt at Meerut and Delhi, Nana Sahib was very sympathising. He not only repeated his protestations of friendship towards the English, but actually organised a Mahratta force for their protection at Cawnpore.

Subsequently there was an alarm that the Sepoys at Cawnpore were about to mutiny; and as there was an exceptionally large number of English ladies and children, General Wheeler moved them into some old barracks, and tried to entrench the building. In June the Sepoys broke out in mutiny, and went off towards Delhi; but Nana Sahib pursued them and brought them back. It turned out that Nana Sahib was dreaming of recovering the throne of the Peishwas of Poona, which had been subverted forty years before; and that he was tempting the rebel Sepoys to rally round him as Peishwa, in preference to rallying round the Great Moghul at Delhi. The Sepoys cared neither for the Nana nor for Padishah or Peishwa, but were induced to return to Cawnpore by fabulous stories of the treasures that lay hidden in the barracks which had been entrenched by General Wheeler.

The assumption of Nana Sahib bordered on insanity. He besieged the little garrison in the old barracks at Cawnpore, as if it represented the British empire; and he seems to have supposed that if the barracks fell the British empire would follow. Whether Scindia or Holkar were likely to acknowledge his Suzerainty as Peishwa, or what he was to do with the Great Moghul after he had conquered the Governor-General, seems never to have crossed his mind.

For sixteen days the little English garrison under General Wheeler held out in the old barracks at Cawnpore against an overwhelming force of rebel Sepoys. At the end of that time, however, the barracks were found to be untenable. The English would have cut their way through the Sepoys, or perished sword in hand whilst making the attempt, but they could not abandon the ladies and children. Accordingly General Wheeler gave ear to certain proposals that were made by the Nana.

The Mahratta Brahman offered to provide forty boats to carry the whole of the besieged, numbering 450 souls, down the river Ganges from Cawnpore to Allahabad, provided that General Wheeler would surrender the barracks. The terms were accepted. Men, women and children moved to the river at early morning on the 27th of June, and embarked on board the boats. Everything was ready for the start, when the soldiers of the Nana opened a heavy fire upon the helpless voyagers. Hundreds were killed or drowned. The survivors were dragged ashore, and all the men were shot dead by another volley. The women and children were lodged in a neighbouring house to the number of 200 souls.

Of all the fugitives on board the boats, only four men escaped to tell the story.

On the 1st of July Nana Sahib left Cawnpore and returned to his palace at Bithoor, and was proclaimed Peishwa of the Mahrattas. Meanwhile an avenging column, under General Havelock, was advancing from Bengal towards Cawnpore. The Nana vainly endeavoured to oppose him, but was driven back with heavy loss. In wild desperation the bloodthirsty coward ordered the women and children to be slaughtered and thrown into the well at Cawnpore. Havelock reached Cawnpore, but only in time to see the bleeding remains of the victims.

The massacre at Cawnpore was the crowning tragedy in the Sepoy mutiny. It sent a thrill of horror through the civilised world. During July and August the British government began to put forth its strength to trample out a rising which had culminated in such revolting crime. John Lawrence, Lieutenant Governor of the Punjab, was distracted by the necessity of keeping enough troops and guns for the protection of his province against the mutinies of the Bengal Sepoys within his jurisdiction, whilst responding to the imperial demands for soldiers and artillery for the siege of Delhi. At the same time Lord Canning was burdened with the cares and anxieties which beset the British empire in India. The high road from Calcutta to Delhi was blocked up by mutiny and insurrection, whilst the telegraph wires had been cut immediately after the revolt at Meerut; and Lord Canning was forced to concentrate all his efforts in sending Europeans and other levies towards the north-west to avenge the massacre at Cawnpore, relieve the beleaguered garrison at Lucknow, and crush the rebellion in Oude.

The siege of Delhi was the all important event of the war.

In Europe, as well as in India, every eye was intent on the progress of events in the old capital of the Moghul empire. As early as June, the month after the revolt, a British force advanced towards the city, and occupied the old cantonment on the Ridge; but for many weeks they were unable to attempt siege operations, and were chiefly occupied in defending their position against repeated assaults. The city was strongly fortified, and abundantly supplied with provisions; whilst the garrison numbered 30,000 strong, amply provided with arms, artillery and ammunition, and recruited by the frequent arrival of fresh bands of mutineers.

The British camp on the Ridge presented a striking picture. There were long lines of European tents, thatched hovels of native servants, rows of horses, parks of artillery, English soldiers in grey linen coats and trousers, Sikhs in blue and red turbans, Afghans in gay head dresses, and Ghorkas in Kilmarnock hats. There were but few Hindu Sepoys in the British ranks, but native servants were very numerous. From the summit of the Ridge it was easy to see the river Jumna winding along the left of the city, the towers of the old Moghul palace, the minarets of the great mosque of the Jumma Musjid, the house roofs and gardens, and the picturesque fortifications with batteries here and there sending forth white clouds of smoke and flashes of flame.

In August, Brigadier John Nicholson came from the Punjab, with a brigade of troops and a siege train; and other reinforcements of men and guns began to join the British force on the Ridge. On the 8th of September fifty-four heavy guns were brought into position, and four batteries poured a constant storm of shot and shell upon the doomed city. On the 13th the breaches were practicable. On the 14th the

Cashmere gate was blown up with gunpowder, and the British troops rushed in. The advancing column was met by a ceaseless fire from houses, mosques, and other buildings, and Nicholson received a mortal wound. Then followed six days of desperate fighting. Women and children, and other inoffensive inhabitants were spared; but rebels with arms in their hands received no quarter. On the 20th the fortified palace of the Moghul was captured, but the royal family had fled in terror and despair.

The old representative of Moghul royalty, with other rebel princes, had sought an asylum in the tomb of Humayun, the father of Akbar. This splendid mausoleum is a vast quadrangle, larger than any at Oxford or Cambridge, and is raised on terraces and enclosed by walls. It contains buildings, towers, and monumental marbles in memory of different members of the Moghul family, as well as extensive gardens and fountains, surrounded with cloistered cells for the accommodation of pilgrims.

On the 21st of September, Captain Hodson rode out to the tomb of Humayun, and brought the Moghul king to Delhi, and lodged him in the palace. The next day he went out again, and arrested two rebel princes, and brought them away in a carriage; but as he returned to the city he was surrounded by a tumultuous crowd, and prevented an attempt at rescue by shooting the princes dead, and placing their bodies in a public place upon the walls.

The capture of Delhi in September, 1857, was the turning point of the Sepoy mutinies. On the 25th of the same month, four days after the capture of the Moghul at Delhi, Generals Havelock and Neill relieved the British Residency at Lucknow after a siege which had lasted four months. Next after the capture of Delhi, the relief of Lucknow was the most important event of the war. The British force was obliged to cut its way through the disaffected city of Lucknow before it could reach the Residency, and as it approached the British entrenchment, an enthusiastic excitement was displayed which has but few parallels in history. The pent-up feelings of the garrison burst forth in deafening cheers; even the wounded soldiers in hospital crawled out to join in the chorus of welcome. The bearded warriors, who had just fought their way through the city, shook the hands of the soldiers of the garrison with frantic joy, and took the infants out of their mothers' arms, and kissed them with tears running down their cheeks; whilst they thanked God that they had come in time to save the survivors from the fate that had befallen the victims at Cawnpore.

The British Residency was relieved, but the siege was not raised, and General Neill was shot dead in the moment of victory. Indeed, the relief was only a reinforcement, for the Residency was besieged for two months longer, whilst the city of Lucknow still remained in the hands of the rebels.

At last, in November, 1857, Sir Colin Campbell advanced on Lucknow, and brought away the beleagured garrison; but General Havelock died of dysentery, in the moment of victory and deliverance, and was buried in the garden of Alumbagh.

Meanwhile General Windham had been left in charge at Cawnpore, and met with a sad disaster. A clever Mahratta Brahman, named Tantia Topi, had left the Nana and made his way to Scindia's capital at Gwalior, and persuaded the Gwalior contingent to break out in revolt and advance to Cawnpore. By some mischance, General Windham was out-generalled by Tantia Topi, and compelled to abandon the city to the rebels and retire within the entrenched barracks. The Gwalior rebels, however, were routed in their turn by Sir Colin Campbell, and driven out of Cawnpore. Tantia Topi made his escape, and during several months gave considerable trouble, but was at last taken prisoner, and executed for his complicity in the massacre.[1]

The fall of Delhi and relief of Lucknow brought the Sepoy revolt very nearly to a close; but the troubles were not quite over, and Oude was still in a state of insurrection. Sir Colin Campbell, afterwards Lord Clyde, completed the conquest of Oude, and restored order and law; and a column from Bombay, under Sir Hugh Rose, and another from Madras, under General Whitlock, carried out a similar work in Central India and Bundelkund.

Meanwhile the Nana must have discovered that his cause was hopeless, and his life in sore peril; and it is supposed that he fled away to the Himalayas, and perished miserably in the jungles of Nipal.

By November, 1858, the last spark of mutiny had been trampled out of the land, and the proclamation of Her Majesty Queen Victoria announced the transfer of the government of India from the East India Company to the Crown of Great Britain.

---

[1] The defeat of Windham was severely criticised at the time. During the following night Major Adye, of the Royal Artillery, re-entered the city with a small party, and recovered two guns which had fallen into the hands of the rebels. It is thus evident that had General Windham beaten up the enemy's quarters at midnight he might have retrieved his disaster. Major Adye is now General Sir John Adye, and Surveyor-General of the Royal Artillery. In the "Short History of India" it is said that Major Adye lost the two guns, but this is a mistake. He only recaptured two guns which had been lost by others.

XVII.—*India under the Crown*

1858 to 1876.

THE Sepoy mutinies of 1857-58 have always been a mystery. It is easy to understand that the Sepoys at Barrackpore mutinied against the greased cartridge. Indeed the idea of forcing Hindus to abandon their religion by causing them to eat impure food had long been familiar to the people of India. Under Muhammadan rule hundreds and thousands had been compelled to swallow beef, which destroyed their caste, and left them no alternative but to accept the religion of their conquerors. Thousands of Brahmans were converted in this fashion by Tippoo Sultan of Mysore.

But whilst the greased cartridge might account for the mutinies, it could not account for other phenomena, such as the revolt at Delhi, and the proclamation of the Sovereignty of the Great Moghul. Neither could it account for the fact that many Hindus and Muhammadans joined in the rebellion, or carried on secret intrigues with the rebel leaders, who were not Sepoys and could not have been in any way inspired by fear of loss of caste through biting greased cartridges.

As far, however, as Delhi and the Moghul are concerned, the action of the Sepoys may perhaps be explained. At

Barrackpore the mutiny was suppressed, and the Sepoys of the disbanded regiment disappeared from the scene, and so far nothing more was heard of them. The circumstances later on, which induced the Sepoy mutineers to rush to Delhi and proclaim the Moghul, may be explained by reference to the facts. At Barrackpore the Sepoys never seem to have had any other object than to get rid of the greased cartridges; all their associations were bound up with Calcutta and the East India Company. Many of them had been recruited in Oude, and when they were disbanded they no doubt returned to Oude, and helped to swell the army of rebels that besieged Lucknow. But there was nothing to suggest to the Sepoys at Barrackpore the wild idea of setting up a moribund Moghul as a possible rival to the British government. As for the Sepoys at the other military stations, they were disaffected, but like Natives in general, they were irresolute and infirm of purpose; they waited for events to tell them what to do.

It was the mutiny at Meerut that worked all the mischief. The station was only forty miles from Delhi, and was closely associated with memories of the Moghul. The whole country round about was crowded with relics of Moghul rule, and glorified by traditions of the palmy days of the Moghul empire, when there was no discipline or drill. Accordingly, after the mad excitement of that terrible Sunday at Meerut, when their fury was spent and a panic had begun, they had no alternative but to run away from Meerut to escape the vengeance of the Europeans; and there was no place to go to but Delhi, and no standard to rally round save that of the Moghul. The example once set was then followed at every cantonment in Northern India.

Had the Europeans fallen upon the Sepoys before they left

Meerut, the mutiny would have been crushed at the outset, and the other stations might have been saved. Had the European cavalry followed them on the road to Delhi, the mutineers might have been cut off or brought back as prisoners, for they must have been worn out with the debauch and riot of the day. As it was, the Sepoys probably slept off their intoxication, and were refreshed by the morning air; and on reaching Delhi they set an example which the Sepoys at the other stations blindly followed without regard to consequences.

As regards the Hindus and Muhammadans, who were not Sepoys, and yet were more or less implicated in the rebellion, some had grievances, real or imaginary, like those of Nana Sahib; whilst many decayed families were doubtless yearning for a return of the days when their ancestors were magnates in the land, and may have sympathised with the rebels, although they could scarcely hope to profit by the rebellion. One or two Native rulers were suspected of secret misdoings; but they were probably only anxious to keep on good terms with the rebels in the event of any revolutionary change in the government of the country, such as the transfer of the Suzerainty of India to any Native power. It is also possible that some Native potentates may have felt alarm at the annexations of Lord Dalhousie, and feared that a day might come when their own principalities might share the same fate. But even in Native States the rebellion was mostly confined to the Subsidiary armies, where the Sepoys shared in the panic about the greased cartridges, and broke out against their English officers exactly as they had done in British territory.

Indeed it is extremely difficult to associate the Sepoy mutinies with the annexations of Lord Dalhousie. As a matter of fact, Hindus and Muhammadans have been accustomed for ages to conquests, annexations, changes of empires and dynasties, absorption of principalities, and violations of hereditary rights, real or adopted; and the masses, whether in towns or villages, have accepted the change of masters, without any manifestation of feeling either one way or the other, beyond a natural desire to propitiate the conquerors, or to welcome those who were most likely to protect and befriend them. Native armies have never mutinied except from want of pay, or from having been bought over by the enemy; whilst the people of India have only rebelled, as they rebelled against Aurangzeb, on account of religious persecution, and especially when such persecution took the form of taxation, as in the case of the Jezya. In a word, popular rebellions on mere questions of policy, apart from religion or taxation, are absolutely unknown in India.

The Sepoy revolt swept away the East India Company; but there were a number of other concurrent causes, all tending to the same result, which were at work both in India and England. The rule of the Company was not without its faults, but it was well adapted to the wants of the people during the early years of British administration. It was conservative as regards Native institutions and usages, and such conservatism was most desirable during the transition period between the dead stagnation of the eighteenth century, and the slow awakening to a national life and aspirations which characterised the nineteenth. Under old John Company the people of India rested and were thankful. They were not exposed to premature reforms that might have excited undue alarm; and so long as they remembered the old days of oppression and misrule, they were grateful for the protection they received from the British government, and happy and contented under the Company's Raj.

But contentment ceases to be a virtue when it is a bar to progress. By the middle of the nineteenth century, the rising generation of Hindus had forgotten the old anarchy and devastations, and could not remain as satisfied with their lot as their more ignorant and apathetic fathers. Railways, telegraphs, English education, and the overland route were awakening new ideas of life, and preparing the way for social and political developments upon English lines.

All this while there was discontent in Great Britain at the government of the East India Company, and a growing sentiment that the people of India ought to be brought under the more immediate cognisance of the British Parliament and nation. As far back as 1833 the trade monopoly of the East India Company was abolished. In 1853, or twenty years later, the Civil Service of India was taken out of the patronage of the Court of Directors, and thrown open to the general public under a system of competitive examinations. Finally, in 1858, the Court of Directors and Board of Control were moulded into one body under the form of a Secretary of State for India in Council; whilst the Governor-General of India became the direct representative of Her Majesty the Queen under the title of Viceroy.

The transfer of the conduct of Indian affairs from the Company to the Crown was accompanied by other changes. The British nation was as much opposed to the annexations of Lord Dalhousie as it had been to the conquests of Lord Wellesley, but nevertheless they were more or less justified by results. The condition of Oude under its Muhammadan rulers had been lawless and oppressive; and all attempts at reform had been paralysed by the corruption which pervaded every branch of the Native administration. In Nagpore and one or two other dependent principalities the ruler had died without leaving any sons, real or adopted; and Lord Dalhousie refused to permit the widow to adopt a son to enable her to act as Regent mother during the minority.

The question of adoption has caused much bitter controversy. According to Indian usage, a man might adopt a son to perform the Sraddha of his new father, but it by no means followed that it invested the stranger with a right to succeed to a principality. Lord Dalhousie, however, denied any intention of prohibiting the adoption of a successor in those Mahratta and Rajput principalities which had been always treated as "protected allies;" and he only refused it to those Native rulers who had been set up by the British government, and were regarded as "dependent princes." But nevertheless Lord Canning conceded the right of adoption to all Native principalities without distinction; and no doubt this concession has been regarded as a boon; whilst evil results, such as transpired in Jeypore and the Punjab during a minority, have been obviated by the appointment of a Council of Regency, and the careful education of the infant who is destined to occupy a throne.

Lord Canning left India in 1862, but died the same year, and was buried in Westminster Abbey.

Lord Elgin succeeded Lord Canning as Viceroy, but died in 1863. His administration had not lasted two years, but was characterised by two important events—namely, a mountain expedition against some hill tribes on the north-west, and a war against Bhutan.

The hill tribes along the whole line of frontier from the Punjab to Burma have always proved troublesome neighbours, and have occasionally committed raids on British territory, or kidnapped British subjects, which called for immediate punishment. The hill tribes which provoked the expedition in question occupied the neighbourhood of the Mahabun mountain, about forty miles westward of Peshawar. A body of Wahabi fanatics had settled at Sitana on this mountain, and stirred up the hostility of the tribes against the British government. In 1863—64, a British expedition was sent against this quarter, which ended in a better understanding with the tribes.

The people of Bhutan are ignorant barbarians inhabiting the Himalaya mountains to the eastward of Nipal. They follow a corrupt form of the Buddhist religion, but are dirty savages in comparison with the Burmese. Thousands of idle monks waste their lives in secluded monasteries, doing nothing for the welfare of the people, or the education of the rising generation; whilst the masses are abandoned to a gross immorality, and constantly engaged in civil broils. For many years the Bhutanese committed raids on British territory, and were deaf to all remonstrances. In 1863 an Envoy was sent to lay a complaint before the Bhutanese authorities at the capital; but was dismissed with insult. War was declared in 1864, and lasted over two years, owing to the difficulty of carrying on hostilities in a country of ravines and precipices. In the end the Bhutanese released all the British subjects they had carried into slavery, and pledged themselves to abstain from all raids for the future. Since then the Bhutanese have proved better neighbours.

In 1864 Sir John Lawrence succeeded to the post of Viceroy. About this time the progress of events in Afghanistan was pressed upon the attention of the British government. Old Dost Muhammad Khan, who fought against the English during the first Cabul war, had concluded treaties of friendship in 1855 and 1856; and during the Sepoy mutinies of 1857 he loyally withstood the entreaties of his leading Sirdars to attempt the invasion of the Punjab. During 1862 and 1863 he was engaged in reducing a disaffected son-in-law who had rebelled in Herat; but he died in 1863, just as he had re-established his dominion.

The death of Dost Muhammad Khan was followed by the accession of Shere Ali Khan, who was a younger son, but had been nominated his successor through the influence of a young and favourite wife, just as a younger son had obtained the throne in the old traditions of the Maha Bharata and Ramayana. Shere Ali Khan was recognised as Ameer by the British government, but the elder brethren rebelled against the younger, and a war broke out for the succession which devastated Afghanistan for nearly four years. Trade was stopped, caravans were plundered, and the whole country was a prey to robbery and murder. Sir John Lawrence declined to interfere, and the Afghans were left to settle their own quarrels; and nothing was done by the British government beyond recognising the man who got the uttermost as the Ameer of Afghanistan for the time being, and granting stipends to the defeated rivals, who found a refuge in British territory.

At last, in 1868, after a series of fortunes and misfortunes, defeats, treacheries, desertions, and unexpected victories, Shere Ali Khan recovered his throne at Cabul, chiefly by the help of his eldest son, Yakoob Khan, and was duly recognised by the British government as Ameer of Afghanistan.

In 1869 Sir John Lawrence returned to England. His administration as Viceroy of India had been as successful as his previous administration as Lieutenant-Governor of the Punjab. Accordingly he was rewarded with a peerage, and spent the remainder of his life in works of usefulness in England. He died in 1879, and was buried in Westminster Abbey.

Lord Mayo succeeded Lord Lawrence, and filled the post of Viceroy from 1869 to 1872. In 1869 he held a conference with Shere Ali Khan at Umballa, about a hundred and twenty miles to the north-west of Delhi, and succeeded in winning the confidence of the Ameer. But Shere Ali Khan wanted the British government to protect him against all enemies and rivals, whilst Lord Mayo refused to send a British force beyond the frontier.

In 1872 Lord Mayo undertook a visit to Rangoon, and was received by the Burmese inhabitants with a spontaneous enthusiasm which proved the attachment of the people to British rule. From Rangoon he paid a flying visit to Maulmain, and thence steamed to the Andaman Islands to inspect the penal settlement at Port Blair. There he was suddenly assassinated by an Afghan, who had been condemned to penal servitude for life on account of a murder, and took advantage of the dusk of the evening to inflict a mortal stab on the Viceroy as he was about to leave the settlement.

Lord Northbrook succeeded Lord Mayo as Viceroy of India, and filled the post from 1872 to 1876. In 1873—4 Bengal was visited by a famine, which is worthy of note from the unprecedent efforts that were made to relieve it, and the vast expenditure which it entailed.

About this time the vicious courses and mal-administration of the Guicowar of Baroda were forced on the attention of the British government. An investigation took place and ended in the deposition of the worthless ruler, and the adoption of a boy to succeed to the throne, with a Council of Regency to conduct the administration during the minority.

In 1875—6 His Royal Highness the Prince of Wales paid a visit to India, and was received by all classes of people, Native and European, with universal loyalty and devotion.

In 1876 Lord Lytton succeeded Lord Northbrook as Viceroy of India, and the history of India entered on a new phase.

XVIII.—*Imperial Assemblage at Delhi.*

1877.

ON the 1st of January, 1877, Her Majesty Queen Victoria was proclaimed Empress of India by Lord Lytton at an Imperial Assemblage of all the potentates and princes of the Empire, which was held at Delhi. The event is a landmark in Indian history, and also serves to introduce Native rulers to English readers, whilst awakening memories of the times that have passed away.

The city of Delhi has already been described in dealing with the accession of Aurangzeb; and to this day, seen from a distance, it presents one of the loveliest landscapes in the Oriental world. Mosques and palaces,—towers, domes and fortifications,—are half hidden by the foliage of trees and gardens. On one side is the old palace of the Moghul, on the bank of the Jumna, which was the focus of rebellion during the mutiny. In the middle of the city is the great mosque of the Jumma Musjid, built on a rocky eminence, ascended by broad flights of steps;—a stately temple of red sandstone, with pulpit and floor of white marble, standing on the side of a quadrangle with a marble fountain in the centre for true believers to perform their ablutions before entering the sacred walls.

The Imperial Assemblage was not held at the close of the Sepoy mutiny, and consequently was not associated with the story of treachery and revolt; nor will it recall the sarcasm which a Queen of Portugal once levelled against a Viceroy of Goa, that he had fought like a Christian and triumphed like a Pagan. It was held at a time of peace, when there were no conquests or defeats to cloud the rejoicings; and princes who had never before seen each other, and whose fathers had fought against each other for generations, met together as friends under the shadow of British Suzerainty, to celebrate the proclamation of Her Majesty the Queen as Empress of India.

The different potentates and princes that attended the Imperial Assemblage were lodged, with their retinues and guests, in tented pavilions outside the city, after the old Oriental fashion, in which Chenghiz Khan and Timur feasted their lords and ladies. The English camps were like streets, each one consisting of two rows of tents with a pavilion of canvass at one end; and by a curious coincidence these camps were pitched on the site occupied by the British army during the siege of Delhi. The Hindu and Muhammadan camps were radiant in blue and scarlet, ornamented with gold knobs and other ornaments like the pavilions of Ahasuerus and Aurangzeb.

The 23rd of December, 1876, was fixed for the public entry of the Viceroy. From early dawn the whole city was astir. There were strangers from every land and representatives of every race. Stalwart Afghans with burly frames and ruddy faces; Beluchis from Khelat with long black locks and flowing beards; Hindustanis in quilted jackets of green and yellow; Bengalis in shawls and round flat hats; Burmese in silks and satins; Ghorkas and Siamese in European uniforms. Indeed, every variety of colour and costume was to be seen in the vast multitude, from the calicoes and muslins of the common people to the jewelled turbans and rich attire of Rajput and Mahratta Rajas.

The line of route was nearly six miles long, and was thronged on either side. There were retinues of Native Chiefs with richly caparisoned elephants and howdahs of gold and silver, and troops and officials of all descriptions bearing insignia of Native sovereignty and effigies of demigods and heroes. Perhaps the grandest sight of all was the war elephants mounted by Hindu warriors in chain mail, armed to the teeth with weapons of all ages, from the battle axe to the dagger, and recalling pictures of ancient times, when Porus went out to fight Alexander on the banks of the Jhelum, and the Rajputs fought against Mahmud of Ghuzni in the valley of Peshawur. The strangest sight, however, was two pieces of cannon from Baroda, one of silver with carriage and wheels of gold, and the other of gold with carriage and wheels of silver:—eminently the outcome of oriental imagination, combining the love of jewellery with the most terrible artillery of war.

The procession lasted for three hours. It was a long array of English governors and other leading officials from the Viceroy downwards, riding on elephants in Oriental fashion, followed by troopers on horseback and a battery of horse artillery. The procession moved from the railway station towards the great mosque of Jumma Musjid, and then through the famous street of jewellers and shawl dealers, known as the Chandni Chouk. This is the street through which Lalla Rookh is said to have been conducted, when she left the palace of Aurangzeb to become the bride of the Sultan of Samarkand. Here, too, the little mosque is still standing, in which Nadir Shah was seated on that dreadful day when the inhabitants of Delhi were slaughtered by the Persian soldiery. Leaving the Chandni Chouk, the procession went out of the city by the Lahore gate, and passed through the suburb where many a hard battle was fought during the siege of 1857; then along the Ridge, and near the Flagstaff Tower; and then past the pillar of Asoka, with its inscription of twenty-two centuries old, until it finally reached the camp of the Viceroy.

There were sixty-three ruling Chiefs at Delhi during the Assemblage, and three hundred titular Chiefs. Amongst the former were the Muhammadan Nizam of Hyderabad, a boy of eleven or twelve; and the Rajput princes, including the Maha Rana of Oodeypore, whose ancestors were Suzerains of Rajputana; the Maha Raja of Jeypore, who died in 1880; and the Maha Raja of Jodhpore. Besides these were the Jhat Maha Raja of Bhurtpore, whose father was restored to the throne by the English in 1826; the Nawab of Tonk, and the Begum of Bhopal. There were also the three Mahratta princes, whose ancestors are famous in Indian history, namely, Scindia of Gwalior, Holkar of Indore, and the Guicowar of Baroda. To these must be added the Maha Rajas of Cashmere and Mysore.

The proclamation of Her Majesty the Queen as Empress of India was made on the 1st of January, 1877. The Viceroy, Lord Lytton, was seated in a throne pavilion facing an amphitheatre of potentates and princes, European and Native, in which governors, lieutenant-governors, members of council, chief commissioners, secretaries, and other English officials and functionaries were mingled with the Hindu and Muhammadan princes and nobles of India. The ceremony concluded with a salute of a hundred and one guns and *feux des joie*.[1]

---

[1] The arrangements at the Imperial Assemblage were carried out under the direction of Colonel Sir Owen Burne, at that time Private

The Imperial Assemblage at Delhi was unpopular with some, chiefly on account of the change of title. The name of Queen is dear to every Englishman, and the symbol of all that is great and good. But this is not the case in India, nor in other Asiatic countries, where power is estimated by title. Moreover, amidst the social convulsion that accompanied the decline and fall of the Moghul empire, some of the Native clerks in public offices assumed the title of Raja, or purchased such title from the pageant king at Delhi; and Zemindars often called themselves Maha Rajas, whilst their wives were addressed as Queens. Indeed, so general has been the feeling that no other term but Empress could express the Sovereignty of India, that the title was in common use long before it was proclaimed to the world.

The Imperial Assemblage was attended by an important result. The East India Company was an abstraction which no Asiatic could understand; but the proclamation of the Empress has associated the Sovereignty of India with the British Crown in the mind of every Oriental. It was carried out moreover at a happy moment. The visit of His Royal Highness the Duke of Edinburgh to India in 1869—70, and above all the visit of his Royal Highness the Prince of Wales in 1875—76, stirred up the loyalty and devotion of the people of India to a degree which would be scarcely credible in Europe, and thus prepared the way for the Imperial Proclamation.

In 1880 Lord Lytton was succeeded by Lord Ripon as Viceroy and Governor-General of India.

Secretary to Lord Lytton, and now Political Secretary to the Home Government.

XIX. *Four Asiatic Empires: Persia, Russia, Turkey, and China.*

Ante 1881.

THE Imperial Assemblage at Delhi was followed by new developments of policy. The political relations between the British government and Native principalities have continued to run in the same grooves as of old; but more attention has been turned to the progress of foreign affairs outside the British frontier. Accordingly, it may be as well to tell something of the modern history of Persia, Russia, Turkey, and China, with especial reference to the course of events in Afghanistan, and what is known as the Eastern question.

Afghanistan is our next door neighbour, and separates us from Persia on the west. Northward of Afghanistan, and northward of the river Oxus, are the three Usbeg principalities of Khiva, Bokhara, and Khokand, which used to separate us from Russia. The whole territory is known as Central Asia. Accordingly, the relations of the British government with Central Asia have become mixed with Persian and Russian affairs.

The present kingdom of Persia was founded in the beginning of the sixteenth century, about fifty years before the establishment of the Moghul empire in India by Akbar. It is Muhammadan, like its Turkish and Afghan neighbours; but the Persians are Shiahs, and consequently hostile to Turks and Afghans, who are mostly Sunnis.

The early Shahs or sovereigns of Persia were half warriors and half saints, known as Sufis. They were enthusiastic followers of Ali, the husband of Fatima, the daughter of the Prophet, and their two sons, Hassan and Hussein. The hero of the Persian empire was Shah Abbas the Great, a contemporary of Akbar and Jehanghir, of Queen Elizabeth and James the First.

In the days of Shah Abbas, Afghanistan was a bone of contention between Persia and the Moghul power in India. During the seventeenth century Persia was content to hold Candahar, whilst Cabul remained in the possession of the Moghul. But so long as Persia and the Moghul were real powers this distribution of territory was productive of frequent wars. The Punjab was exposed to Persian invasion *viâ* Candahar, whilst the Moghul often found it difficult to maintain his authority in Cabul.

Between 1715 and 1725 the Afghan chiefs and people of Candahar broke out in revolt against the Persian rule. All the Persians in Candahar were massacred, and an overwhelming army of Afghans advanced westward to Ispahan, and committed every conceivable atrocity, culminating in the murder of the last Shah of the Sufi dynasty, and the establishment of an Afghan ruler on the throne of Persia.

At this period Russia was becoming a strong power under Peter the Great, who reigned between 1689 and 1725; and during the Afghan troubles the Czar Peter appropriated some of the Persian territories on the Caspian. But after the death of Peter, in 1725, Nadir Shah appeared upon the stage, the same who afterwards invaded Hindustan.

Nadir Shah rose to power by feigning to espouse the cause of a son of the murdered Shah. He drove the Afghans out of Persia, and conquered Central Asia, including the Afghan and Usbeg principalities. He then usurped the throne of Persia, defeated the Turks, recovered the territories appropriated by Russia, and founded a new Persian empire as vast as that of Cyrus and Darius Hydaspes. Unfortunately for him, he meddled in religious matters. He tried to force the Persians to become Sunnis, in order that all his subjects might be of one religion; and by his efforts in this direction he stirred up so much fanatical hatred against himself, that in 1747 he was murdered by assassins.

For fifty years after the death of Nadir Shah, Persia was distracted by civil wars between the Zends and Kajars, and was of no account in Asiatic politics. The Zends were the most illustrious of the old Persian tribes; whilst the Kajars were a Turkish tribe who had settled in the mountains to the south of the Caspian. In the end the Kajars got the mastery; and from 1797 down to the present day a Kajar Shah has sat upon the throne of Persia.

But Persia never regained her old importance, and has suffered so much in wars with Russia that she has lost much of her independence. The Afghans, however, recovered their independence after the death of Nadir Shah, and have never been reconquered by Persia. In 1837 Persia laid siege to Herat, but was compelled to withdraw; and about the same time Russia was advancing towards the Usbeg states on the north of Afghanistan. It was these events which brought about the Afghan war of 1838—42. In 1856, after the Crimean war, Persia again endeavoured to occupy Herat, but a British expedition was sent to the Persian Gulf, and the Persian army was compelled to retire.

The Crimean war, in 1854—56, had been brought about by the Eastern question. The Turkish empire had been founded in the fourteenth and fifteenth centuries on the ruins of the old Greek empire of Roum or Byzantium. It reached its zenith under Suleiman the Magnificent in the sixteenth century, but then began to decline; and during the eighteenth century it seemed to be tottering before the arms of Russia and Austria. But in the nineteenth century the Eastern question has saved it from destruction. Ever since the establishment of a Muhammadan dominion over a decayed Christian empire, the Christian populations of Turkey have suffered from the oppressions of their Turkish rulers. Russia has long been anxious to take the Christian populations under her own protection; whilst during the present century Great Britain and France have been anxious that the Sultan should carry out the necessary reforms without the intervention of Russia, which would destroy the independence of Turkey and upset the balance of power.

The war of Great Britain and France against Russia was brought to a close in 1856, and followed by a calm; but Turkey remained in the hands of weak and sensual rulers, who borrowed money under various pretences, and spent it on their pleasures, whilst the Christian populations were as much oppressed as ever.

In 1875 Europe was awakened from its dream of repose, and the Eastern question burnt more fiercely than ever. The Christian populations of Bosnia and Herzegovina, in the north-western quarter of Turkey in Europe, broke out in revolt. The powers of Europe put their demands in the shape of a Memorandum, and it was on the eve of being presented at Constantinople when action was stayed by a tragedy within the Seraglio that filled all Europe with horror. On the 4th of June, 1876, the Sultan was dead; and whilst it was reported that he had committed suicide, a great fear was abroad that he had perished by the hands of assassins.

Another Sultan was placed upon the throne, but proved to be an utter imbecile. After three wretched months he was forced to abdicate, and the present Sultan, Abdul Hamid, became the ruler of the Turkish empire.

By this time the Eastern question had assumed unexpected dimensions. There was an insurrection in Bulgaria, on the northward of the Balkan mountains; and the Turks tried to suppress it by committing frightful atrocities. The Christians of other provinces took a part in the revolt, and in July, 1876, Servia and Montenegro declared war against Turkey on behalf of the Bulgarians. Russia was preparing for war, but in December, 1876, a conference of the Great Powers was held at Constantinople to avert it, when proclamation was suddenly made that the Sultan was about to introduce a representative government into Turkey, which would doubtless carry out every reform that Europe could desire.

The proclamation appeared at the time to have saved the Turkish empire. A Senate was nominated by the Sultan, and a House of Deputies was elected by the people, but the experiment proved a failure. The new constitution was unmanageable and revolutionary; and the House of Deputies was finally dissolved in February, 1878, and nothing more has been heard of it.

In April, 1877, Russia declared war against Turkey, and by the end of January, 1878, had brought it to a triumphant close. In March, 1878, a treaty between the Czar and the

Sultan was signed at San Stefano, but in the following July was modified by the Congress at Berlin.

Meanwhile, the progress of affairs in Afghanistan had attracted the attention of the British government. Ever since the death of Lord Mayo, in 1872, the Ameer, Shere Ali Khan, had grown more and more estranged from Great Britain, and was supposed to be secretly courting the protection of Russia. He had quarrelled with his eldest son, Yakoob Khan, to whom he was indebted for the recovery of his throne in 1868; and he had appointed his youngest son, Abdulla Jan, to be heir apparent to the throne, to the exclusion of his firstborn. In 1874 he placed Yakoob Khan in confinement on charges of rebellion and disloyalty, and was offended with Lord Northbrook for trying to bring about a reconciliation.

In September, 1878, Major Cavagnari was sent by Lord Lytton on a mission to Shere Ali Khan at Cabul, but was refused admittance into Afghanistan. Subsequently it transpired that the Ameer had publicly received a Russian mission at Cabul. Accordingly the British government declared war against the Ameer, and a British column, under the command of General Sir Frederick Roberts, was sent up the Kurram Valley towards Cabul.

Shere Ali Khan made a futile attempt to resist the advance of General Roberts, and then fled northward towards Russian territory, leaving Yakoob Khan in command at Cabul. Shortly afterwards it was known that Shere Ali Khan was dead; and as Abdulla Jan had died a short time previously, Yakoob Khan succeeded to the throne of Afghanistan.

On this occasion General Roberts did not advance to Cabul, but halted about half way; whilst another British force, under General Stewart, advanced to Candahar, *viâ*

Quetta, and took possession of the city. Meanwhile, Yakoob Khan came to terms, and in May, 1879, a treaty was signed at Gandamak, about half way between Cabul and Jellahabad, under which Yakoob Khan was accepted by the British government as ruler of Cabul, and agreed to receive a British Resident, who should permanently reside at Cabul.

In July, 1879, Sir Louis Cavagnari reached Cabul as British Resident, and was received with a great show of cordiality by Yakoob Khan. On the 3rd of September, however, the Residency was attacked by an overwhelming force of Afghans, and Cavagnari and all his escort perished fighting sword in hand.

On hearing of this disaster, General Roberts advanced towards Cabul, and after some sharp fighting entered the citadel known as the Bala Hissar on the 12th of October. Subsequently it was discovered that Yakoob Khan was more or less implicated in the attack on Cavagnari; but he abdicated the throne, and was transferred to British territory.

Since these events the British government has been anxious to withdraw its armies from Afghanistan, and leave the country in the hands of Afghan rulers, provided the chiefs could agree to accept governors who would prove faithful to the British alliance. Abdur Rahman Khan, a nephew of the late Shere Ali Khan, has been accepted as Ameer of Cabul; but treachery has been at work at Candahar. The enemies of the English have been suitably punished, and the rapid march of General Roberts from Cabul, and splendid victory at Candahar, has restored British *prestige;* but the future of Afghanistan is a disturbing problem which time alone can solve.

The British government has now withdrawn from Afghanistan, and left the chiefs and people to settle their own quarrels. The question of the retention of Candahar has been hotly discussed, and the question has been embittered by the jealousies of nations, which cannot as yet be kept under the restraint which is generally observed in the jealousies between individuals. To occupy Candahar as a menace to Russia could scarcely have been attended with beneficial results; but to occupy Candahar as the only possible means of keeping the peace in Afghanistan may yet prove to be a necessary measure.

The last of the Asiatic empires that calls for special notice is that of China. Very little is known of the past history and present condition of this interesting, but mysterious, people. That China has an important part to play in the future cannot be doubted by those who are familiar with the energy and enterprise of Chinamen; but at present the country is barred off from India by the remote territories of Thibet and Upper Burma. The latest accounts from Pekin would seem to show that the imperial government is somewhat distracted. The present Emperor is an infant, and the administration has been conducted since 1874 by two rival queens, surrounded by intriguing eunuchs and ambitious princes; whilst the death of one of the queens in April last has been recently announced in the "Times." Fortunately for China, the plots and explosions which distract the court are but little felt in the provinces; and to all appearance the country is more prosperous and contented at the present moment than at any other period since its conquest by the Manchus, and nothing is wanting but railway communication to bring it into direct intercourse with Europe and India.

XX. *India: Past and Future.*

THE annals of India have now been told. Between the eleventh and seventeenth centuries Hindu kingdoms were brought more or less under the dominion of Muhammadan rulers; but since the middle of the eighteenth century the Moghul empire has fallen to pieces before the repeated assaults of the Mahrattas; and the English have been forced to assume the government of provinces in order to preserve their trading settlements, and then to exercise a paramount power in order to keep the peace between the princes of India.

Little, however, has been said of the history of the people of India as distinguished from their rulers. Indeed, there are few, if any, materials for such history like those which are available in almost every European nation. There have been no struggles between the masses and a feudal nobility; no developments of a representative government and parliamentary system for the protection of the national liberties, and the promotion of the moral and material advancement of the community at large. Hindu literature is chiefly concerned with religious doctrines and metaphysical speculations; and the pictures of ancient life which appear in Sanskrit epics and dramas are as much wanting in historical accuracy as Tennyson's "Idylls of the King," or Shakespeare's tragedies of "Macbeth" and "King Lear."

The history of the people of India, apart from religious developments, would lie in a nutshell. The Rajputs conquered the aboriginal tribes, and formed them into kingdoms and empires. The Brahmans distributed them into castes, and rivetted the fetters of caste by associating them with the worship of the gods and religious obligations. Buddhism flourished in India, but failed to break up the caste system. The Muhammadans came and established their empire, and then tried to force the Hindus to abandon Brahmans and idols, and embrace the religion of the Koran. But the persecutions of Aurangzeb were followed by the rebellion of the Hindus, the uprising of the Mahrattas, and the decay and dismemberment of the Moghul empire. Finally the English have appeared upon the scene, and delivered the people of India from the oppression of anarchy, and established the reign of order and law.

The people of India are now awakening from the ignorance and torpor of centuries. The higher classes are no longer contented to live in the same hereditary grooves of profession and caste as those which satisfied their fathers, and are beginning to yearn for some higher good than even the protection of person and property. Education in government colleges and schools is opening out a new world to the imagination of the people. Railways and telegraphs are revealing the resources of their own country. Above all, a voyage to Europe, and association with Europeans on equal terms, have perhaps done more than anything else to awaken a few of the natives of India to a sense of their own deficiencies. Indeed, there is so vast a difference between the native of India who has spent a year or two in England and the general mass of his fellow countrymen, that the former appears to be a changed man; and travelled Hindus are the men who are yearning for a higher life, in which infant marriages shall cease to be the rule, and householders may have a voice in the government of their country and in the promotion of its moral and material welfare.

These aspirations, however, are only confined to a very small minority, mere knots of young men in the English capitals. The rural populations are either contented with their lot, or only anxious to better the circumstances of their individual families, and to secure position and advancement for the rising generation of sons. At present there is a broad separation between the masses, who live in the same grooves as their fathers, and those who have been educated in colleges and taken university degrees; whilst, as already stated, those who have been to England seem to have been half transformed into Europeans. These data are of importance, as showing the sources of those aspirations which may be expected in course of time to work out the social reformation of their fellow countrymen.

Few Hindus can doubt, and certainly not those who have visited Europe, that the English people are at least as anxious to promote the welfare of their Indian empire as the people of the country. At the same time, very much depends upon the spontaneous action of the people themselves. The fundamental principle of the British government is a universal toleration in matters of religion. Unlike Muhammadan rulers of the stamp of Aurangzeb, the British government has never appropriated the revenues of India for the destruction of any form of religious belief, or the promulgation of Christian doctrines amongst its Hindu and Muhammadan subjects. Practices which are opposed to the common instincts of all civilised nations, such as widow burning, infanticide, and self-torture, have been suppressed by legislative enactment, with the approval of the Native population; but there are other usages not so directly opposed to civilisation, and notably that of infant marriages, which have never been brought under legislative restrictions, and which, indeed, belong to that family life which is always sacred so long as it is not opposed to the moral sense of the civilised world, and can only be altered by the will of the people themselves.

Family life and political life have always gone hand in hand in the progress of nations. The seclusion of the women and the institution of slavery retarded the political development of the Greeks; and negro slavery proved for many years the stumbling-block in the way of political progress in the United States. In India, as yet, the masses of the people show no inclination to accept such social reforms as will work out their own political development; and thus it is difficult to see how British rulers can make a move in the direction of political progress until there is some indication that the people at large are prepared for its reception.

But not even in India can humanity remain stationary. There have been religious and social revolutions working more or less beneath the surface at different intervals in past ages, and such revolutions are doubtless at work in the nineteenth century. The Greek accounts of India at the time of the invasion of Alexander the Great, in the fourth century before Christ, would seem to indicate that to all outward appearance the people of India were much the same then as they are in the present day—distributed into castes and hereditary trades and professions, and governed by Brahmanical institutions and usages. Yet it has been proved beyond all doubt that a great revolution was already at work under the name of Buddhism, which was undermining the caste system, and for centuries afterwards was spreading abroad education, stimulating the practice of medicine, maintaining public hospitals, and encouraging the study of every branch of science which was considered in those early days to be likely to promote the moral and material welfare of all classes of the community, without regard to caste or creed.

Any attempt to deal with the religious history of India would be out of place in the present volume. The legend of Gotama Buddha, and the conflict between Brahmanism and Buddhism, has been dealt with in larger histories, and may be brought under review hereafter in a separate publication; but there is one institution associated with Buddhist rule which might possibly be adopted in the present day, or at any rate would furnish practical hints to Native reformers. Every year all the wise men of the kingdom were summoned to meet the Maha Raja at the gate of the city, and formed what was known as the Great Assembly; and there all those who had made any discoveries, and committed them to writing, which might tend to the improvement of the earth and of the human race and other animals who lived upon it, were expected to declare them openly.

That something might be done in this direction by the spontaneous action of the better educated natives of the larger towns and villages can scarcely be denied. At present, however, there is little immediate hope of carrying out such a project for the well-being of the public at large, although it could scarcely fail to add something authentic to the stock of information respecting the Native population which is already at the disposal of the British government. As a matter of fact, based on the authority of personal experience, it may be broadly stated that of all the thousands of petitions that are poured in every year upon the British government, there are but very few, if any, that refer to the general welfare of the people of India. There are complaints of all kinds against Native rulers and English officials; also against obnoxious cesses, and notably against the income-tax, which was repealed a few years ago. There are also petitions for the redress of grievances, or grant of rewards to particular individuals or individual families; and occasionally there are petitions from some particular class, trade, or profession. But the few that have been presented by Native philanthropists have been mostly impracticable, like the measure for abolishing the consumption of beef throughout British India, which has been pressed more than once upon the British government; or they have been attended with no appreciable result, like the legislative enactment permitting the re-marriage of Hindu widows, which as far as the masses are concerned is a dead letter to this day.

The present tales and sketches of India and its people may here be brought to a close, not, however, without an expression of faith and hope in the India that is to be. A new era is dawning upon this great empire, which the present generation cannot hope to see in the full light of day. When the railway unites India with Europe, when every Native prince, nobleman, or wealthy merchant sends his sons to be educated in an English university, and when representatives from India take their seats in one or other of the national assemblies at Westminster, generations yet unborn will be married at suitable ages, and those affections which impart freedom to family life, and find expression in a constitutional government, will have full and healthy play, beyond what Hindus have ever dreamed from the days of Manu until now.

A CATALOGUE

OF

THACKER, SPINK & CO.'S

PUBLICATIONS.

July, 1881.

5 AND 6, GOVERNMENT PLACE, CALCUTTA.

CORRESPONDING HOUSES.

THACKER & CO. (LIMITED), BOMBAY.

W. THACKER & CO., 87, NEWGATE ST., LONDON.

A LIST OF

WORKS IN GENERAL LITERATURE

PUBLISHED OR SOLD BY

THACKER, SPINK AND CO.,

5 & 6, Government Place, Calcutta.

HISTORY, BIOGRAPHY, POLITICS, &c.

Bellew.—THE RACES OF AFGHANISTAN; being a Brief Account of the principal Nations inhabiting that Country. By Surgeon-Major H. W. BELLEW, C.S.I., late on special Political Duty at Cabul. 8vo., cloth. Rs. 3-8.

Aberigh-Mackay.—THE SOVEREIGN PRINCES AND CHIEFS OF CENTRAL INDIA. By G. R. ABERIGH-MACKAY, Principal, Residency (Rajcoomar) College, Indore, Central India. Illustrated with Portraits and Views. Volume I. Royal 8vo., cloth, extra gilt, and gilt top. Rs. 12.

NOTES ON WESTERN TURKISTAN. Some Notes on the Situation of Western Turkistan. By G. R. ABERIGH-MACKAY. 8vo. Rs. 2-8.

McCrindle.—ANCIENT INDIA AS DESCRIBED BY MEGASTHENES AND ARRIAN; being a Translation of the fragments of the "Indica of Megasthenes," collected by DR. SCWAUBECK; and a Translation of the first part of the "Indica of Arrian," with Introduction, Notes, and a Map of Ancient India. By J. W. McCRINDLE, M.A., Principal of Patna College. 8vo. Rs. 2-8.

THE COMMERCE AND NAVIGATION OF THE ERYTHRÆAN SEA; being a Translation of Periplus Maris Erythræi by an Anonymous Writer, and of Arrian's Account of the Voyage of Nearkhos from the mouth of the Indus to the head of the Persian Gulf. With Introduction, Commentary, Notes, and Index. By J. W. McCRINDLE, M.A., Principal of the Government College, Patna. 8vo. Rs. 3.

Wilkins.—A HANDBOOK OF HINDU MYTHOLOGY. Vedic and Puranic. Illustrated.

Sherring.—HINDU TRIBES AND CASTES. Vol. III. Together with three Dissertations: on the Natural History of Hindu Caste; the Unity of the Hindu Race; and the Prospects of Indian Caste. Including a General Index of the three Volumes. By the Rev. M. A. SHERRING, M.A., LL.B. Demy 4to., cloth. Rs. 16.

This Volume contains the Tribes and Castes of Rajputana, the Madras Presidency, Mysore, Travancore, &c.

Baness.—INDEX GEOGRAPHICUS INDICUS: being a Statistical, Political, and Descriptive Account of the several Provinces and Administrations of the Empire, and the Independent, Feudatory, and outlying Native States; and the Foreign and Colonial Possessions in the East. Together with a Glossary, Statistical Tables, the Religions and Peoples of India, and an Alphabetical List of the Principal Places in Her Majesty's Indian Empire. With 8 Maps, drawn on a scale of 64 miles=1 inch. By J. FREDERICK BANESS, F.R.G.S. Royal 8vo., half-bound. Rs. 12; post free 12-8.

THE IMPERIAL GAZETTEER OF INDIA. Nine volumes. Half morocco. Rs. 40.

"The Imperial Gazetteer will be the condensation and fruit of a series of Statistical Surveys of each of the administrative or political divisions of India, specially and minutely compiled within moderate limits of time."

Wheeler.—TALES FROM INDIAN HISTORY: being the Annals of India retold in Narrative. By J. TALBOYS WHEELER.

Wheeler.—EARLY RECORDS OF BRITISH INDIA, a History of Early English Settlements as told in Government Records, old Travels, and contemporary documents down to the rise of British Power in India. By J. TALBOYS WHEELER. Royal 8vo., cloth. Rs. 5.

Sherring.—HINDU TRIBES AND CASTES; Vol. II. together with an Account of the Mahomedan Tribes of the North-West Frontier and of the Aboriginal Tribes of the Central Provinces. By the Rev. M. A. SHERRING, M.A., LL.B. Demy 4to., cloth. Rs. 16.

This Volume contains an account of the Tribes of the Punjab and its Frontiers, Central Provinces, and Berar; Bombay Presidency, and Frontiers of Scind

McMahon.—THE KARENS OF THE GOLDEN CHERSONESE. By Lt.-Col. A. R. MCMAHON, F.R.G.S. With Maps. Demy 8vo., cloth. Rs. 12-14.

Mead.—SEPOY REVOLT: its Causes and its Consequences. By H. MEAD. 8vo., cloth. Rs. 4.

Wyllie.—ESSAYS ON THE EXTERNAL POLICY OF INDIA. By W. S. WYLLIE M.A. Edited, with a Memoir and Notes, by W. W. HUNTER, B.A., LL.D. With Portrait. 8vo. Rs. 10.

Rajendra Lala Mittra.—THE PARSIS OF BOMBAY: a Lecture delivered on February 26, 1880, at a Meeting of the Bethune Society. By RAJENDRA LALA MITTRA, LL.D., C.I.E. 8vo., sewed. Re. 1.

Conran.—AUTOBIOGRAPHY OF AN INDIAN OFFICER. By Major H. M. CONRAN. 8vo., cloth. Rs. 3-8.

Hunter.—THE INDIAN MUSSULMANS. By Dr. W. W. HUNTER. Second Edition. 8vo. Rs. 7-8.

A LIFE OF THE EARL OF MAYO, fourth Viceroy of India. With a Narrative of his Indian Administration. By W. W. HUNTER. 2 vols. demy 8vo. Rs. 17-2.

A STATISTICAL ACCOUNT OF BENGAL. By W. W. HUNTER. 20 vols. 8vo., half bound. Price per volume, Rs. 4.

ANNALS OF RURAL BENGAL. By W. W. HUNTER. Fifth Edition. 8vo., cloth. Rs. 12 4.

ORISSA; or, the Vicissitudes of an Indian Province under Native and British Rule. With Engravings and Map. By W. W. HUNTER. 2 vols. demy 8vo., cloth. Rs. 22 8.

Valbezen.—LES ANGLAIS ET L'INDE (nouvelles Etudes). By E DE VALBEZEN. 2 vols. 8vo., stitched. Rs. 9.

Briggs.—THE NIZAM: his History and Relations with the British Government. By HENRY GEORGE BRIGGS. With Portrait. 2 vols. 8vo. Rs. 15.

Thorburn.—BANNU; or, Our Afghan Frontier. By S. S. THORBURN, C.S., Settlement Officer. With Map. 8vo., cloth. Rs. 12-14.

Laurie.—SKETCHES OF SOME DISTINGUISHED ANGLO-INDIANS, with an account of Anglo-Indian Periodical Literature. By Col. W. F. B. LAURIE. With Portrait of Sir John Kaye. 12mo., cloth. Rs. 3-6.

The Rajatarangini.—KINGS OF KASHMIRA; being a Translation of the Sanskrit Work, Rajatarangini of Kahlana Pandita. By JOGESH CHUNDER DUTT. Small 8vo. Rs. 2.

Smith.—MOHAMMED AND MOHAMMEDANISM: Lectures delivered at the Royal Institution of Great Britain in February and March, 1874. By R. BOSWORTH SMITH. Second Edition, revised, with considerable additions. 8vo., cloth. Rs. 6-2.

Muir.—THE LIFE OF MAHOMET, from Original Sources. By Sir WILLIAM MUIR. New and cheaper Edition, in one vol. With Maps Demy 8vo., cloth. Rs. 10.

The Original Edition, in four volumes 8vo. Rs. 30.

Haggard.—ENGLAND AND ISLAM. By A. H. HAGGARD, B.C.S. 8vo. Re. 1.

Syed Ameer Ali.—A CRITICAL EXAMINATION OF THE LIFE AND TEACHINGS OF MOHAMMED. By SYED AMEER ALI. Post 8vo., cloth. Rs. 6-8.

CENTRAL ASIAN QUESTIONS FROM AN EASTERN STAND-POINT. 8vo., stitched. Rs. 1-8.

Malcolm.—A MEMOIR OF CENTRAL INDIA, including Malwa and adjoining Provinces, with the History, and Copious Illustrations, of the past and present conditions of that Country. By Major-General Sir JOHN MALCOLM, G.C.B., K.L.S. Reprinted from the Third Edition. With Map. In 2 vols. crown 8vo. Rs. 7.

Fytche.—BURMAH, Past and Present. With personal Reminiscences of the Country. By Lieut.-Genl. E. A. FYTCHE. Illustrated. 2 vols. 8vo. Rs. 21-8.

Haughton.—CHAREEKAR and Service there with the 4th Goorkha Regiment (Shah Shooja's Force), in 1841. An Episode of the First Afghan War. By Col. HAUGHTON, C.S.I. 8vo., sewed. As. 8.

Goldsmid.—LIFE OF LIEUTENANT-GENERAL SIR JAMES OUTRAM. By Major-General Sir FREDERIC J. GOLDSMID, C.B., K.C.S.I. With Illustrations and Maps. 2 vols. 8vo. Rs. 23.

TRAVELS, GUIDE-BOOKS, &c.

Keene.—A HANDBOOK FOR VISITORS TO AGRA AND ITS NEIGHBOURHOOD. By H. G. KEENE, C.S. Fourth Edition, revised. Maps, Plans, &c. Fcap. 8vo., cloth. Rs. 2-8.

A HANDBOOK FOR VISITORS TO DELHI AND ITS NEIGHBOURHOOD. By H. G. KEENE, C.S. Third Edition. Maps, Fcap. 8vo., cloth. Rs. 2.

A HANDBOOK FOR VISITORS TO ALLAHABAD, CAWNPORE, AND LUCKNOW. By H. G. KEENE, C.S. Second Editon, re-written and enlarged. Fcap. 8vo., Rs. 2-8,

Ince.—THE KASHMIR HANDBOOK; a Guide for Visitors. With Map and Routes. By JOHN INCE, M.D. Third Edition. Rs. 5.

CALCUTTA TO LIVERPOOL, BY CHINA, JAPAN, AND AMERICA, IN 1877. By Lieut. General Sir HENRY NORMAN. Second Edition. Fcap. 8vo., cloth. Rs. 2-8.

HOW WE DID "THE LIONS" OF THE NORTH-WEST: a Trip in the Durga-Pujahs to Lucknow, Delhi, Agra. By F. O. B. Re. 1.

Bholanath Chunder.—TRAVELS OF A HINDU TO VARIOUS PARTS OF BENGAL AND UPPER INDIA. By BHOLANATH CHUNDER. With an Introduction by J. TALBOYS WHEELER. 2 vols. small 8vo., cloth. Rs. 12.

Stephen.—THE DELHI HANDBOOK. By CARR-STEPHEN. Stitched. Rs. 8.

THE ARCHÆOLOGY AND MONUMENTAL REMAINS OF DELHI. By CARR-STEPHEN. Royal 8vo., cloth. Rs. 10.

Villeroi.—A TRIP THROUGH CENTRAL ASIA. By BERNARD DE VILLEROI. 12mo. Re. 1.

Cornish. — UNDER THE SOUTHERN CROSS. By HENRY CORNISH. Second Edition. Revised. enlarged, and illustrated. 8vo. Rs. 3.

Vaughan.—THE MANNERS AND CUSTOMS OF THE CHINESE OF THE STRAITS SETTLEMENTS. By J. D. VAUGHAN, Barrister-at-Law. 8vo., stiff cover. Rs. 3.

NATURAL AND PHYSICAL SCIENCES.

Clarke.—COMPOSITÆ INDICÆ DESCRIPTÆ ET SECUS GENERA BENTHAMII ORDINATÆ. By C. B. CLARKE, M.A. Demy 8vo. Rs. 1-8.

ROXBURGH'S FLORA INDICA; or, Descriptions of Indian Plants. Reprinted literatim from Carey's Edition. 8vo., cloth. Rs. 5.

Gregg.—A TEXT-BOOK OF INDIAN BOTANY; Morphological, Physiological, and Systematic. Profusely illustrated. By W. H. GREGG, B.M.S., Lecturer on Botany at the Hugli Government College. Chapters I. and II. in part. Crown 8vo. Re. 1. The completion of the work is in active preparation.

Day.—REPORT ON THE FRESH WATER FISH AND FISHERIES OF INDIA AND BURMAH. By J. DAY. 8vo., boards. Rs. 2.

Kurz.—FOREST FLORA OF BRITISH BURMAH. By S. KURZ, Curator of the Herbarium, Royal Botanical Gardens, Calcutta. 2 vols. demy 8vo., cloth. Rs. 15.

Beavan.—HANDBOOK OF THE FRESH WATER FISHES OF INDIA. Giving the characteristic peculiarities of all the Species at present known, and intended as a guide to Students and District Officers. By Capt. R. BEAVAN, F.R.G.S. Twelve full Plates. Demy 8vo. Rs. 7-8.

Theobald.—DESCRIPTIVE CATALOGUE OF THE REPTILES OF BRITISH INDIA. By W. THEOBALD, Geographical Survey. 8vo., cloth. Rs. 10.

Nevill.—A CATALOGUE OF MOLLUSCA IN THE INDIAN MUSEUM. By G. NEVILL. Demy 8vo., stitched. Rs. 2.

Dobson.—A MONOGRAPH OF THE ASIATIC CHIROPTERA AND CATALOGUE OF BATS IN THE COLLECTION OF THE INDIAN MUSEUM, CALCUTTA. By G. S. DOBSON. Demy 8vo., cloth. Rs. 6.

Gore.—A GLOSSARY OF FOSSIL MAMMALIA. For the use of Students of Palæontology. By J. E. GORE. Fcap. 8vo., cloth. Rs. 1-8

SOUTHERN STELLAR OBJECTS between the Equator and 55° South Declination. By J. E. GORE. 8vo., cloth. Rs. 2-8.

Jerdon.—THE BIRDS OF INDIA: being a Natural History of all the Birds known to inhabit continental India, a Manual of Ornithology specially adapted for India. By the late T. C. JERDON, to which is added his Supplementary Notes published in the "Ibis." 3 vols. 8vo., cloth. Rs. 30.

Blanford.—THE INDIAN METEOROLOGIST'S VADE MECUM. Part I.—Instructions to Meteorological Observers in India. Part II. —Meteorology of India. With Tables for the reduction of Meteorological Observations in India. By H. F. BLANFORD. 2 parts, large 8vo., cloth. Rs. 10.

RAINFALL TABLES. Table of Average Monthly and Annual Rainfall in Northern India, &c. One Sheet. As. 4.

McGregor.—PROTECTION OF LIFE AND PROPERTY FROM LIGHTNING DURING THUNDER-STORMS. By W. MCGREGOR. Second Edition, enlarged. Stitched. Re. 1.

Archibald.—THE RAINFALL OF THE WORLD in connection with the eleven-years period of Sunspots. With an Introduction and Appendix. By E. D. ARCHIBALD, B.A., F.M.S. Demy 8vo., stitched. Rs. 2.

Elson.—THE SANDHEADS SAILING DIRECTORY; or, The Sub-Marine Hooghly Delta; its Marks and Deeps, its Winds, Weather, Tides, and Currents, being an Epitome of useful information for Ship-masters, also a Handy Book of Reference for Pilots. By SAMUEL R. ELSON, Senior Master Pilot, Author of the "Morse Universal Marine Flashing Signal," "The Sailors' East Indian Sky Interpreter," "Circular Diagram for Compass Deviation" and the "Bengal Pilot's Code of Signals."

THE SAILOR'S EAST INDIAN SKY INTERPRETER AND WEATHER BOOK; being a Description of the Phenomena and Prognostics of the Bay of Bengal October-Cyclones, as experienced at the Pilot Station off the mouth of the Hooghly. By S. R. ELSON. 8vo. Re. 1.

THE MORSE UNIVERSAL MARINE FLASHING SIGNALS, for use, with the Commercial Code Signal Book in foggy weather, Night Signalling, &c., with a selection of twenty-one handy Night Towing Signals. By S. R. ELSON, Licensed Hooghly Pilot. 8vo., sewed. As. 12.

Yonge.—LATITUDE AND LONGITUDE WITHOUT INSTRUMENTS; being a Chart for finding the Hour of Sunrise and Sunset for every day in the year, at every place in the Northern or Southern Hemisphere. By Capt. W. L. YONGE, R.A. On paper, Re. 1; on India-rubber, Rs. 2-8.

FINANCE, PRODUCE, &c., OF INDIA.

Seyd.—THE FALL IN THE PRICE OF SILVER; its Causes, its Consequences, and their possible Avoidance, with special reference to India. By ERNEST SEYD, F.S.S., 8vo. Rs. 1-12.

MONETARY RELIEF THROUGH THE PARIS INTERNATIONAL CONFERENCE. By NEMO. 8vo. Pamphlet. 8 an.

Hector.—CURRENCY CONSIDERED WITH SPECIAL REFERENCE TO THE FALL IN THE VALUE OF SILVER AND ITS CONSEQUENCES TO INDIA. By J. HECTOR. 8vo. Pamphlet. Rs. 1-6.

Smeaton.—THE CURRENCY OF INDIA: an Examination of the reasons for change of the present Standard of Value and of the mode of effecting it. By D. MACKENZIE SMEATON, Bengal Civil Service. Demy 8vo., stitched. Re. 1.

Oakeley.—REMARKS ON MR. WILSON'S MINUTE ON THE INTRODUCTION OF A GOLD CURRENCY IN INDIA. By H. E. OAKELEY, M.A. 8vo. Pamphlet. Re. 1.

Lees.—THE DRAIN OF SILVER TO THE EAST, AND THE CURRENCY OF INDIA. By Colonel W. NASSAU LEES, LL.D. Demy 8vo., cloth. Rs. 5.

MEMORANDUM WRITTEN AFTER A TOUR THROUGH THE TEA DISTRICTS IN EASTERN BENGAL IN 1864-65. By Colonel W. NASSAU LEES, LL.D. Rs. 5.

THE LAND AND LABOUR OF INDIA, a Review. By Colonel W. NASSAU LEES, LL.D. 8vo., cloth. Rs. 4.

Smith.—SILVER AND THE INDIAN EXCHANGES; a Remedy for its Depreciation, in seven Essays. By Colonel J. T. SMITH, R.E., F.R.S. Demy 8vo., boards. Rs. 1-8.

Baildon.—TEA IN ASSAM. A Pamphlet on the Origin, Culture, and Manufacture of Tea in Assam, with an Appendix—Rural Life amongst the Assamese. By S. BAILDON. Demy 8vo. Rs. 2.

Hem Chunder Kerr.—REPORT ON THE CULTIVATION OF, AND TRADE IN, JUTE IN BENGAL, and on Indian Fibres available for the Manufacture of Paper. By HEM CHUNDER KERR. Fcap. folio. Paper boards. With Map. Rs. 8.

Hughes.—NOTES ON THE COST OF CARRIAGE BY RAIL AND WATER IN THE UNITED STATES OF AMERICA. With Maps and Statistical Plans. By A. J. HUGHES, C.E. Demy 8vo., boards. Rs. 3-8.

Stoker.—MANAGEMENT OF THE TEA PLANT. By T. STOKER. 8vo., stitched. Rs. 2.

Watson.—REPORTS ON COTTON GINS and on the Cleaning and Quality of Indian Cotton. By D. FORBES WATSON. Part II.—Detailed Description with Records of the Cotton Gin. Trials at Manchester, Dharwar, and Broach (published by order of the Secretary of State for India in Council). Imperial 8vo. Rs.

Digby.—FAMINE CAMPAIGN IN SOUTHERN INDIA (Madras and Bombay Presidencies and Province of Mysore), 1876–78. By WILLIAM DIGBY, Hony. Secy., Indian Famine Relief Fund. Two vols. Demy 8vo., cloth. Rs. 16.

Money.—CULTIVATION AND MANUFACTURE OF TEA. By Lieut.-Col. EDWARD MONEY. Prize Essay. Third Edition, corrected and much enlarged. Demy 8vo., cloth. Rs. 5-6.

Hull.—COFFEE PLANTING IN SOUTHERN INDIA AND CEYLON; being a Second Edition, revised and enlarged, of "Coffee," its Physiology, History, and Cultivation. By E. C. P. HULL. 12mo., cloth. Rs. 6.

Schrottky.—MAN, PLANT, AND SOIL, AND THEIR CORRELATIONS. By EUGENE C. SCHROTTKY. 8vo., paper. Re. 1.

MILITARY WORKS.

Barrow.—THE SEPOY OFFICER'S MANUAL; a Book of Reference for Officers of the Bengal Native Infantry. By Lieut. E. G. BARROW, 7th N. I. Pocket. Rs. 2-8.

BENGAL ARMY REGULATIONS. Revised Army Regulations corrected to 1880. Regulations and Orders for the Army of the Bengal Presidency. 8vo., cloth. Rs. 4. Interleaved copies, Rs. 5.

BENGAL ARMY LIST. The Official Quarterly Army List of H.M.'s Forces in Bengal, exhibiting the Rank, Dates of Commission, and present Location of every Officer in the Bengal Army. Published January, April, July, and October in each year. Each Rs. 1.

Bell.—INSTUCTIONS IN CAVALRY DRILL. Part III.—Skirmishes, Scouts, Advance, Rear and Flank Guards, Outposts and Patrols. By C. W. BOWDLER BELL. Fcap. 8vo., stiff cover. Rs. 1-12.

Sterndale.—MUNICIPAL WORK IN INDIA; or, Hints on Sanitation, General Conservancy, and Improvement in Municipalities. Towns and Villages. By REGINALD CRAUFUIRD STERNDALE. Crown 8vo., cloth. Rs. 5. *(Shortly.*

PAY CODE. Revised Code of existing Orders regarding Pay, Pension, and Promotion of the Military Services in India. Corrected to 1st May, 1876. Royal 8vo., cloth.

Vol. I.—British Troops, including Officers and Men, Indian Army. Rs. 4.

Vol. II.—Native Troops, including Followers of British and Native Troops. Rs. 2.

Furse.—STUDIES ON MILITARY TRANSPORT. By G. A. FURSE, Major, 42nd Royal Highland Regiment. 8vo., stitched. Rs 3.

Schmid.—THE SOLDIER IN THE FIELD. A Guide to the Theoretical Instruction of Non-Commissioned Officers and Soldiers in Picquet and Outpost Duties. By Major A. SCHMID. Sewed. Re. 1.

Stubbs.—HISTORY OF THE ORGANIZATION, EQUIPMENT, AND WAR SERVICES OF THE REGIMENT OF BENGAL ARTILLERY. Compiled from Published Works, Official Records, and various private sources, by Colonel FRANCIS W. STUBBS. With numerous Illustrations and Maps. Demy 8vo., cloth. 2 vols. Rs. 23.

Trench.—SHORT SERVICE AND DEFERRED PAY. By Captain F. CHENEVIX TRENCH. Second Edition, revised and enlarged. 8vo., stitched. Rs. 2-8.

Voyle.—A MILITARY DICTIONARY, comprising Terms, scientific and otherwise, conected with the Science of War. By Major-General G. E. VOYLE. Third Edition (London, 1876). 8vo. Rs. 7-8.

Broome.—THE RISE AND PROGRESS OF THE BENGAL ARMY. Maps and Plans. By General A. BROOME. Vol. I. (all published). 8vo., cloth. Rs. 5.

TARGET PRACTICE. The Soldiers' and Volunteers' Handbook. How to Shoot straight. 12mo. Rs. 2.

VETERINARY WORKS, SPORTS, &c.

Humfrey—THE STEEPLECHASE HORSE: how to Select, Train, and Ride Him. With Notes on Accidents and Diseases, and their Treatment. By Capt. J. HUMFREY. Cloth, limp. Rs. 3-8.

Hayes.—VETERINARY NOTES FOR HORSE-OWNERS. With Hindustani Vocabulary; an every-day book. By Capt. M. HORACE HAYES. Illustrated. Crown 8vo. Second Edition, enlarged. Rs. 7.

A GUIDE TO TRAINING AND HORSE MANAGEMENT IN INDIA. With a Hindustanee Stable and Veterinary Vocabulary and Calcutta Turf Club Tables of Weight for Age and Class. By Capt. M. HORACE HAYES, Author of "Veterinary Notes for Horse-Owners." New Edition, re-arranged and much enlarged. Crown 8vo. Rs. 5.

RIDING ON THE FLAT AND ACROSS COUNTRY. A Guide to Practical Horsemanship. By Captain M. HORACE HAYES. Handsomely illustrated and bound. Rs. 7.

THE ORIENTAL SPORTING MAGAZINE FROM JUNE 1828 TO JUNE 1833. In two volumes 8vo. Rs. 7-8; cash 6-12.

Sanderson.—THIRTEEN YEARS AMONG THE WILD BEASTS OF INDIA; their Haunts and Habits, from the Personal Observation: with an account of the Modes of Capturing and Taming Wild Elephants. By G. P. SANDERSON, Officer in Charge of the Government Elephant Keddahs at Mysore. With 21 full-page Illustrations and three Maps. Second Edition. Fcap. 4to. Rs.

INDIAN NOTES ABOUT DOGS; their Diseases and Treatment. Compiled by Major C. ——, author of "Horse Notes." Fcap. 8vo., cloth. Re. 1-8.

Baldwin.—THE LARGE AND SMALL GAME OF BENGAL AND THE NORTH-WESTERN PROVINCES OF INDIA. By Capt. J. H. BALDWIN. With numerous illustrations. 4to., cloth. Rs. 15.

Kinloch.—LARGE GAME SHOOTING IN THIBET AND THE NORTH-WEST. By Capt. ALEX. A. KINLOCH, C.M.Z.S., 60th Royal Rifles. Illustraated by Photo. tint. Second Series, in demy 4to., cloth, gilt. Rs. 15.

Sterndale.—SEONEE; OR, CAMP LIFE ON THE SAPTURA RANGE. A Tale of Indian Adventure. By ROBERT A. STERNDALE, F.R.G.S. Illustrated by the Author. Demy 8vo. Rs. 15.

DOMESTIC ECONOMY AND MEDICINE.

Birch.—GOODEVE'S HINTS FOR THE MANAGEMENT AND MEDICAL TREATMENT OF CHILDREN IN INDIA. By EDWARD A. BIRCH, M.D., Surgeon-Major. Seventh Edition. Crown 8vo., cloth. Rs. 7.

"I have no hesitation in saying that the present one is for many reasons superior to its predecessors. It is written very carefully, and with much knowledge and experience on the author's part, whilst it possesses the great advantage of bringing up the subject to the present level of Medical Science."—Dr. GOODEVE.

GOODEVE'S HINTS FOR THE GENERAL MANAGEMENT OF CHILDREN IN INDIA in the absence of Professional Advice. Entirely re-written by JOSEPH EWART, M.D. Limp cloth. Rs. 2.

THE INDIAN COOKERY BOOK: A Practical Handbook to the Kitchen in India, adapted to the three Presidencies; containing original and approved Recipes in every Department of Indian Cookery; Recipes for Summer Beverages and Home-made Liqueurs; Medicinal and other Recipes; together with a variety of things worth knowing. By A THIRTY-FIVE YEARS' RESIDENT. Crown 8vo. Rs. 3.

Riddell.—INDIAN DOMESTIC ECONOMY AND RECEIPT BOOK. With Hundustani Names. By Dr. R. RIDDELL. Eighth Edition. Royal 12mo. Rs. 6.

Duke.—QUERIES AT A MESS TABLE: What shall we eat? What shall we drink? By JOSHUA DUKE, Surgeon, 3rd Punjab Cavalry, Author of "Banting in India." Fcap. 8vo., cloth, gilt. Rs. 2-4.

HOW TO GET THIN; or, Banting in India. By J. DUKE. 12mo., stiff cover. Re. 1.

Hogg.—PRACTICAL REMARKS CHIEFLY CONCERNING THE HEALTH AND AILMENT OF EUROPEAN FAMILIES IN INDIA, with special reference to Maternal Management and Domestic Economy. By FRANCIS R. HOGG, M.D., Surgeon-Major. Demy 8vo., boards. Rs. 2.

Hunter.—MEDICAL HINTS FOR THE DISTRICTS, AND COMPANION TO THE DISTRICT MEDICINE CHEST, arranged for Government Officials, their Families, and Camp-followers, and for all who are cut off from oral Medical Advice. By GEORGE YEATES HUNTER, Surgeon, Bombay Army. Fcap. 8vo., cloth. Rs. 3-8.

HEALTH IN INDIA; Medical Hints as to who should go there; how to retain Health there and on returning Home. By GEORGE YEATES HUNTER. 16mo., cloth, gilt. Rs. 2.

GARDENING.

Firminger.—A MANUAL OF GARDENING FOR BENGAL AND UPPER INDIA. By T. A. C. FIRMINGER, Honorary Member, Agri.-Horti. Society. Third Edition. 8vo., cloth, gilt. Rs. 10.

THE AMATEUR GARDENER IN THE HILLS: being Hints taken from various works by Authorities on Garden Management, and adapted to the Hills; to which are added a few Hints on Fowls, Pigeons, and Rabbit keeping; and various Recipes connected with the above subjects, which are not commonly found in Receipt Books. By AN AMATEUR. Crown 8vo. Rs. 3.

Graham.—THE CULTURE OF EXOTIC ROSES IN INDIA MADE EASY: Practical Directions for their improved Training, Propagation, and General Treatment. New Edition, revised by JAMES GRAHAM. Fcap. 8vo., cloth. Rs. 2-8.

Lowis.—FAMILIAR INDIAN FLOWERS. Thirty coloured plates and descriptive letterpress. By LENA LOWIS. 4to., cloth. Rs. 22-8.

MEDICAL WORKS.

Russell.—MALARIA; ITS COURSE AND EFFECTS. Injuries of the Spleen: an Analysis of Thirty-nine Cases. By E. G. RUSSELL, M.B., B.Sc., London. Demy 8vo., cloth gilt. Rs. 8.

"Discusses most exhaustively the subject of Malaria and its effects, and the work should be read by all who are liable to be called upon to treat the conditions to which it gives rise. . . . We leave Dr. Russell's volume commending it to the notice of our readers as a book full of facts and of clinical research, and which must be considered as an authority on the subject."—*The Lancet.*

"Besides the results of his personal observations, he summarises the views of recognised authorities on his subject, and thus presents to his readers a convenient epitome of previous investigations."—*Medical Press and Circular.*

Hall.—CAUSES OF BLINDNESS IN INDIA, Treatment and Cure, with an Appendix on Hypermetropia, Diagnosis, &c. By Surgeon GEOFFREY C. HALL, Indian Medical Service. Fcap. 8vo., cloth, gilt. Rs. 2.

Roy.—THE CAUSES, SYMPTOMS, AND TREATMENT OF BURDWAN FEVER: or, The Epidemic Fever of Lower Bengal. By GOPAUL CHUNDER ROY, M.D., F.R.C.S., London (Exam.) 8vo., cloth. Rs. 3-6.

Dutt.—THE MATERIA MEDICA OF THE HINDUS. Compiled from Sanscrit Medical Works by UDOY CHAND DUTT; with a Glossary of Indian Plants, by G. KING, M.B., F.L.S. Demy 8vo., cloth. Rs. 6.

Hutchinson.—A GLOSSARY OF MEDICAL AND MEDICO-LEGAL TERMS, including those most frequently met with in the Law Courts. Compiled by R. F. HUTCHINSON, M.D., Surgeon-Major, Bengal Army. Fcap. 8vo., cloth. Rs. 3.

Ranking.—HIDAYAT-UL-HUKUMA. A Hindustani Manual for the use of Indian Medical Officers, Native Doctors, and others. By GEORGE S. A. RANKING, B.A., M.B., Cantab., Surgeon, 6th Bengal Cavalry. 18mo., sewed. Rs. 1-4.

Barnard.—CHOLERA MALIGNA is a Specific Acute Inflammation of the Mucous Tissue of the Small Intestines. By G. BARNARD. 8vo. Pamphlet. Re. 1.

Billing.—THE NATURE AND TREATMENT OF ASIATIC CHOLERA. By ARCHIBALD BILLING. 12mo. Re. 1.

THE INDIAN ANNALS OF MEDICAL SCIENCE. Nos. XXVIII. to XXXVII., January, 1877. Rs. 4 each.

Munro.—LEPROSY. By W. MUNRO, M.D., C.M. 8vo., boards. Rs. 3-4.

Chevers.—A PRACTICAL TREATISE ON THE MANAGEMENT OF THE DISEASE OF THE HEART AND OF AORTIC ANEURISM, with especial reference to the Treatment of those Diseases in India. By Dr. NORMAN CHEVERS. Demy 8vo., cloth. Rs. 2-8.

Bose.—PRINCIPLES OF RATIONAL THERAPEUTICS, commenced as an Inquiry into the relative value of Quinine and Arsenic in Ague. By BHOLANATH BOSE, M.D. Crown 8vo. Rs. 3-4.

A NEW SYSTEM OF MEDICINE, entitled Recognizant Medicine or, The State of the Sick. By BHOLANATH BOSE. 8vo. Rs. 7-8.

O'Shaughnessy.—THE BENGAL DISPENSATORY. Compiled chiefly from the works of Roxburgh, Wallich, Royle, Ainslie, Wight, Arnoll, Pereria, Fee, Richard, and Lindlay, including the Results of numerous Special Experiments. By W. B. O'SHAUGHNESSY. Large 8vo., cloth. Rs. 8.

Martin.—THE NATURE OF THE TISSUE-CHANGE KNOWN AS FATTY DEGENERATION OF THE HEART. By J. MARTIN, Medical Department. 8vo., cloth. Re. 1.

Playfair.—A TREATISE ON THE SCIENCE AND PRACTICE OF MIDWIFERY. By W. S. PLAYFAIR, M.D. 2 vols. 8vo. Rs. 20.

Ram Narain Dass.—A MONOGRAPH OF TWO HUNDRED AND FORTY-EIGHT CASES OF LATERAL LITHOTOMY OPERATIONS performed in the North-Western Provinces during a period of twelve years, by RAM NARAIN DASS. Illustrated by 256 Diagrams of Calculi, showing exterior and section, executed in Lithography. Pp. viii., 94. 8vo., cloth. Rs. 10.

SURVEYING, ETC.

Thuillier.—MANUAL OF SURVEYING FOR INDIA. Detailing the mode of operations on the Trigonometrical, Topographical, and Revenue Surveys of India. By Col. H. L. THUILLIER and Col. SMYTH. Revised and enlarged. Royal 8vo., cloth. Rs. 12.

Mackesy.—UNIVERSAL SCANTLING DIAGRAM. By Col. MACKESY. Price Rs. 4, in case, 4-8. Gives on inspection the correct dimensions for all kinds of timber beams to one tenth of an inch.

Scott.—NOTES ON SURVEYING. For the use of Schools. By J. MIDDLETON SCOTT, C.E. Second Edition. 8vo., stitched. Re. 1.

Kelly.—HANDBOOK OF PRACTICAL SURVEYING FOR INDIA. Especially designed as a Guide and Book of Ready Reference for District Officers, Planters, Municipalities, Courts of Wards and Landholders and for the use of Surveying Classes. Illustrated with Plans, Dirgrams, &c. By F. W. KELLY. Second Edition. Rs. 6.

THEOLOGICAL.

Welland.—EARTHLY AND HEAVENLY TRAINING; Sermons preached to the Calcutta Volunteers. By Rev. JAMES WELLAND. Paper, sewed. Re. 1.

Banerjee.—THE ARYAN WITNESS; or, The Testimony of Aryan Scriptures in Corroboration of Biblical History and the Rudiments of Christian Doctrine, including Dissertations on the Original Home and Early Adventures of Indo-Aryans. By Rev. K. M. BANERJEE. 8vo., paper, Rs. 3-4; cloth, Rs. 4.

Macdonald.—THE VEDIC RELIGION; or, The Creed and Practice of the Indu-Aryans, three thousand years ago. By the Rev. K. S. MACDONALD, M.A. 8vo., pp. 164, sewed. Rs. 1-8.

Slater.—GOD REVEALED. An Outline of Christian Truth, being Sunday Afternoon Lectures delivered to Educated Hindus. By Rev. T. E. SLATER, London Mission, Madras. Re. 1.

Temple.—THE LORD'S PRAYER TRANSLATED INTO THE BOJINGIJIDA, or South Andaman Language. By E. H. MAN. With Preface, Introduction, and Notes by Lieut. R. C. TEMPLE, 21st R. N. B. Fusiliers. Demy 8vo., cloth. Rs. 3-8.

Long.—SCRIPTURE TRUTH IN ORIENTAL DRESS; or, Emblems Explanatory of Biblical Doctrines and Morals. With Parallel or Illustrative References to Proverbs and Proverbial Sayings in the Arabic, Bengali, Canarese, Persian, Russian, Sanskrit, Tamil, Telegu, and Urdu Languages. By Rev. J. LONG. Half bound. Re. 1.

POETRY AND MISCELLANEOUS LITERATURE.

Aliph Cheem.—LAYS OF IND; Poems, Grave and Gay. Sixth Edition, enlarged, with additional Poems and Illustrations by the Author. Cloth, gilt. Rs. 7.

"BASIL ORMOND," and "Christabel's Love:" Metrical Tales of English Life. By ALIPH CHEEM, Author of "Lays of Ind." Rs. 3-8.

THE MEMOIR OF THE LATE JUSTICE ONOOCOOL CHUNDER MOOKERJEE. A Verbatim Reprint. 12mo. Rs. 1-8.

Ghose.—LIBERAL EDUCATION IN INDIA. A Paper read at a Meeting of the Bethune Society on the 21st March, 1878. By NAGENDRA NATH GHOSE, Barrister-at-Law. 8vo., sewed. Re. 1.

INDIAN VIEWS OF ENGLAND: the Effects of Observation of England upon Indian Ideas and Institutions. By NAGENDRA NATH GHOSE. Demy 8vo., stitched. Re. 1.

Long.—THREE THOUSAND BENGALI PROVERBS AND PROVERBIAL SAYINGS ILLUSTRATING NATIVE LIFE AND FEELING AMONG RYOTS AND WOMEN. By Rev. J. LONG. 12mo., paper. As. 8.

Maine.—THE EFEECTS OF OBSERVATION OF INDIA UPON MODERN THOUGHT. By Sir HENRY SUMNER MAINE, K.C.S.I., LL.D., the Rede Lecture, 1875. 8vo. Re. 1.

Dutt.—A VISION OF SUMERU AND OTHER POEMS. By SHOSHEE CHUNDER DUTT. With Portrait of the Author. 8vo., cloth. Rs. 5.

DURGESA NANDINI; or, THE CHIEFTAIN'S DAUGHTER. A Bengali Romance by BANKIM CHANDRA CHATTERJEE. Translated into English Prose by CHARU CHANDRA MOOKERJEE. 8vo., cloth. Rs. 2-8.

STORIES OF THE INDIAN OPERAS. 8vo., stitched. Rs. 2.

Tawney.—TWO CENTURIES OF BHARTRIHARI. By C. H. TAWNEY, Professor, Presidency College, Calcutta. 12mo., cloth. Rs. 2.

Sterndale.—THE AFGHAN KNIFE. By ROBERT ARMITAGE STERNDALE, F.R.G.S., Author of "Seonee, or Camp Life on the Satpura Range." Post 8vo. Rs. 4-4.

LIFE IN THE MOFUSSIL; or, the Civilian in Lower Bengal. By an EX-CIVILIAN. 2 vols. Rs. 10.

Mitchell.—IN INDIA. Sketches of Indian Life and Travel from Letters and Journals. By Mrs. MURRAY MITCHELL. Sq. 16mo., cloth. Rs. 2-8.

Day.—GOVINDA SAMANTA; or, The History of a Benga Ryot. By the Rev. LAL BEHARI DAY. Crown 8vo. Rs. 4-4.

Mackay.—SERIOUS REFLECTIONS AND OTHER CONTRIBUTIONS. By late G. ABRIGH MACKAY, under the *nom de plume* of "Our Political Orphan." Crown 8vo., cloth. Rs. 3.

DURGESHA NANDINI. Itibritta Mulak Upanays. Shri Bankimchandra Chattopadhyaya Pranita. Roman Akshare Mudrita. Cloth, boards. Price Re. 1, post free Re. 1-3.

This is the first attempt to print a Bengali work in the Roman character. It has been set in type direct from the Bengali original.

SKETCHES IN INDIAN INK. By JOHN SMITH, Jun., Colonel (Retired List). Crown 8vo., cloth. Rs. 5.

Grant.—RURAL LIFE IN BENGAL, illustrative of Anglo-Indian Suburban Life; the Habits of the Rural Classes; the varied Produce of the Soil and Seasons, and the Culture and Manufacture of Indigo. By C. GRANT. Illustrated with 166 Engravings. Royal 8vo., cloth. Rs. 6-8.

ANGLO-INDIAN DOMESTIC LIFE. By the Author of "Rural Life in Bengal." Profusely illustrated. A new Edition abridged and re-written with the Original and other Illustrations selected by the late COLESWORTHY GRANT. *(In preparation.*

DIRECTORIES, EXAMINATION MANUALS, COMMERCIAL TABLES, &c.

THACKER'S BENGAL DIRECTORY, Comprising, amongst other information, Official Directory; Military Directory; Mofussil Directory; Commercial Directory; Trades Directory; Street Directory, Calcutta; Alphabetical List of Residents in Bengal Presidency. Seventeenth Annual Publication. Royal 8vo., cloth, Rs. 14 cash; Rs. 16 credit.

BENGAL OBITUARY; a Compilation of Tablets and Inscriptions; with Directory, Biographical Sketches, and Memoirs. Royal 8vo., cloth. Rs. 2-8.

CIVIL LIST FOR THE LOWER PROVINCES OF BENGAL, Published quarterly. Rs. 3.

CALCUTTA UNIVERSITY CALENDAR, containing the Acts incorporating the University and authorizing it to grant Degrees—Bye-Laws—Regulations for all the Examinations, with lists of subjects and Text-Books—The University List of Fellows, Affiliated Institutions, Graduates, &c., and Papers set at the last Examinations in all Degrees. Demy 8vo., cloth. Rs. 5.

Grimley.—RULES FOR THE DEPARTMENTAL EXAMINATIONS OF JUNIOR MEMBERS OF THE COVENANTED CIVIL SERVICE, the Subordinate Executive Service, the Non-Regulation Commission, Police and Opium Departments; including a Selection of Examination Papers, in which are incorporated specimens of questions in Bentham's Theory of Legislation, Political Economy, History of India. For the Examination of Candidates for admission into the Staff Corps, and of Officers in the Political Department. By W. H. GRIMLEY, C.S., Secretary to the Central Examination Committee. 8vo., boards. Rs. 5.

GUIDE TO THE SUBORDINATE CIVIL SERVICE EXAMINATIONS, including a Selection from the Questions set in previous Examinations and the Orders of Government on the subject. By W. H. GRIMLEY. 8vo., boards. Rs. 4.

THE HUNDRED YEARS' ANGLO-CHINESE CALENDAR, from 1776 to 1876. 8vo., stitched. Rs. 7.

Jarrett.—A MANUAL OF REFERENCE TO THE EXAMINATIONS IN ORIENTAL LANGUAGES HELD THROUGHOUT THE BENGAL PRESIDENCY, containing the latest Orders of Government of India, establishing the Tests for Civil and Military Officers, Graded Officers of the Educational Department, and of the Uncovenanted Service, with Specimens of Test Papers for the various Examinations. By H. S. JARRETT, Secretary to the Board of Examiners. Stitched. Rs. 2-8.

Tables.

Merces.—TABLES OF EXCHAGE. A New Edition, showing the Conversion of English Money into Indian Currency and *vice versâ*, calculated for every 16th of a Penny, from 1*s.* 5*d.* to 2*s.* 3*d.* per Rupee. By F. A. D'MERCES. 8vo. Rs. 8.

TABLES OF INTEREST, showing the Interest of any sum from 3 pie to 100,000 rupees, at any rate from 1 to 15 per cent. per annum, reckoning 360 and 365 days to the year. By F. A D'MERCES. New Edition. Demy 8vo., bound. Rs. 4.

TABLES OF INCOME, WAGES, RENTS, &c., for months of 28, 29, 30, and 31 days; from 4 annas to 10,000 rupees, advancing by 1 rupee to 100 rupees. By F. A. D'MERCES. Fcap. 8vo. Rs. 1-4.

THE HANDY CALCULATOR, showing the cost of goods by number, per dozen, per hundred, per pound, per maund, and at so many seers and chittacks per rupee; also containing Tables of Income, Wages, &c., and Weights. By F. A. D'MERCES. 12mo., pp. 264. Rs. 3.

Spens.—THE INDIAN READY-RECKONER. Containing Tables for ascertaining the value of any number of Articles, &c., from 3 pies to 5 rupees, also Tables of Wages, from 4 annas to 25 rupees, and other useful Tables. By Capt. A. T. SPENS. Rs. 1-12.

Todivala.—MERCHANTS' AND BANKERS' COMPANION; or, Tables for calculating Interest and Commission, Freight and Exchanges between India, England, and China, in Rupees, Sterling, and Dollars. With Tables to show the Rates of Exchange and Prices of Bullion. By MANEKJI KAVASJI TODIVALA. Royal 8vo. Rs. 12.

THE LANGUAGES OF INDIA.

Kayathi.

(The language lately ordered to be adopted in the Courts of Behar.)

A HANDBOOK TO THE KAYATHI CHARACTER. By G. A. GRIERSON, Esq., C.S., late Sub-Divisional Officer of Madhubani Tirhoot. Royal 4to., cloth. Rs. 7-8.

The works contains thirty plates of facsimile handwriting in various styles of writing, with transliteration and translation to each.

Hindustani.

ARAISH-I-MAHFIL. Printed in Urdu. For the use of the Junior Members of Her Majesty's Indian Civil and Military Services. Fourth Edition. Revised and corrected by W. NASSAU LEES, LL.D. 8vo., paper. Rs. 6.

FISANAH-I-AJAIB OF MIRZA ALI BEG SURER. New and Revised Edition. For Examination for Degrees of Honour in Urdu. 8vo. Rs. 4.

Lower Standard.—HINDUSTANI COLLECTIONS FOR THE LOWER STANDARD EXAMINATION: being Selections from the Bagh-o-Bahar and History of India. 8vo. Rs. 2-8.

Higher Standard.—HINDUSTANI SELECTIONS FOR THE HIGHER STANDARD; being Selections from the Bagh-o-Bahar and Premsagur. 8vo., stitched. Rs. 4-8.

IKHWAN-US-SAFA, IN URDU. Fourth Edition, revised and corrected. For Examination, High Proficiency in Urdu. 8vo. Rs. 3.

NUZR-I-BE-NUZEER, IN URDU. Third Edition, revised and corrected. For Examination, High Proficiency in Urdu. 8vo. Rs. 3.

NAZR-I-BI-NAZIR. Translated from Urdu by C. W. BOWDLER BELL. 8vo., stitched. Rs. 4-8.

NAZR-I-BI-NAZIR; or, The Incomparable Prose of Meer Hussen. Literally translated by Capt. M. H. COURT. 8vo., stitched. Rs. 5-8.

Stapley.—GRADUATED TRANSLATION EXERCISES. Part II—English-Urdu, Urdu-English. With Rules, and Remarks for the guidance and assistance of Native Teachers and Students. By L. A. STAPLEY. 8vo., paper. Ans. 6.

KULLIYAT-I-SAUDA OF MIRZA RAFI-US-SAUDA, Extracts from, in Urdu. For Examination for Degrees of Honour in Urdu. 4to. Rs. 4.

MUSNAWIYAT OF MIRZA RAFI-US-SAUDA. For Candidates for the High Proficiency Examination in Urdu. Sewed. As. 12.

Court.—SELECTIONS FROM THE KULLIYAT-I-SAUDA. The parts appointed for the High Proficiency Examination. Literally translated by Capt. M. H. COURT. 8vo., paper. Rs. 3.

Yates.—INTRODUCTION TO THE HINDUSTANI LANGUAGE. Eighth Edition, improved. By Rev. W. YATES. In Roman Character, Rs. 5. In Persian Character, Third Edition, Rs. 6.

URDU ENTRANCE COURSE. Selections appointed by the Calcutta University. Poetry, As. 12; Prose, As. 10.

THE PEOPLE'S DICTIONARY IN ENGLISH AND ROMAN URDU. An Etymological, Idiomatic, and Illustrated Dictionary. 8vo., boards. As. 8; post free 9.

THE ROYAL SCHOOL DICTIONARY IN ENGLISH AND ROMAN URDU. Etymological, Pronouncing (English), and Idiomatic. Crown 8vo., boards. Re. 1; post free, 1-2.

Jarrett.—TRANSLATION OF THE HINDU PERIOD OF MARSHMAN'S HISTORY for the Lower Standard Examination. By Major H. S. JARRETT. 8vo. Rs. 1-4.

Bell.—THE RAJNITI OF LALLU LALA. Translated from the Braj Bhasha by C. W. BOWDLER BELL. 8vo., stitched. Rs. 6.

BYTAL PACHEESEE: or, The Twenty-five Tales of a Demon. Reprinted from the New Edition of Eshwar Chandra Vidyasagar in Hindi. Second Edition. Rs. 3.

Thompson.—A DICTIONARY IN HINDI AND ENGLISH. Compiled from approved Authorities. Second Edition. By J. T. THOMPSON. Royal 8vo., paper. Rs. 10.

Sanscrit.

Tawney.—UTTARA RAMA CHARITTA, a Sanscrit Drama by Bhavabhute. Translated into English Prose by C. H. TAWNEY, Professor, Presidency College, Calcutta. Sewed. Rs. 1-8.

THE MALAVIKAGNIMITRA: a Sanscrit Play by Kalidasa. Literally translated into English Prose by C. H. TAWNEY, Professor, Presidency College, Calcutta. 12mo., cloth. Rs. 2.

TWO CENTURIES OF BHARTRIHARI. By C. H. TAWNEY, Professor, Presidency College, Calcutta. 12mo., cloth. Rs. 2.

Banerjee.—BHUTTI KAVYA: Poem on the Actions of Rama. The first five Books, with Notes and Explanations. By Rev. K. M. BANERJEE. 8vo., paper. Rs. 2.

KUMAR SAMBHAVA OF KALIDASA. With Notes and Explanations in English. By Rev. K. M. BANERJEE. Third Edition, revised. 8vo., paper. Rs. 2-8.

RAGHUVANSA BY KALIDASA. With Notes and Grammatical Explanations. By Rev. K. M. BANERJEE. 8vo. paper. No. 1 (Cantos 1—3), Rs. 2. No. 2 (Cantos 4—9), Rs. 3. The two parts together, Rs. 4.

Ram Jasan.—A SANSCRIT AND ENGLISH DICTIONARY; being an abridgment of Professor Wilson's Dictionary. With an Appendix explaining the use of Affixes in Sanscrit. By PANDIT RAM JASAN. Royal 8vo., cloth. Rs. 10.

WILSON'S DICTIONARY IN SANSCRIT AND ENGLISH; translated, amended, and enlarged from an original Compilation prepared by learned Natives fof the College of Fort William. Third Edition. By JAGUN MOHANA TARKALANKA and KHETTER MOHANA MUKERJEE. 4to., bound. Rs. 16.

Persian.

A'ARAS-I-BOZORGAN; being an Obituary of Pious and Learned Moslims, from the beginning of Islam to the middle of the 12th Century of the Hijirah. Edited in Persian by Col. W. N. LEES and KABIR ALDIN AHMED. 8vo., paper. Rs. 2-8.

GULISTAN OF SADY. Edited in Persian, with Punctuation and the necessary Vowel-marks. Third Edition, revised and corrected. By Col. W. N. LEES. For Examination, High Proficiency in Persian. 8vo. Rs. 5.

IQD-I-GUL; being a Selection from the Gullistan and Anwari Sohaili. For Examination, Higher Standard. Rs. 3.

IQD-I-MANZUM; being a Selection from the Bostan of Sadi. Edited by KABIR ALDIN AHMED. Second Edition. For Examination, Higher Standard. 8vo. Rs. 2.

SELECTIONS FROM THE SHAH NAMAH. For the Degree of Honour Examination in Persian. For Officers in the Military and Civil Services. By Major H. S. JARRETT. Published by Authority.

Lee's Persian Series:—

I.—ZAWABIT-I-FARSI; or, A Persian Grammar in Oordoo. Prepared by ABD-UL-HUQQ. Seventh Edition. 12mo. As. 5.

IV.—IQD-I-LAALI; or, A Persian Poetical Reader, No. 1, containing the Pand-Nama or Karima and the Tarjiband, called Mamoquiman. Second Edition. 12mo. As. 4.

V.—IQD-I-MARJAN; or, Persian Poetical Reader, No. 2, containing the Pand-Nama of Farid Aldin Attar and the Quiccah-i-Yoosof; being an extract from Jami's Poem Yoosof and Zalaikha. Second Edition. 8vo. As. 8.

MODERN PERSIAN PHRASES. By an Officer of the Hyderabab Contigent. Revised by AKA MIRZA ZENUL ARIDEES SHEERAZEE. 8vo., cloth. Rs. 5.

PERSIAN SELECTIONS FOR FIRST ART COURSE, Rs. 1-4; For B.A. Course, Rs. 2-8.

Arabic.

ALIF LAILA (THE): or, Book of the Thousand Nights and one Night. Edited by Sir W. H. MACNAGHTEN. 4 vols. royal 8vo., (all remaining copies soiled). Rs. 25.

ARABIC SELECTIONS FOR THE ENTRANCE EXAMINATION entitled Sullam-ul-Adah. 8vo., cloth. Rs. 3-8.

ARABIC SELECTIONS FOR THE FIRST ARTS EXAMINATION, 8vo., cloth. Rs. 2-8.

Hayes.—SYNOPSIS OF THE GRAMMAR OF MODERN ARABIC. With a Vocabulary and Dialogues. By Capt. F. F. C. HAYES. Fcap. 8vo., paper. Rs. 2.

KALUBI, IN ARABIC. Edited by Col. W. N. LEES and MAULAVI ABD-UL-HUQQ. 8vo. Rs. 2.

KASHAF; being the Commentary on the Koran. By ABL-KASIM MUHMAD. 2 vols. 4to. Rs. 25.

Lee's Arabic Series:—

I.—ARABIC INFLECTION. 12mo. As. 4.

II.—ARABIC SYNTAX. 12mo. As. 4.

III.—TUHFAT-UL-TALIBIN. 12mo. As. 4.

Pukshto.

Bellew.—A DICTIONARY OF THE PUKHTO OR PUKSHTO LANGUAGE. In which the words are traced to their sources in the Indian and Persian Languages. By H. W. BELLEW. 4to., cloth. Rs. 21.

A GRAMMAR OF THE PUKHTO OR PUKSHTO LANGUAGE on a new and improved system, combining brevity with practical utility, and including Exercises and Dialogues intended to facilitate the acquisition of the Colloquial. By H. W. BELLEW. 4to., cloth. Rs. 10-8.

Vaughan.—A GRAMMAR OF THE PUKSHTO LANGUAGE as spoken in the Trans-Territories under British Rule. By Capt. J. L. VAUGHAN. 8vo., paper. Rs. 4.

Bengali.

STAPLEY'S GRADUATED TRANSLATION EXERCISES adapted to the Bengali Language. 8vo. As. 8.

THE LITERATURE OF BENGAL, from the earliest times to the present day. By ARCYDAE. With Extracts. 12mo., stitched Re. 1.

Mendes. — ABRIDGMENT OF JOHNSON'S DICTIONARY, English and Bengali. Second Edition. By JOHN MENDES. 8vo., cloth. Rs. 5.

YATES'S INTRODUCTION TO THE BENGALI LANGUAGE, Edited by J. WENGER. Vol. I.—Grammar and Reader, 8vo., cloth. Rs. 5; Vol. II.—Selection from Bengali Literature. 8vo. Rs. 5.

Glossaries.

Carnegy. — KACHARI TECHNICALITIES; or, A Glossary of Terms—Rural, Official, and General—in daily use in the Courts of Law, and in illustration of the Tenures, Customs, Arts, and Manufactures of Hindustan. By P. CARNEGY. Demy 8vo., cloth. Rs. 12.

Durga Prasad.—A GUIDE TO LEGAL TRANSLATION; or, A Collection of Words and Phrases used in the Translation of Legal Papers from Urdu to English. By DURGA PRASAD. 8vo., cloth. Rs. 5.

Rajenda Lala Mittra.—A SCHEME FOR THE RENDERING of European Scientific Terms into the Vernacular of India. By RAJENDRA LALA MITTRA. Demy 8vo., stitched. As. 8.

Robinson.—DICTIONARY OF LAW AND OTHER TERMS commonly employed in the Courts of Bengal, including many Commercial Words and Idiomatic Phrases, in English and Bengali. By JOHN ROBINSON. 8vo. Rs. 6.

EDUCATIONAL WORKS.

Including Macmillan & Co.'s English Series of "Text books for Indian Schools" (English prices at the Exchange of the day).

ENGLISH LANGUAGE.

MILTON'S ODE ON THE MORNING OF CHRIST'S NATIVITY With Notes (Todd's). Fcap. 8vo., limp. As. 4.

A GUIDE TO ENGLISH PARSING. By H. P. JACOB. Fcap. 8vo. As. 4.

LAMB'S TALES FROM SHAKESPEARE. Thacker, Spink & Co.'s School Edition. Fcap., cloth. As. 12.

SELECTIONS FROM MODERN ENGLISH LITERATURE. By E. LETHBRIDGE. 8vo., cloth. Rs. 2.

FIRST ARTS COURSE FOR 1881. Authorized by the Calcutta University. 8vo., cloth. Rs. 5.

ENGLISH CLASSICS FOR INDIAN SCHOOLS: Goldsmith's Deserted Village. Edited by G. W. FORREST and STORR. As. 12.

EASY SELECTIONS from Modern English Literature. By E. LETHBRIDGE. 1*s.* 6*d.*

A SERIES OF SIX ENGLISH READING-BOOKS. For Indian Children. By PEARY CHURN SIRCAR. Revised by E. LETHBRIDGE. First 5*d.*; Second 6*d.*; Third, 8*d.*; Fourth, 1*s.*; Fifth, 1*s.* 2*d.*; Sixth, 1*s.* 3*d.*

HINTS ON THE STUDY OF ENGLISH. By F. J. ROWE and W. T. WEBB. Demy 8vo., cloth. Rs. 2-8.

A COMPANION READER to "Hints on the Study of English." Demy 8vo., paper. Rs. 1-4.

THE STUDENT'S COMPANION TO ENGLISH GRAMMAR. Compiled from University Examination Papers. By J. TANNOCK, Nizamut College, Moorshedabad. 8vo., stitched. As. 8; Supplement, 1876.

A KEY TO TANNOCK'S STUDENT'S COMPANION TO ENGLISH. By G. A. LORRIMER. 8vo., sewed. As. 8.

ENGLISH PEOPLE AND THEIR LANGUAGE. Translated from the German of Loth by C. H. TAWNEY. Stitched. As. 8.

A PRIMER OF ENGLISH GRAMMAR. For Indian Students. By the Rev. R. MORRIS, M.A., LL.D. 1*s.*

A SHORT HISTORY OF ENGLISH LANGUAGE. By THOMAS EDWARDS, F.E. Fcap. 8vo. Rs. 1-4.

GEOGRAPHY.

A GEOGRAPHICAL READER AND COMPANION TO THE ATLAS. By C. B. CLARKE, M.A. 2*s.*

PHYSICAL GEOGRAPHY. For Indian Students. By H. F. BLANFORD, Associate of the Royal School of Mines, Director-General of the Indian Meteorological Department. 2*s.* 6*d.*

THE INDIAN ATLAS OF THE WORLD. By JOHN BARTHOLOMEW. Coloured. 16 Maps—the World, Mercator's projection; the World in Hemispheres; Asia; Europe; Africa; N. America; S. America; Oceania; Turkey in Asia, Persia, Arabia; China and Japan; Indian Empire; Bengal, N. W. Provinces; Punjab, Sindh, Rajputana; Bombay, Berar, &c.; Madras, Hyderabad, Mysore; British Isles. As. 6, post free 6½.

INDIAN SERIES OF MAPS. Imperial 4to., prepared from the best authorities, and printed in colours. Price one anna each; or the set, post-free, for one rupee. List of Maps.—Hemispheres; Europe; Asia; Africa; North America; South America; British Isles; England and Wales; Persia, Afghanistan, and Beloochistan; India; North West Provinces; Punjab, &c.; Chinese Empire and Japan; Palestine; United States.

HISTORY.

THE WORLD'S HISTORY. Compiled under the direction of E. LETHBRIDGE, M.A. Second Edition. 1*s.*

AN EASY INTRODUCTION TO THE HISTORY OF INDIA. Second Edition. By E. LETHBRIDGE, M.A. 1*s.* 6*d.*

A HISTORY OF ENGLAND. Second Edition. Compiled under the direction of E. LETHBRIDGE. M.A., 1*s.* 6*d.*

AN EASY INTRODUCTION TO THE HISTORY AND GEOGRAPHY OF BENGAL. Second Edition. By E. LETHBRIDGE, M.A. 1*s.* 6*d.*

MATHEMATICS.

EUCLID'S ELEMENTS OF GEOMETRY. Part I., containing the First Four Books, with Notes, &c. By P. GHOSH. Sewed, Rs. 1-4; cloth, Rs. 1-8.

A CHAPTER OF DECIMALS. By J. M. ALDIS, M.A. 16mo. Stitched. Re. 1.

ARITHMETIC FOR BEGINNERS, designed for the use of Junior Classes, to which are appended Exercises in Mental Arithmetic. By CHARLES D'CRUX, Bengal Academy. 16mo. As. 6.

SOLUTIONS OF EXERCISES FROM TODHUNTER'S MENSURATION. Including Surveying, and an Appendix. By P. GHOSH, 12mo. Rs. 1-8

ELEMENTARY TREATISE ON MECHANICS. By F. W. STEPHENSON. Stitched, 8vo. Rs. 2-8.

ARITHMETIC WITH ANSWERS. For Indian Students. By BARNARD SMITH, M.A. 2*s.*

This Edition of Barnard Smith's Arithmetic contains the Indian Tables of Weights, Measures, and Currency, as well as the English Tables; and Examples fully worked out, and very numerous Questions for practice, based on the Tables, have been inserted under each rule.

ALGEBRA. For Indian Students. By I. TODHUNTER, M.A., F.R.S. 2*s.* 6*d.*

THE FIRST FOUR BOOKS OF EUCLID. With Notes, Appendix, and Exercises. By I. TODHUNTER, F.R.S. 2*s.*

ELEMENTARY MENSURATION AND LAND SURVEYING. For Indian Students. By I. TODHUNTER, M.A., F.R.S. 2*s.*

This Edition of Todhunter's Mensuration has been prepared specially for Entrance Candidates, and contains an Appendix on Practicnl Surveying in India.

NOTES ON PRACTICAL GEOMETRY AND THE CONSTRUCTION OF SCALES. By J. M. SCOTT. Second Edition. 8vo., stitched. Re. 1.

THE ELEMENTS OF ALGEBRA, by JAMES WOOD; remodelled, simplified, and adapted for general use in schools, with numerous Exercises and Examination Papers. Part I. For Entrance Candidates. By P. GHOSH. 12mo., cloth. Rs. 1-8.

MISCELLANEOUS ARITHMETICAL QUESTIONS selected from various sources. With neat and concise Solutions. By EDWARD FELL. 12mo. Rs. 2.

ELEMENTARY TREATISE ON PLANE TRIGONOMETRY. With Examination Papers and Examples. Designed for the use of the Government Colleges of India, and Schools affiliated to the University of Calcutta. By E. WILMOT. Pp. 76. 8vo., cloth. Rs. 2-12.

ALGEBRAICAL EXERCISES WITH SOLUTIONS. For Students preparing for the Entrance Examination of the Calcutta University. By SARAT CHANDRA MUKHOPADHYAY, M.A. 12mo., stiff cover. Rs. 1-4.

ELEMENTARY DYNAMICS, with numerous Examples. By W. G. WILLSON. Second Edition, by J. WILLSON. Crown 8vo. Rs. 3-8.

BENGALI.

BENGALI ENTRANCE COURSE. Entrance Examination. Rs. 1-6.

THE WORLD'S HISTORY. Compiled under the direction of E. LETHBRIDGE, M.A. Translated into Bengali. Demy 8vo. As. 8.

AN EASY INTRODUCTION TO THE HISTORY AND GEOGRAPHY OF BENGAL. For the Junior Classes in Schools. By E. LETHBRIDGE, M.A. Translated into Bengali. Demy 8vo, Re. 1.

A PRIMER OF CHEMISTRY. By H. E. ROSCOE. Translated into Bengali. Demy 8vo. As. 7.

STAPLEY'S GRADUATED TRANSLATION EXERCISES, adapted to the Bengali Language. As. 8.

ELEMENTS OF EUCLID. First two Books. With Notes and Exercises. Translated into Bengali. Demy 8vo. As. 6.

MENSURATION FOR BEGINNERS. With numerous Examples. By I. TODHUNTER, M.A., F.R.S. Translated into Bengali. Demy 8vo. As. 12.

EXTRACTED CHAPTERS FROM THE RUDIMENTS OF PHYSICAL GEOGRAPHY FOR INDIAN SCHOOLS. By H. F. BLANFORD. Translated into Bengali by BABOO PURNA CHANDRA DATTA for the Author. As. 10.

AN EASY INTRODUCTION TO THE HISTORY OF INDIA. By E. LETHBRIDGE, M.A. Translated by BABOO RADHIKA PRASANNA MUKERJEE. Demy 8vo. Re. 1.

METAPHYSICS.

THE ELEMENTS OF THE PSYCHOLOGY OF COGNITION. By R. JARDINE. Crown 8vo. 6*s.* 6*d.*

ANALYSIS OF SIR WILLIAM HAMILTON'S LECTURES ON METAPHYSICS., with Dissertations and Copious Notes. By W. CAREY FINK. Author of "Analysis of Dr. Thos. Reid's Inquiry into the Human Mind." Rs. 2.

ANALYSIS OF REID'S INQUIRY INTO THE HUMAN MIND. By W. C. FINK. With Notes. Second Edition. 8vo., stitched. Rs. 1-12.

LECTURES ON METAPHYSICS. By Sir WILLIAM HAMILTON, Bart., 2 vols. 8vo., cloth. Rs. 9.

AN INQUIRY INTO THE HUMAN MIND ON THE PRINCIPLES OF COMMON SENSE. By THOMAS REID, D.D. 8vo., cloth. Rs. 1-4.

LATIN.

SELECTA POETICA. The Selection adopted by the Calcutta University. Part I., Selections from Ovid. 18mo., cloth. Re. 1. Translation. Re. 1.

SELECTA POETICA. The Selections adopted by the Calcutta University. Part II., Selections from Catullus, Tibullus, Propertius, Martial, Aulus, Persius, Juvenal. 18mo., cloth. Re. 1. Translation. Re. 1.

ARNOLD'S ECLOGÆ OVIDIANÆ. A Translation. Fcap. 8vo., sewed. Re. 1.

INDIAN LAW PUBLICATIONS.

Civil Procedure.

Code of Civil Procedure (The); being Act X. of 1877. With Notes and Appendix, containing Charters of all the High Courts, Privy Council Appeals, Orders, Rules, the Limitation and Specific Relief Acts; with Copious Index. By L. P. DELVES BROUGHTON, assisted by W. F. AGNEW and G. S. HENDERSON. Royal 8vo. Reduced to Rs. 18. Appendix, Act XII. of 1879. Rs. 1.

Evidence.

The Law of Evidence (Act I. of 1872, with Amendments). With a Commentary, Notes, &c. Third Edition. By C. D. FIELD. Demy 8vo., cloth. Rs. 18.

Contracts.

The Indian Contract Act (IX. of 1872). With a Commentary, critical, explanatory, and illustrative. By C. C. MACRAE. 8vo., cloth. Rs. 10.

The Indian Contract Act (IX. of 1872), and the Specific Relief Act (I. of 1877). With a full Commentary. By D. SUTHERLAND. Royal 8vo., cloth. Rs. 10.

The Contract Act (IX. of 1872). With an Introduction and Explanatory Notes. By the Hon. H. S. CUNNINGHAM, M.A., and H. H. SHEPHARD, M.A. Third Edition. Demy 8vo., cloth. Rs. 14.

Criminal Law.

The Indian Penal Code Act (XLV. of 1860), and other Laws and Acts of Parliament relating to the Criminal Courts of India. With Notes containing the Rulings of the Nizamut Adawlut on points of Procedure and Decisions of the High Court of Calcutta. By J. O'KINEALY. Second Edition. Royal 8vo. Rs. 14.

The Indian Magistrate's Guide: an Introduction to the Judicial Duties of Magistrates and Justices of the Peace in India. By Sir BENSON MAXWELL. Edited for India by L. P. DELVES BROUGHTON, B.A., Barrister-at-Law. 8vo., cloth. Rs. 12.

The Penal Code Act (XLV. of 1860) (Fifth Edition), as amended by later Enactments. With Rulings of all the High Courts and Chief Courts in India. By FENDALL CURRIE. 8vo., cloth. Rs. 8.

The Indian Code of Criminal Procedure. With Rulings of all the High Courts in India and the Chief Courts of the Provinces. With a copious Index. (Fifth Edition.) By FENDALL CURRIE. 8vo., cloth. Rs. 10-8.

Pocket Penal, Criminal Procedure, and Police Codes; Acts XLV. of 1860, X. of 1872, V. of 1861, VI. of 1864, XXXI. of 1867, and XXVII. of 1870. Limp cloth. Rs. 4.

Divorce.

The Law of Divorce in India; being the Indian Divorce Act. With Notes and Forms of Pleadings. By C. C. MACRAE. Cloth. Rs. 10.

Joint Stock Companies.

The Indian Companies' Act, 1866 (Act X. of 1866). With an Appendix and Notes. By WHITLEY STOKES. Royal 8vo. Rs. 8.

Succession.

The Indian Succession Act, 1865 (Act X. of 1865). With a Commentary, and the Parsee Succession Act, 1865, Acts XII. and XIII. of 1855, and the Acts relating to the Administrator-General. With Notes. By WHITLEY STOKES. 8vo. Rs. 10.

The Probate and Administration Act; being Act V. of 1881. With Notes. By W. E. H. FORSYTH, Esq. Edited with Index by F. J. COLLINSON, Esq. Demy 8vo., cloth. Rs. 5.

Mortgages.

Law of Mortgage in Bengal and the North-West Provinces. By A. G. MACPHERSON, Judge of the High Court of Judicature. Sixth Edition. Demy 8vo. Rs. 10.

Registration.

The Indian Registration Act (III. of 1877). With Notes (fourth edition of the Notes). By CARR-STEPHEN, Barrister-at-Law. Demy 8vo., cloth. Rs. 5.

Landlord and Tenant.

Revenue Sale Law of Lower Bengal, comprising Act XI. of 1859: Bengal Act VII. of 1868; Bengal Act VII. of 1880. (The Public Demands Recovery Act), and the Unrepealed Regulations and the Rules of the Board of Revenue on the subject. With Notes. Edited by WILLIAM E. H. FORSYTH. Demy 8vo., cloth. Rs. 5; post free Rs. 5-4.

The Rent Law of Bengal, L. P. (Act VIII. 1869, B.C.). with all important Rulings and Notes. By JOGINDRA CHANDRA MAULIK. 8vo., cloth. Rs. 4.

The Law of Landlord and Tenant as administered in Bengal. By H. BELL, C.S. Second Edition. Cloth, large 8vo. Rs. 4.

Miscellaneous.

A Treatise on the Law of Bills of Lading. Comprising the various Incidents attaching to the Bill of Lading, the Legal Effects of the Clauses and Stipulations, the Rights and Liabilities of Consignors, Consignees, Indorsees, and Vendors, under the Bill of Lading. With an Appendix, containing Forms, &c. By EUGENE LEGGETT, Solicitor. 8vo., cloth. Rs. 10; post free 10-8.

Law of Indian Railways and Common Carriers. A Commentary upon the Indian Railway Act of 1879, the Carriers' Act of 1865, and the Act known as Lord Campbell's Act (XIII. of 1855). Together with such Sections and Quotations from the Merchant Shipping Act, the Contract Act, the Railway and Canal Traffic Act, Civil Procedure Code, Court Fees Act, and the Statute of Limitations, as apply to Carriers by Land and Water. By W. G. MACPHERSON. 8vo., cloth. Rs. 12.

The Indian Law Examination Manual. Second Edition. Revised with all the new Laws. By FENDALL CURRIE. 8vo. Rs. 5.

The Sea-Customs Law, 1878, and Tariff Act; with Notes and Appendices. By W. H. GRIMLEY, Esq., B.A., LL.B., C.S. Demy 8vo., cloth, Rs. 7-8; Interleaved, Rs. 8-8.

Legislative Acts.

Bengal Acts: the Legislative Acts (Unrepealed) of the Lieutenant-Governor of Bengal in Council. From 1862 to the present. Annotated and edited with Index, by FRED. CLARKE, Esq., Barrister-at-Law. Rs. 12.

Legislative Acts published annually in continuation of Mr. Theobald's Edition. Royal 8vo., cloth—1872, Rs. 8; 1873, 1874, 1875, Rs. 5 each; 1876, Rs. 6; 1877, Rs. 10; 1878, Rs. 5; 1879, Rs. 5; 1880, Rs. 4.

Chronological Tables of Acts of Parliament. Regulations of the Bengal Code, Acts of the Governor-General of India in Council, and Acts of the Lieutenant-Governor of Bengal in Council, with Remarks. By H. S. CUNNINGHAM, Esq., one of the Judges of the High Court of Judicature, Bengal.

Reports.

Indian Law Reports, published under Authority. The Reports appear in Monthly Parts, at Calcutta, Madras, Bombay, and Allahabad, and comprise four Series.—The Cases heard by the Privy Council on appeal from each High Court are reported in the Series for that High Court. Annual Subscription, Rs. 47-8.

Judgments of the Privy Council on Appeals from India. 1831 to 1877. By D. SUTHERLAND. In paper cover, Rs. 16. Vol. II., 1868 to 1877, Rs. 20. Vol. III., Rs. 20. The three vols. together, Rs. 40.

Moore's Indian Appeals, a Reprint, 14 vols. half-bound, Rs. 210.

Digests.

The Indian Digest: a complete Index to the Reported Cases of the High Courts established in India. Second Edition. By H. COWELL, Barrister-at-Law. Royal 8vo., cloth. Reduced to Rs. 12.

The Digest of Indian Law Reports: a Compendium of the Rulings of the High Court of Calcutta from 1862, and of the Privy Council from 1831 to 1876. By D. SUTHERLAND, Esq., Barrister-at-Law. Impl. 8vo. Rs. 20.

Tagore Law Lectures.

The Hindu Law; being a Treatise on the Law administered exclusively to Hindus by the British Courts in India. (1870.) By HERBERT COWELL. Royal 8vo., cloth. Rs. 12.

The Hindu Law; being a Treatise on the Law administered exclusively to Hindus by the British Courts in India. (1871.) By HERBERT COWELL. Royal 8vo., cloth. Rs. 8.

History and Constitution of the Courts and Legislative Authorities. (1872.) By HERBERT COWELL. Royal 8vo., cloth. Rs. 8.

Mahomedan Law; a Digest of the Laws applicable to the Sunnis of India. (1873.) By SHAMA CHURN SIRCAR. Royal 8vo., cloth. Rs. 9.

Mahomedan Law; being a digest of the Sunni Code in part, and of the Imamyah Code. (1874.) By SHAMA CHURN SIRCAR. Royal 8vo., cloth. Rs. 9.

The Law relating to the Land Tenures of Lower Bengal. (1875.) By ARTHUR PHILLIPS. Royal 8vo., cloth. Rs. 10.

The Law relating to Mortgage in India. (1876.) By RASH BEHARI GHOSE. Royal 8vo., cloth. Rs. 10.

The Law relating to Minors in Bengal. (1877.) By E. J. TREVELYAN. Royal 8vo., cloth. Rs. 10.

The Hindu Law of Marriage and Stridhana. (1878.) By GOOROO DOSS BANERJEE. Royal 8vo., cloth. Rs. 10.

The Law relating to the Hindu Widow. (1879.) By TRAILOKYANATH MITTRA, M.A., D.L. Royal 8vo., cloth. Rs. 10.